Princeton Theological Monograph Series

Dikran Y. Hadidian

General Editor

WITHDRAWN

47

HISTORY AND THEOLOGY

Walter Schmithals On The Unity
of the New Testament

HISTORY AND THEOLOGY

WALTER SCHMITHALS ON THE UNITY OF THE NEW TESTAMENT

PIET B. BOSHOFF

PICKWICK PUBLICATIONS
SAN JOSE, CALIFORNIA

Copyright © 2001 by Piet B. Boshoff

Published by
        Pickwick Publications
        215 Incline Way
        San Jose, CA 95139-1526

All rights reserved. No part of this book may be reproduced, stored in a retrieval system, or transmitted, in any form or by any means, electronic, mechanical, photocopying, recording, or otherwise, without the written permission of the publisher.

Printed on Acid Free Paper in the United States of America

Library of Congress Cataloging-in-Publication Data

Boshoff, Piet B.
    History and theology : Walter Schmithals on the unity of the
      New Testament / Piet B. Boshoff.
        p.   cm. -- (Princeton theological monograph series ; 47)
    Includes bibliographical references.
    ISBN 1-55635-039-2
    1. Bible. N.T.---Hermeneutics.
    2. Schmithals, Walter.   I. Series.

BS2331 .B67 2001
225.6'092--dc21
                                                2001036485

CONTENTS

Acknowledgements ix

Abbreviations x

Chapter 1 *Introduction*

Chapter 2 *Schmithals's Debut: "Die Gnosis in Korinth"*
   2.1 Introduction 5
   2.2 Literary analysis 6
   2.3 The antagonists 7
   2.4 Christology 8
   2.5 Gnosis 10
   2.6 Anthropology 12
   2.7 Ethics 18
   2.8 Eschatology 21
   2.9 Ecclesiology 24
   2.10 Paul and the Historical Jesus 29
   2.11 Closing Remarks 32

Chapter 3 *Pointers in the Theological Interpretation of the New Testament*
   3.1 Introduction 33
   3.2 The Gospel 34
   3.3 The Word 41
   3.4 The Canon of Scripture 46
   3.5 The Historical Critical Method 49
   3.6 The The Doctrinal Method 61
   3.7. Closing Remarks 63

Chapter 4 *Early Christianity*
   4.1 Introduction 65
   4.2 The Office of the Apostle 65
   4.3 Comparative Exegesis 68

4.4 Early Christianity 71
4.5 Q and Q1 76
4.6 *Aposunagogos* 80
4.7 The Emperor Cult 85
4.8 Fundamental Gospel (*Grundevangelium*) and
    Gospel (*Evangelium*) 87
4.9 The Prologue 94
4.10 The Beloved Disciple Editing 95

Chapter 5 *The relationship between the "proclaimer and proclaimed" as the main problem in the theological understanding of the New Testament*
5.1 Introduction 101
5.2 Bultmann and the Main Problem 102
5.3 Discontinuity 114
5.4 Continuity 117
5.5 The Historical Jesus Tradition 119
5.6 Peter and Jesus 122
5.7 The Historical Jesus 125
5.8 The Decisive Question 131
5.9 Jesus is God 137
5.10 Closing Remarks 141

Chapter 6 *The Theological History of the New Testament*
6.1 Introduction 143
6.2 The Relationship between the New Testament and the
    Old Testament 144
6.3 Eschatology and Apocalyptic 154
6.4 Paul's Theology of Conversion (Damascus) 161
6.5 The Theology of Antioch 165
6.6 Paul's Original Theological Ideas 169
6.7 Theological Additions to Paul's Letters by Editors 171
6.8 Closing Remarks 171

Chapter 7 *Theory and Practice of Preaching in the New Testament*
7.1 Introduction 173
7.2 Theory of Preaching 174
7.3 Meditation: The Listener 185
7.4 The Role of the Historic Situation of the Text in Preaching.189
7.5 Closing Remarks 194

Chapter 8 *Ethics*
    8.1 Introduction 197
    8.2 Public Worship 198
    8.3 The Church and the Christian 202
    8.4 The Foundation of Ethics 209
    8.5 Creature and Creation 219
    8.6 Closing Remarks 221

Chapter 9 *Conclusion* 223

Works Consulted 225

Scripture References 235

Topic References 239

Addendum: *Bibliography of Walter Schmithals 1993-1998* 243

ACKNOWLEDGEMENTS

I wish to recognize my debts to patient helpers: Klaus Schmitz, Willem Oliver, Adri Goosen, Annette van der Walt and Tim Groenewald. My thanks are due also to the decision to publish the work and the technical assistance of the publisher, Pickwick Publications, especially to their General Editor, Dr. Dikran Y Hadidian. Still another vote of thanks goes to Andries van Aarde who encouraged me during the writing process and believed that it should be published. As research associate in the research project "Biblical Theology and Hermeneutics," directed by Prof. Dr. A. G. van Aarde, I hereby acknowledge the support of the Department of New Testament Studies at the University of Pretoria.

Piet B. Boshoff

November 2001

ABBREVIATIONS

EdF	Erträge der Forschung
Epd	Evangelischer Pressedienst
EZS	Evangelische Zeitstimmen
GTB	Gütersloher Taschenbücher Siebenstern
HTS	Hervormde Teologiese Studies
FRLANT NF	Forschungen zur Religion und Literatur des Alten und Neuen Testaments Neue Folge
GPM	Göttinger Predigtmeditationen
KEK	Kritisch-exegetischer Kommentar über das Neue Testament
KiZ	Die Kirche in der Zeit
NTD	Das Neue Testament Deutsch Neues Göttinger Bibelwerk
ÖTK	Ökumenischer Taschenbuchkommentar zum Neuen Testament
RGG	Religion in Geschichte und Gegenwart
RKZ	Reformierte Kirchenzeitung
ThEh NF	Theoligische Existenz Heute Neue Folge
ThLZ	Theologische Literaturzeitung
ThRs	Theologische Rundschau
Th Viat	Theologia Viatorum
TRE	Theologische Realenzyklopädie
UTB	Uni-Taschenbücher
VDK	Volksbund Deutsche Kriegsgräberfürsorge
VuF	Verkündigung und Forschung
WdF	Wege der Forschung
ZBK	Zürcher Bibelkommentare
ZGP	Zeitschrift für Gottesdienst und Predigt
ZKG	Zeitschrift für Kirchengeschichte
ZNW	Zeitschrift für die Neutestamentliche Wissenschaft
ZThK	Zeitschrift für Theologie und Kirche
ZZ	Zwischen den Zeiten

CHAPTER 1

INTRODUCTION

Schmithals (1971b:50, 1996a:24) tells the story of how he accidentally attended Rudolf Bultmann's lectures. Having completed his studies at the theological school of Wuppertal, he travelled to the Philipps University at Marburg in March 1948 to complete his studies and obtain the necessary ecclesiastical recognition. He did not go to Marburg because of any acquaintance with Bultmann or for the reason that he wished to study under Bultmann. According to him, he, in fact, arrived there in spite of Bultmann. What drew him was the availability of lodgings at a former hunters' barracks.

Schmithals attended Bultmann's lectures on the theology of the New Testament, the history of the investigation of the life of Jesus and on the interpretation of 1 Corinthians and 2 Corinthians. He also took part in two seminar lectures directed by Bultmann on Pauline Theology in the 1948/9-winter semester and on the Johannine epistles in the summer semester of 1949. Bultmann (1950) reported as follows: "Herr Schmithals ist mir als Mitplied des neutestamentlichen Seminars in mehreren Semestern als ausgezeichnet begabt und als sehr fleissig bekannt."

Because of the storm resulting from Bultmann's ideas on the demythologization of the New Testament kerygma, a group was formed which initially discussed exegetical problems in the light of existential interpretation and, later, works on dogmatic theology under the leadership of Bultmann on a monthly basis. Bultmann (1967b:33) noted, with respect to Schmithals, that as a pastor, he made the effort to travel from Raumland to attend these gatherings and that, later as lecturer in Marburg, he became a tower of strength within this group.

Schmithals was fascinated by the fact that Bultmann treated the divine acts of salvation in Christ seriously and yet attempted to apply historical exegesis with a radical authenticity, making the Biblical and reformational dogma understandable by employing historical science.

Establishing the unity between historical and theological interpretation is regarded by Schmithals to be the task of the modern theologian. Historical consciousness came to the fore and theology should acknowledge this fully, while remaining faithful to the dogma. This is the only way in which theology can today be seen as a reliable expression of the word of God.

Schmithals regards this as the direction in which theology should move and his theological work aims at making a contribution in this respect.

Schmithals is a prolific writer. The published list of his publications, from 1952 to 1982, contains four hundred and sixty-eight entries (cf. Schmithals 1983:185-208). By the end of 1997 (cf. Schmithals 1993a:1095; Addendum p.142), this number has reached eight hundred and ninety six, which includes independent publications, articles, reviews, homilies and sermons. The flow of publications is still continuing.

It is my aim to classify, in the most suitable manner, the main themes appearing in Schmithals' work, to develop these themes and establish a relation between them. This will enable the reader to view his work as a whole. Schmithals' work may truly be regarded as a unit, because he, even more than Bultmann, has established the unity between the historical and theological interpretation of the New Testament. It thus appears to be reasonable to raise the question of Schmithals' theological contribution, as Bultmann is generally regarded as the New Testament scholar of our age. It is not my aim to evaluate Schmithals' viewpoints regarding specific themes.

With regard to the organization of the book, I have decided to place at the beginning a chapter on Schmithals' first theological work on Gnosticism. This chapter proves that Schmithals speaks in this contribution, *Die Gnosis in Korinth*, his own mind. Moreover, a significant part of his work cannot be understood without a thorough exposition of his views regarding Gnosticism. The following chapter serves as an introduction to the remainder, paving the way for a theological understanding of the New Testament. It is clear that the next step should be to account for the historical situation of Early Christianity in order to arrive at the main problem of New Testament theology, namely the question of the relationship between the proclaiming 'Jesus' and the 'proclaimed Christ.' When this matter has been put into perspective, the history of theology in the New Testament is considered, which concludes the preparatory work leading to the theory and practice of preaching. The chapter on ethics serves as an indication of the ethical relevance of Schmithals' theological thoughts with regard to everyday life. Although the translation of the New Testament texts has been strongly influenced by Schmithals' understanding of these texts, I must accept responsibility for it.

Bultmann's legacy is most visible in the introductory chapter, which deals with the method of theologizing, offering pointers to the historical and theological interpretation of the New Testament. Regarding the remainder of Schmithals' theological thought, he follows his own star to a greater or lesser degree. Schmithals was able to develop in greater detail, the unity of an historical and theological interpretation of the New Testament. This is what he appreciated in Bultmann's work, especially with regard to historical interpretation. To me, he is more successful than Bultmann in making the subject matter of the New Testament accessible on a historical critical level. He describes in much greater detail the historical basis of the unity of historical and theological interpretation.

With regard to the main question of New Testament

theology, we must note that such a fundamental problem cannot be solved by means of a formula. A formula would be much too simple a solution to the question regarding the relationship between the historical Jesus and the kerygmatic Christ. The importance of such a fundamental problem lies in the challenge that one should regard it existentially. In other words, it is far more than an intellectual issue. The problem should become a quest. This is exactly what Walter Schmithals made it. The main question of New Testament theology became his quest. In the execution of this task he stood alone. He should be regarded as someone who performs a task and not as someone who yearns for achievement and recognition.

CHAPTER 2

SCHMITHALS' DEBUT: "DIE GNOSIS IN KORINTH"

2.1 INTRODUCTION

In 1948/49 Schmithals attended the lectures given by Bultmann on 1 and 2 Corinthians. These lectures awakened his interest in the Corinthian letters and in the gnostic antagonists with whom Paul had to contend in Corinth. He says that he later proposed to Bultmann that "Die Gnosis in Korinth" should be the title of his (Schmithals') thesis, and that Bultmann inquired whether this would not be too limiting for a thesis. According to Bultmann, there was very little Gnosticism in Corinth and he proposed that Schmithals should rather use the title *Die Gnosis in Neuen Testament*. Schmithals agreed, but resolved to retain his original title, as he suspected that Gnosticism exerted a much greater influence in Corinth. He decided to record the theology of Paul's gnostic antagonists in Corinth. Here, in persevering with his chosen theme, Schmithals displays the character of a researcher with his own originality.

In his report on the thesis, Bultmann wrote that Schmithals' work speaks of his uncommon powers of independent thought. Bultmann often experienced tension in following the precise exposition and strict train of thought. *Im Thick auf die Energie und Originalität des Denkens und die Konsequenz der Gedankenführung könnte man versucht sein, die geradezu als glänzend zu bezeichnen* (Bultmann 1954). Although Bultmann was not in agreement with all the details, the end result convinced him. New light was shed on many texts, and questions previously unanswerable were now answered. Bultmann proposed *magna cum laude* for the thesis.Three German editions of *Die Gnosis in Korinth* appeared. It was also published in English in 1971. Schmithals used the later editions to introduce corrections and additions to the text, and to react to comments his work had elicited.

2.2 LITERARY ANALYSIS

In his thesis, Schmithals (1969:84-94; 1984a:19-20) reaches the conclusion that 1 and 2 Corinthians are the reflection of a lively discussion between Paul and the church in Corinth. According to him, 1 and 2 Corinthians constitute a collection of the essential parts of Paul's letters written to the church in Corinth over a period of six to eight months. In his thesis, Schmithals (1969:84-94) expresses the opinion that Paul wrote six letters to the Corinthians; later Schmithals (1973d) changed it to nine, and even later (Schmithals 1984a:19-85 cf. 1996c:77 footnote 92) to thirteen. He also attempts to reconstruct the original correspondence a reconstruction that includes a literary-critical analysis of the letters and a representation of the course of events.

The guidelines he follows in rearranging the letters are the two themes of polemics against heresy and Paul's vindication of his apostleship. Where these themes are absent or weakly represented, he believes that this indicates earlier correspondence, as Paul initially might have thought that there was a relapse into heathendom, although he later realized that, in fact, there was a specific heresy. When Paul reacts to the changes in the cult and dogma, the heretics do not answer him, but skillfully launch an attack by disputing Paul's apostleship (Schmithals 1984a:21-85).

Schmithals (1973d:280-282; 1984a:21) commences Paul's correspondence with: "I find it praiseworthy that you remember me in everything and hold to the teachings as I have passed them on to you" (1 Cor 11:2). At this stage, Paul does not realize that the tension in the church was caused by the heretics. He is therefore tolerant and constructive in his criticism: "No doubt there have to be differences among you to show which of you are genuine" (1 Cor 11:19).

Schmithals (1984a:28) finds the first indication of heretics in the church in 1 Cor 15:12: "But if it has been preached that Christ has been raised from the dead, how can some of you say that there is no resurrection of the dead?" In the subsequent letter, of which 1 Cor 12:1-3 forms a part, it becomes clear that the heretics in Corinth are *pneumatics*, in other words Gnostics, as they are the ones who can say: "Jesus be cursed" (Schmithals 1984a: 34). The heretics now attack Paul. In his next letter he answers the accusation that he is not preaching words of "wisdom" to the Corinthians: "For Christ did not send me to baptize, but to preach the gospel not with words of human wisdom, lest the cross of Christ lose its power" (1 Cor 1:17; see Schmithals 1984a:48).

Paul devotes the very next letter to his personal apologia by beginning with the following words (cf. Schmithals 1984a:57):

> All men should regard us as servants of Christ and as managers of the secret things of God. It is furthermore required that managers must prove to be faithful. I care very little if I am judged by you or by any human court; indeed, I do not even judge myself.
>
> (1 Cor 4:1-3)

In his last letter, the so-called letter of joy (*Freudenbrief*), Paul can joyfully mention that the church has remained devoted to him and what he taught them (cf. Schmithals 1984a:79): "I did not write to you on account of one who did wrong or on account of the injured party, but to show how devoted to us you are before God. And by this we are greatly comforted" (2 Cor 7:12-13a).

2.3 THE ANTAGONISTS

From the heretics' attack on the apostleship of Paul, one can assume that they wished to reserve to themselves the office of apostle. Paul also mentions this when he calls them "so-called apostles" (2 Cor 11:5). They, like Paul, travelled to do missionary work and also had a new message to deliver to the Christian churches. They did not receive or expect any material support from these churches (Schmithals 1969:108). 2 Cor 11:22: "Are they Hebrews? So am I. Are they Israelites? So am I. Are they Abraham's descendants? So am I". Which leads Schmithals (1969:32) to conclude that these apostles were of Jewish descent. This combination of apostleship and Jewish descent, leads Schmithals (1969:32) to describe their system of convictions as a pre-Christian Jewish Gnosticism (Schmithals 1969:32). "Christ" was the point of contact with the ecclesiastic kerygma. Christ was adopted from the Jewish tradition and pneumaticized in a Christian Gnosis.

2.4 CHRISTOLOGY

To Schmithals (1969:117-122) the exposition of 1 Cor 12:1-3 represented a breakthrough in determining who Paul's antagonists in Corinth were and what their theology entailed. The Corinthians made enquiries regarding the pneumatics, the spiritual people who walked in their midst and who drew a sharp distinction between "Christ according to the Spirit" and "Christ according to the flesh." Paul and the church also knew of the distinction that existed between the incarnate Christ and Christ the Lord. However, they did not regard this distinction as a disagreement; the crucified Jesus is also the risen Lord Jesus. But the pneumatics in Corinth went further and exclaimed: "Jesus be cursed!" The church was unsure whether this was permissible, and in reply to their enquiry in this regard, Paul answers:

> Regarding the pneumatics, brothers, I do not want you to be ignorant. You know that when you were pagans, you were influenced and led astray to dumb idols. Therefore I tell you that no one who is speaking through the Spirit of God says, "Jesus be cursed!" and no one can say, "Jesus is Lord" except through the Holy Spirit.
>
> (1 Cor 12:1-3)

Schmithals presumes that the phrase "Jesus be cursed" was uttered during a church gathering, and furthermore that the church was uncertain whether such a curse could be reconciled with Christianity. The uncertainty of the church may be an indication of the fact that there was a Christian school of thought in which it was quite possible simultaneously to profess Christ and to call Jesus accursed. Which Christian school of thought can incorporate such a paradox? Who can proclaim "Jesus be cursed!" at a meeting of Christians who come together for worship?

In order to answer this question, Schmithals refers to the heresy against which 1 John is directed and which denies that Jesus is the Christ (1 Jn 2:22). A Jew may also deny that Jesus is the Christ. However, unlike the case of the Jews, this heresy does not deny that the Messiah has come. What is denied is that Jesus has come in the flesh: "This is how you can recognize the Spirit of God: He who acknowledges that Jesus is the Christ, who has come in the flesh, is from God" (1 Jn 4:2). The heretics deny Christ's incarnation (cf. Eichholz 1960:13). They accept that Christ came by water, but deny that Christ came "by water and blood" (1 Jn 5:6). In this instance we should regard "blood" as the reality of the physical body, Jesus the son of man. The Gnostics spread this heresy. They believed that the heavenly Christ revealed himself during the baptism in the Jordan and came to live in Jesus' body, without committing himself to the flesh. Christ remains the Savior who comes from above and does not truly become part of the son of man, Jesus.

Schmithals (1969:120) declares that the Gnostics

who were active in Corinth were of the same type as those against whom 1 John polemicizes. During divine worship they could proclaim ecstatically that Jesus was cursed. They passed as Christians because they professed Christ, but they denied that he became human, in other words, came "by blood." And it was this denial they voiced strongly with "Jesus be cursed!"

Schmithals emphasizes that, like Paul, the church in Corinth also distinguished between Christ according to the flesh and Christ according to the Spirit. This distinction featured in their conversations. By "Christ according to the flesh" one should understand the appearance of the Savior (of whom we know very little) on earth. The Savior became flesh; he became human. Christ came by blood. As regards the "spiritual Christ," we should understand the heavenly Savior, as opposed to the earthly form he assumed. Christ came by water.

The Gnostics in Corinth could not accept that there is both unity and continuity between Christ according to the flesh and Christ according to the Spirit; that he came by water and by blood. They took offence at the humanness of Jesus the man. The curse was not directed at the heavenly Christ, but by this curse they wished to deny that the Savior's appearance on earth, the blood, the cross and his humiliation were of any significance. However, this denial of the significance of the cross goes beyond what is acceptable to the church and, thus, the Corinthians question it.

2.5. GNOSIS

When attempting to identify "the different gospel" (2 Cor 11:4) that the antagonists of Paul preach, Schmithals is confronted by the problem that Paul does not use the term *gnosis* but the term *sophia* when he states his basic views in 1 Cor 1:17-2:5. If it were really the Gnostics against whom Paul defined his position, one would expect at least a direct reference to *gnosis*. Initially Schmithals (1969:135, 335) explained the use of *sophia* as being here a more comprehensive term than *gnosis*. Furthermore, Paul wishes to put a name to the whole of the sectarian preaching, and at this stage he was not very well acquainted with the Corinthian heresy (Schmithals 1969:29, 135). On the basis of literary criticism, Schmithals (1982b:68-69; 1984a: 49-50; 1989a:48; 1994a:127-130, 149-154) later came to the conclusion that 1 Cor 1:18-25 and 1:26b-29, 30 were dogmatic texts quoted by Paul, and thus not aimed specifically at the situation in Corinth. In this doctrinal text regarding the "message of the cross," Paul contrasts the Christian point of view with Hellenistic wisdom in general. The actual term used in Corinth to describe this doctrine is *gnosis* or *knowledge*. Schmithals (1969:134-135; 1989a: 480) finds an indication of this in 1 Cor 8:1, in which Paul quotes verbatim from the enquiry by the church: "We all possess the knowledge." Although the text is concerned with the eating of food sacrificed to idols, "we all" are characterized as people who possess "knowledge" 1 Cor 13:8-13 supports Schmithals'(1969:135-136) belief that the Corinthian heretics regarded *gnosis* as the way to salvation. In this passage, Paul shows knowledge to be imperfect, while faith, hope and love, by contrast, are perfect and enduring. Man's salvation is not to be found in knowledge, but in his faith in God. In 1 Cor 8:1 love is also contrasted with knowledge: "Knowledge puffs up, but love builds up."

In order to identify Paul's antagonists in Corinth, 2 Cor 11:4-6 is also of major importance:

> For if someone comes to you and preaches a Jesus other than the Jesus we preached, or if you receive a different spirit from the one you received, or a different gospel from the one you accepted, you put up with it easily enough. Nevertheless, I do not think I am in the least inferior to those super apostles: I may not be a trained speaker, but I do have knowledge. We have made all clear to you.

Schmithals (1969:137) shows that the *gnosis* in verse 6 is the main idea of the intruders in the congregation. The pseudo-apostles in Corinth used the term *gnosis*, and, in that situation, Paul justifies himself by using this very term.

2.6 ANTHROPOLOGY

Paul, in his own words, sketches the circumstances of his writing on the resurrection: "... how can some of you say that there is no resurrection of the dead?" (1 Cor 15:12) The apocalyptic event of the resurrection falls beyond the scope of that which is familiar and humanly possible. Moreover, Schmithals (1969:147; 1994a:57) is certain that Paul was under the impression that the Corinthians had denied all hope of a transcendental reality. The hope these people put in Christ was empty (1 Cor 15:19). Nothing remains but to enjoy the present: "Let us eat and drink, for tomorrow we die!"

Paul, however, was not well informed regarding the views of the Corinthians, as is apparent in 1 Cor 15:29: "What do those who are baptized for the dead expect? If the dead are not raised at all, why are people baptized for them?" There is no sense in practicing vicarious baptism if the dead are not raised. In addition "those who are baptized for the dead" are the same church members who said "that there is no resurrection of the dead." If this were not the same group, Paul would not have been able to contrast their behavior with their views (Schmithals 1969:146).

Using this premise, Schmithals (1969:147) deduces that the Corinthian group disputed the resurrection of the dead, but that they did not regard themselves as being without hope as they had an expectation of spiritual transcendence. Gnosticism comes to the fore in the identification of a group holding these views, because, to the Gnostic, the denial of the resurrection of the body was a fundamental dogma. They saw the physical body as a despicable prison from which the true man had to be set free. The Gnostic does not pin his hopes on the resurrection he is already in possession of his salvation (Schmithals 1969:148-149).

In 2 Cor 4:7 Paul uses the following peculiar image: "But we have this treasure in jars of clay." The apostle's knowledge of the glory of God or of the gospel he preaches is a treasure. The treasure is found in "jars of clay" so that people will know that the power of this preaching is from God and not from the weak apostle. The peculiarity lies in the fact that the weak, concrete, human body contains the apostle's abstract knowledge. Schmithals (1969:151) seeks to find the origin of this expression in the controversy against Gnosticism in which the apostle was engaged. Dualism of body and soul was a characteristic of Gnosticism. From the weakness of the body the fragility of the clay jar, they deduced that man was deficient and inadequate. The jar of clay is fragile in order to show the all-surpassing power of the *pneuma* or spirit. In Gnosticism the all-surpassing power of the human spirit, the essence of man, is preached. They regard the human *pneuma* as their treasure. Paul takes over his opponents' dualism formally and, in terms of the duality of the treasure and the clay jar, the mortal body is according to him the vessel of that which he believes and preaches. However, Paul does not regard the body as the despicable, external part of man. To him it represents the totality of the existence of the human being. Human weakness constitutes no reason for rejecting the human body. It should rather be retained to signify man's dependence on the mercy of God. Salvation coming from outside man that is from God is the all-surpassing power. Human weakness and divine power are supplementary. In stead of the gnostic dualism, Paul preaches a tension-filled unity, consisting of the human being that is allowed to live before God.

Schmithals' exposition of 1 Cor 15, according to which the Gnostics in Corinth deny the resurrection, agrees to their rejection of the mortal body on the grounds of its weakness, as is evident in 2 Cor 4:7. The Gnostics see the body as week and objectionable. Paul's anti-dualistic viewpoint is reflected clearly in the above-mentioned texts, as well as in 2 Cor 12:9-10, which is regarded as a fine example:

> However, he said to me, "My grace is sufficient for you, my power is made perfect in weakness. Therefore I will boast all the more gladly of my weaknesses, so that Christ's power may rest in me. That is why, for Christ's sake, I delight in weaknesses, in insults, in hardships, in persecutions, in difficulties. For when I am weak, then I am strong."

Paul once again emphasizes physical weakness. Schmithals (1969:154) finds no reference whatsoever to the antagonists making an issue of any physical weakness on Paul's side. Nowhere is his illness held against him and the pseudo-apostles do not indicate that they rely on their own physical strength.

If Paul placed such emphasis on the mortal body, in contrast to the intruders in the congregation who despised the body, what then did they regard as the essence of human existence? Schmithals (1969:160-161) finds some indication of the answer to this question in 1 Cor 7:40, where Paul has to reiterate that he possesses the Spirit of God: "... and I think that I too have the Spirit of God." Paul emphasizes the fact that not only they, but he also, has the Spirit. From this, Schmithals deduces that Paul's opponents bore witness that they possess the Spirit of God. In addition, although these few words do not constitute an extensive discussion of pneumatology, they neatly tie in with the gnostic pneumatic dogma, in accordance with which each pneumatic accounts for the *pneuma* part of his being. He regards it as a divine gift to an unworthy soul, which equips him for his task as an apostle.

With regard to 1 Cor 12:1, exegetes do not agree as to whether it should be read as "about spiritual gifts" or "about spiritual people." Schmithals (1969:161-162; 1984a: 40) opts for the latter reading. These words identify a group of inspired pneumatics in Corinth who believed that their possession of *pneuma* distinguished them from others.

Paul neutralizes this privileged position of pneumatics by stating pertinently in 1 Cor 12:9 that faith is also a spiritual gift (Schmithals 1969:163). Faith should not be interpreted as having a different meaning here from Paul's normal usage. If faith is also a spiritual gift, all members of the church are equally inspired; those who preach as well as those who only believe. All these gifts come from one and the same Spirit. Not only those of the pneumatics, but all the spiritual gifts, are useful (Schmithals 1969:162-163, 344).

The pneumatics most outstanding gift was glossolalia or speaking in tongues (Schmithals 1969:164-165). They attributed such importance to this gift because they believed that the *pneuma* excluded all the believer's other spiritual functions, while speaking in tongues was the proof of the *pneuma* at work. Glossolalia served as irrefutable proof of ecstatic religiosity.

Schmithals (1969:166-167) also finds in 2 Cor 10: 1-10 indications of the accusations levelled at Paul by the intruders in Corinth. It is the gnostic pneumatics who say that he is "timid" when he is face to face with them, but "bold" when away; that his letters are readable and worthwhile, but his conduct weak and unimpressive. An expression in Paul's letters, such as "I thank God that I speak in tongues more than all of you" (1 Cor 14:18), makes them acceptable and meaningful to the pneumatics. 1 Cor 2:6-3:3 is another section which would suit the pneumatics. Another pronouncement that would please the gnostics is "Or do you not know your body is a temple of the Holy Spirit, who is in you, whom you have received from God? You do not belong to yourself" (1 Cor 6:19; cf. Schmithals 1969: 221).

In these sections, the apostle becomes a pneumatic to the pneumatics. However, Paul did not, through his conduct, reinforce the impression created by his remarks. In practice, Paul dispensed with ecstatic tokens of his religiosity and, consequently, he made a pitiful and weak impression on them. To the Gnostics, his kerygma, delivered while he was of sound mind, was of a much lower standard than they had expected. The Corinthian anthropology becomes clearly evident between the lines of 2 Cor 4:2-5

(Schmithals 1969:173-174,180):

> We have renounced secret and shameful ways; we do not use deception, nor do we misuse the Word of God. On the contrary, by revealing the truth plainly we commend ourselves to every man's conscience in the sight of God. Even if our Gospel is veiled, it is veiled to those who are perishing. The God of this age has blinded the mind of unbelievers, so that they cannot see the light of the Gospel or the glory of Christ, who is the image of God. For we do not preach ourselves, but Jesus Christ as Lord, and ourselves as your servants for Jesus' sake.

The passage starts off with Paul defending himself against accusations that he abuses the Gospel for financial gain. Paul continues by commending himself as an apostle, which serves as an answer to the claim of the antagonists in the church that they can show letters of recommendation (cf. 2 Cor 3:1). Paul's recommendation is based on the "manifestation of the truth." Schmithals (1969:180) explains that the expression "manifestation of the truth" is directed against the pneumatics' expression "manifestation of the Spirit" (1 Cor 12:7). In verse 3 Paul defends his Gospel and its mystery against the Gnostics' accusation that his Gospel is veiled.

The pneumatics preached their *pneuma* within them. The Gnostic regards his *pneuma* as naturally divine and he discloses this in the hope that the pneumatic spark will ignite the fire in others. The divine *pneuma* imparts an absolute certainty of salvation to its possessor. The *pneuma* leaves the despicable mortal body of a human being in ecstasy and achieves a state of perfection (Schmithals 1969: 169). Unlike the Gnostic, Paul does not take salvation for granted, nor does he regard it objectively. Salvation is more subjective and dependent upon each person's examining the apostle's message in accordance with his or her own conscience. Nor can Paul use external ecstasies to demonstrate his Gospel, and thus he concedes that it is veiled.

However, the Gospel is veiled only to the unbeliever, not to the believer whose conscience has been persuaded by the message. Christ as the complete and divine truth is the content of this message. Moreover, in this way, Paul becomes a servant who does not preach himself, or his *pneuma* as such but Christ.

The Gnostic and his mythological background provide the reason and regarded it as his natural religious duty to praise and commend himself. The *pneuma* should become generally known. Paul is excluded from such praise and commendation: "For it is not the one who commends himself who is approved, but the one whom the Lord commends" (2 Cor 10:18; cf. Schmithals 1969:176).

In 2 Cor 13:3 Paul once again defends his apostleship. He affirms that Christ is speaking through him: "... since you are demanding proof of the Christ speaking in me, who is not weak in dealing with you, but is powerful among you." Schmithals (1969:183) establishes a connection between the "Christ in me" and the identification of Christ and the *pneuma* in 2 Cor 3:17: "... the Lord is the Spirit (*pneuma*)." In terms of the gnostic myth, the *pneuma* forms but a small portion of the cosmic Christ. In prehistoric times, these small portions came to rest in the mortal bodies of the pneumatics. This Christ is setting free his imprisoned particles (Schmithals 1969:185). Thus the "Christ speaking in me" is the *pneuma* which has come to realize that it has been set free. The ecstatic speaking in tongues is proof of the *pneuma*'s liberation (Schmithals 1969:183). "Christ in me" is the same, although seen from another angle, as "to be from Christ," which is found in 2 Cor 10:7: "... if anyone is confident that he belongs to Christ, he should at the same time consider that we belong to Christ just as much as he." In Gnostic terminology, "to be from Christ" means the same as being aware of the *pneuma* part of "Christ in me." Nevertheless, to Paul this expression simply means "to be a Christian" (Schmithals 1969:186-187). From the insight thus gained, Schmithals (1969:188-199) explains the so-called part of Christ. "What I mean is this: One of you says, 'I follow Paul,' another, 'I follow Apollos,' another, 'I follow Cephas'; still another, "I follow Christ'" (1 Cor 1:12). These words do not denote the existence of four parties. The main principle in this verse is that the apostle group, Paul, Apollos and Cephas, is placed in opposition to the Christ group. The chiastic combination with the subsequent verse leads Schmithals to such a deduction: "Is Christ divided? Was Paul crucified for you? Were you baptized in the name of Paul?" Paul uses the upliftment and work done in the church by Apollos, Cephas and himself as a united front against the gnostic Christ group. The gospel preached by man is in opposition to the "Christ speaking in me."

2.7 ETHICS

With regard to the eating of meat sacrificed to idols, the church in Corinth is of the opinion that they possess sufficient knowledge about it to act accordingly: "We know that we all possess knowledge" (1 Cor 8:1). When using these words, they do not take into account that there may be those amongst them who do not possess this knowledge. In addition, it is typical of Gnosticism to avoid placing any restrictions on such freedom. It could be that their eyes were only opened to the fact that the weak were also amongst them, when Paul directly refuted their claim that all possessed knowledge with the words: "But not everyone knows this" (1 Cor 8:7). Knowledge is not a reflection of a state of affairs. However, one should constantly be made aware of the necessity of taking one's fellow-human being into consideration, and this should be maintained during interaction. Schmithals (1969:217) is of the opinion that the majority of the church accepted Paul's point of view, but that, initially, their call upon knowledge is typically that of Gnosticism with regard to form and content. Schmithals concludes that the true Gnostic remains in the background with regard to this matter. In an earlier letter, where Paul warns against idolatry, they came more clearly to the fore (1 Cor 10:14-22). They participated in the cultic meals offered to idols. From Paul's argument it becomes clear that he is speaking to people who deliberately participate in heathen cultic meals in order to demonstrate that the demons have been conquered. This is a typical gnostic attitude (Schmithals 1969:214). Through these gestures, the Gnostics aim to demonstrate their power. Paul, however, warns that they should not see themselves as being stronger than God is (1 Cor 10:22). The church subscribes to Paul's view by not participating in heathen cultic meals, but now require further information regarding the everyday, noncultic eating of meat sacrificed to idols (1 Cor 8 1).

In addition to the motivation that Gnostics dominate the idols and that they may therefore eat of the sacrificial meal, they despise the mortal body, so that nothing physical can threaten their salvation. Contempt for the body and immunity from demons are also combined in the gnostic practice of prostitution or sexual immorality. In 1 Cor 6:12-20, where Paul deals with this matter, he starts with one of his antagonists' slogans: "Everything is permissible for me." This adage gives expression to the gnostic consciousness of the insignificance of the body and of the pneumatic's power over demons (Schmithals 1969:219).

In the remarkable passage of 1 Cor 6:13-14, the eating of meat sacrificed to idols is combined with sexual immorality: "Food for the stomach and the stomach for food but God will destroy them both. The body is not meant for sexual immorality, but for the Lord, and the Lord for the body. By his power God raised the Lord from the dead, and he will raise us also." The Corinthian Gnostics taught that one could eat everything and practice all types of sexual intercourse without experiencing any remorse, because both the body and the stomach are transient. At a later stage, in 1 Cor 10:28-30, Paul considers the matter in depth:

> But if anyone says to you, "this has been offered in sacrifice," then do not eat it, both for the sake of the person who told you and for conscience's sake. Naturally I mean the other person's conscience, not yours, because my free-

> dom cannot be judged by another's conscience. If I take part in the meal with thankfulness, why am I denounced because of something I thank God for?

At the time when he wrote 1 Cor 6:13-14, however, Paul was unaware of the gnostic background and the Gnostics' views on sacrificial meat, thus he still concedes this point. However, with regard to sexual immorality, he cannot go along with the view that the body is transient and therefore ethically neutral. In contrast, he states that the body is raised from the dead, and therefore immortal (Schmithals 1969:220). Schmithals (1969:222) see 1 Cor 7:1-24 as Paul's reaction to the enquiry by the church, which probably read as follows: "Having sex with a prostitute is forbidden; does this also mean that one should refrain from sexual intercourse within marriage, or even dissolve the marriage and remain unmarried?" In principle Paul is in favor of the unmarried state and abstinence, but in practice this is impossible as not all people possess this gift. The insignificant issue of the head covering which women must wear also gains importance when it features in the controversy between Paul and the pneumatics. The pneumatics demanded the abolition of head covering for women because differences between men and women become irrelevant if the *pneuma* is seen as the essence of a human being. From 1 Cor 11:10, "For this reason, and because of the angels, the woman ought to have a sign of authority on her head." Schmithals (1969:229-230) concludes that the head covering served as a repellent to demonic angel forces. The pneumatic who possesses knowledge, however, has no reason to wear such a head covering as she has been safeguarded against demonic forces. For his part, Paul cannot prove the need for wearing a head covering. After a disappointing attempt, he appeals to the church to co-operate: "Such practice is unknown to us" (1 Cor 11:16). Schmithals explains that the compulsion with which the pneumatics campaigned for the abolition of the head covering alerted Paul to the fact that this was a different gospel being preached. In Paul's view, freedom of belief is lost when the head covering is no longer worn. This freedom should be upheld when concrete decisions are made (Schmithals 1969:228-229). The fundamental differences between the sexes are not at issue, because these differences have been set aside "in the Lord." Paul can even use the gnostic terminology to declare: "There is neither Jew nor Greek, slave nor free, male nor female; for you are all one in Christ" (Gal. 3:28; cf. Schmithals 1969:226-227). While, at the outset, Paul did not object to the conduct of women in the church (1 Cor 11:2-16), he nevertheless later (1 Cor 14:34) invokes tradition in order to silence them. According to Schmithals' (1969:231-232) exposition, Paul realized only later that, on the basis of their libertine beliefs, the Gnostics were agitating that women should take part in worship, and that he wished to prevent this. Thus, it would be non-Pauline for Paul merely to state that women should remain silent in church. This was not his view of Christian freedom. At a later stage Schmithals (1996a:77) came to the conclusion that the editor of the main Pauline letters wrote 1 Cor 14:33b-36.

2.8 ESCHATOLOGY

With regard to the exegesis of the difficult passage in 2 Cor 5:1-10, Schmithals (1969:247-248; 1984d) indicates that Paul is not giving an explanation of what he understood anthropology or eschatology to be. The exegete should not take this to mean that the apostle is voluntarily giving an account of what he believes. His statements are largely dictated by the arguments of his antagonists. His opening words are, "We know." In other words, he is referring to a doctrine that has already been dealt with in the church. This older material has now been challenged and he has to defend it.

Initially Paul was under the impression that the pseudo-apostles in Corinth taught that when we die, all is done and all is lost, because they denied the resurrection. Without the resurrection, eternal life is impossible. However, if this were truly the point of view in Corinth, he only needed to refer to his words in 1 Cor 15. Yet in 2 Cor 5:1-10 he treats the theme of "the eternal" in such a way that it becomes evident that his opponents also subscribe to an "eternal life," even though they deny the resurrection. His antagonists believed in an eternal life in which the true man would be set free from the dwelling of the body he lived in. Thus, the resurrection of the body was quite unnecessary. A heavenly dwelling need not be prepared, as eternal life is possible without a body. Paul regards eternal life without being clothed in a body as a contradiction which he ironically describes as follows in 2 Cor 5:3: "... because when we are clothed, we will not be found naked in eternity." The nakedness associated with being without a physical body (bodilessness), which the Gnostics look forward to, Paul sees as nothing less than death (Schmithals 1969: 251). Paul neither knew nor understood the dualism of the Gnostics. He did not realize that eternal life as presented by the Gnostics arises from the system as a whole. He merely compared their representation of eternal life with his own. He yearned to be clothed with a new body in the hereafter and presumed the same longing in his opponents. He is, however, now informed that they, in fact, expect a bodiless eternal life. He finds it absurd to talk about a bodiless life as this is equivalent to death. Paul indicates this absurdity, but the rest of his words do not find their mark. He cannot see eye-to-eye with his opponents because their views on a bodiless eternal life differ. They see it as life while he regards it as death (Schmithals 1969:251). Paul did realize that his opponents put forward the theological argument that the weakness of the body precludes any physical form in eternal life. In contrast to this, he emphasizes the quality and characteristics of the new body: "... an eternal house in heaven, not built by human hands" (2 Cor 5:1). While living in our "earthly tent" we sigh and long for our heavenly dwelling. The oppressiveness of the earthly dwelling serves as proof to Paul that the longing for the heavenly expansiveness is justified. Our desire is enough to entitle us to be delivered from the earthly and enter our heavenly dwelling (Schmithals 1969:250).

What Paul actually had to prove was that a bodiless life, such as the Gnostics represented, was impossible if he wished to do justice to the true point of view in Corinth. Schmithals (1969:252) is of the opinion that he does not go into the matter because he is unable to prove the impossibility of something which he simply cannot imagine. An inconceivable bodiless life need not be denied because its inconceivability already serves as a denial. Should Paul attempt to prove that life without a body is impossible, his opponents would accuse him of a lack of *gnosis*. They would say that he is unable to make such a representation due to ignorance.

In verse 6 Schmithals (1969:225-256) finds further proof that Paul's arguments were dictated by the pseudo-apostles: "Therefore we are always confident and know that as long as we are at home in the body we are away from the Lord." Paul is no longer thinking of the mortal body, which, without a pause, is swallowed up by the heavenly body. He has made the gnostic expression his own, wherein true man leaves his body behind in order to be with the Lord. According to this terminology, he emphasizes the "not yet" of eschatological anticipation, in contrast to the Gnostic's over-extended eschatological consciousness. We still live within the mortal body, far from the Lord. The Gnostics saw themselves as people who ostensibly lived in mortal bodies, but who were, in fact, already living in the Lord, as part of the cosmic body of Christ.

Schmithals (1969:257-258) explains that Paul should not be presented as someone who was uncertain about man's physical being. He did not hold two different views on this. Paul's pronouncements should be seen against the background of his polemics with the Gnostics. He deals initially, in 2 Cor 5:1-5, with the dualistic desire to be rid of the mortal body. Thereafter, in verses 6-8, he deals with their arrogance, acting as if they were already living in Christ. He accepts his opponents' point of view in order to prevent being rejected right from the outset. Here he is able to do this because, unlike in 2 Cor 5:1-5, it is not the point of departure that is important. Using this commonality, he opposes the gnostic hauteur, which he found particularly annoying. In 2 Cor 5:9-10 Paul applies the preceding and addresses the libertinism of the Corinthians. Even though they might already be with the Lord, they should still strive to be acceptable before the Lord. This naturally applies also to those who are not yet with the Lord. We must all appear before the judgement seat of Christ. Schmithals (1969:26) remarks that this refreshing of the memory with regard to people's responsibility during their earthly life fell on deaf ears in the case of the Gnostics, because they no longer took into account the appearance before the judgement seat of Christ as they were already "in Christ."

2.9 ECCLESIOLOGY

Schmithals (1969:4-42) also employs three steps to explain the structure of pre-Christian Gnosticism: a heavenly being (1) becomes matter, (2) and there he strives to, (3) once again ascend to heaven.

Every person or pneumatic is involved in the struggle to be liberated from matter and to realize himself. Each forms part of the *dunamis* that has to be liberated from matter.

It is said that Dositheus, the tutor of Simon the Sorcerer, who regarded himself as a heavenly being, presented himself as "Christ." Simon, who was called "The Great Power of God" (Acts 8:10), also received the title "Christ" from his followers. They took over the title from the Jews, but relinquished the Jewish content (Schmithals 1969:41). They used the title "Christ" to describe the celestial being of light or the gnostic primordial man. Not only was He born of woman, but also He had appeared previously and will appear again, while He also is presented as one who has been born and is still to be born. Christ is not a specific person, but as *dunamis* he is divided among many people for all time. He has committed himself to matter and must be liberated. He awakens the dormant particles of power so that they may be released (Schmithals 1969:45-46). He was also identified as *pneuma* during the pre-Christian period (Schmithals 1969:53). It is against the background of this mythological-gnostic terminology that expressions such as "Christ in us" and "we in Christ" should be viewed. "Christ in us" describes the division of Christ into many *pneuma* particles, while "we in Christ" places the emphasis on the collecting of the scattered particles of power. Paul, however, simply uses "in Christ" and "of Christ" to describe the believers without the constraints of mythological representations (Schmithals 1969:59-60). The celestial Christ-primordial man was also often represented as a cosmic body. The individual *pneuma* particles are used to construct the limbs of the body. Schmithals (1969:60-61; 1994a: 160-161, 184) notes the remarkable formulation used by Paul in 1 Cor 12:12: "The body is a unit, though it is made up of many parts; and though all its parts are many, they form one body. So it is with Christ." Although Paul writes "Christ" he means "church." Schmithals does not doubt the gnostic background to this identification of Christ and the church. Yet Paul is not a party to the beliefs of the Gnostics, (because according to the theology of his conversion) man is not a natural part of this body, but only as a result of personal obedience (Schmithals 1969:62). A comparable passage is to be found in Ephesians 4:11-13:

> It was he who gave some to be apostles, some to be prophets, some to be evangelists, and some to be pastors and teachers, to prepare (God's people) for works of service, so that the body of Christ may be built up until we all reach unity in the faith and in the knowledge of the Son of God and become a complete man, attaining to the whole measure of the fullness of Christ.

According to the interpretation of Schmithals (1969:64), complete man is the primordial man who has reached the fullness of salvation. He is thus equated with Christ. In 1 Cor 10:16b-17, Paul quotes from the gnostic tradition by using a word related to a meal of bread which reminds one of the expression "we in Christ" and "Christ in us": "And the bread that we break: does it not indicate a participation in the body of Christ? Because there is one loaf, we, who are many, are one body, for we all partake of the one loaf." Schmithals (1969:234; 1994a:214-215) is certain that this formula, in gnostic terms, means that the breaking of the bread points at the division of the body of Christ, the primordial man, and that the unity of the bread is indicative of the origin and destination of the *pneuma* particles. Although this reference to the breaking of bread has its origin in the gnostic world, the use of the sacraments is essentially foreign to true Gnosticism. They regard the body as despicable matter. Consequently, a genuine gnostic cult act cannot be based on body and blood. The existence of another sacramental tradition in Gnosticism can only be attributed to the fact that the Gnostics were unable to remain pure in the face of the syncretistic tendencies of the time (Schmithals 1969:233-235).

In respect of the Eucharist, Paul emphasizes that he passed on to the church what he had received from the Lord. This implies that the church partook of bread and wine in a liturgical form. Although the bread was most probably more than the little piece we get during communion today, it was never meant to be a filling meal. Normal eating and drinking must take place at home (Schmithals 1969:238). Reports from the church indicate that a new practice was introduced which involved the replacement of the liturgical meal by a normal meal: When you come together, it is not to eat the Lord's Supper, for when you eat your own food, each of you goes ahead without waiting for anybody else. One remains hungry, another gets drunk. Don't you have homes to eat and drink in?" (1 Cor 11:20-22).

Schmithals (1969:239-341) bases his theory and exposition on the original interpretation that the "own food" was intended to dishonor and desecrate the "Lord's Supper." Such were the extremes. The new supper was not to be any different from a normal meal. This change from the "Lord's Supper" to a normal meal fits in well with the gnostic approach. The Gnostics could not reconcile themselves to a cultic meal through which the death of the crucified, Jesus of the flesh, is preached. They do participate in the Lord's Supper, but in their own way, and probably in order to express their contempt for this transmitted tradition (Schmithals 1969:241).

In 1 Cor 15:29, Paul refers to vicarious baptism, according to which someone has himself baptized in place of an unbaptized deceased person. This was never put into practice in the church, but it was a practice of the Gnostics. They adopted it from the mystery cults, which is simple to explain in view of the fact that the Gnostics were concerned about those who died without *gnosis*. Through the magical act the baptism for the deceased their lack of knowledge is supplemented, and they are liberated from demonic powers to be led into fullness. Schmithals (1969:245) notes that, in terms of gnostic belief, baptism could only be performed with regard to the deceased, because for the living *gnosis* is their salvation and baptism is nothing more than a reflection of such salvation.

In the Corinthian church, it was a foregone conclusion that the authority of the apostle was a necessity of church life. The issue, however, was Paul's right to apostleship. Schmithals (1969:266-267) feels that Paul was not being set off against Apollos and Peter. He does not refer to them with the derisive "super-apostles" (2 Cor 11:5; 12:11) and the cautionary "false apostles, deceitful workmen, masquerading as apostles of Christ" (2 Cor 11:13). The supreme apostles are the pneumatics themselves who, through their ecstatic productions, are able to provide miraculous proof of a *pneuma* that has been awakened: their criterion for a true apostle. To them apostleship is not human strength or power, but the divine *pneuma* that is at work in them. Paul is challenged to react and he quite reluctantly comes to "visions and revelations of the Lord" (2 Cor 12:1). Through this he wishes to show that he too experienced ecstasies. Yet it remains unfamiliar territory, and he consequently adds that he does not wish to be evaluated on the basis of his great revelations, but on the basis of what anyone "sees me do or hears from me" (2 Cor 12:6). Even when Paul describes the "things that mark an apostle" in gnostic terms, he understands them as referring to the miraculous workings of the word: The "things that mark an apostle" signs, wonders and miracles were done among you with great perseverance" (2 Cor 12:12; cf. Schmithals 1969:267-268). Paul does not preach about himself, or about his *pneuma*, but preaches the word, the divine grace that comes to people from outside himself. The gnostic arch-apostles also tried to attack Paul's person by accusing him of planning to use the collection taken for the church in Jerusalem for his personal use. Paul creates the impression that the church does not support him, but he covertly makes use of the collection for this purpose (Schmithals 1969: 266). Paul refers to this in 2 Cor 12:16: "Be that as it may, I have not been a burden to you." Yet, "crafty fellow that I am," "I caught you by trickery!" Paul worried unnecessarily about his position in the church, because they did not believe the accusations levelled against him and supported him to the end (Schmithals 1969:100-101):

> However, God, who comforts the downcast, comforted us by the coming of Titus, and not only by his coming but also by the comfort you had given him. He told us about your longing for me, your deep sorrow about what had happened, how you are defending me, so that my joy was greater than ever.
>
> (2 Cor 7:6-7)

From Paul's remark "since you are zealous for spiritual gifts" (1 Cor 14:12), Schmithals concludes that forms of ecstatic devotion were new to the church in Corinth. Instead of being so enthusiastic about spiritual revelations, Paul would prefer that they be satisfied with the dogma that they, together with all the other churches, had received (Schmithals 1969:269-270).

The Gnostics are the driving force behind this devotion to the Spirit (Schmithals 1969:268-270). This is clearly evident in 1 Cor 14:37: "If anyone thinks himself to be a prophet or spiritual, let him acknowledge that the things which I write to you are the commandments of the Lord." The pneumatic should not be seen as belonging to a category different from that of the prophets. In Corinth the gnostic pneumatics acted as prophets. By virtue of his aroused *pneuma*, every pneumatic is capable of being a prophet in the church and awakening the *pneuma*: "Awake, you who sleep, arise from the dead" (Eph. 5:14; cf. Schmithals 1969:261). The Gnostics called these prophets, who were sent out to preach the gospel, apostles. Paul checks the Gnostics by emphasizing that the interests of the church and its advancement should be the test of spiritual gifts (1 Cor 14:12). He distinguishes between speaking in tongues, where a speaker loses control over his *pneuma* and cannot be understood, and prophecies, where the prophet speaks intelligibly. Only intelligible utterances can be allowed in church services. Schmithals (1969:270) remarks that this offers Paul only a temporary solution of the problem, because a gnostic prophet could also be quite intelligible when uttering the imprecation "Jesus be cursed!" What is indisputable, however, is that Paul wishes to dampen the Spirit in Corinth, as he explains that ecstatic devotion is not the most important gift, but that all spiritual gifts are equally important. To stress this point even more, he regards love as of greater importance than speaking in tongues or prophecy.

2.10 PAUL AND THE HISTORICAL JESUS

Bultmann always had 2 Cor 5:16 in readiness when explaining the problem of the historical Jesus: "So from now on we regard no one from a purely human point of view. Though we once regarded Christ in this way, yet now we know him no longer in terms of the flesh."

Bultmann also interpreted this text as deliberately ignoring the historical Jesus (cf. Valeton 1907:11-12). Paul is not interested in Jesus' personality because this would mean a dual knowledge "in terms of the flesh." In the first place Christ would be known in terms of the flesh as an available world phenomenon. Secondly this knowledge would lead to a physical understanding, in other words, merely taking into account what is worldly and available (Bultmann 1972b:206-207; 1980:239, 294). Neither the personality nor the supposed words of Jesus are of importance any longer, because, according to Paul, he is no longer the messenger or proclaimer, he has become the content of the proclaimed message. Now all that matters is that he specifically, is the messenger of God with the decisive word. His cross, his fate, is the decisive saving act of God (Bultmann 1972b:205). His cross is not just a finalized occurrence, it has the character of an event. In other words, it is proclaimed as God laying claim to man: "My grace is sufficient for you." In examining Paul's use of language, Schmithals (1969:296) concludes that Paul is not referring to the historical Jesus, drawn biographically, when he says "in terms of the flesh." When using the expression concerning Christ "in terms of the flesh" or "Jesus" Paul means the appearance on earth of the Savior, the fact that he existed. This fact of his existence does not include all kinds of biographical details, but it implies that Christ with his wounds (Gal. 6:17) and his resurrection (Rom 8:11) is the essence and foundation of the Christian faith (Schmithals 1969: 124). When using the expression Christ "in terms of the flesh," Paul describes the eschatological qualified fact of Jesus' existence exactly. This was also of great importance to Bultmann. This was the Christ known by Paul.

Now Schmithals tries to find out why Paul says that he does not wish to know this fact. How could Paul write: "So from now on we regard no one from a purely human point of view. Though we once regarded Christ in this way, yet now we know him no longer in terms of the flesh." Particularly when seen against the background of his vehement struggle against the gnostic heresy, it is impossible that he should make this statement. As opposed to the people who could shout in ecstatic rapture, "Cursed be Jesus," he stressed the fact that he was proclaiming Jesus as the crucified one. He does not wish to abandon this Jesus, who as to his human nature was a descendant of David (Rom 1:3; Schmithals 1969:294-295).

The conflict between Pauline theology and the verse in 2 Cor 5:16 forces Schmithals to seek another solution. He explains the verse as a gnostic comment. This gnostic addition implies that no one is known by his or her human existence, not even Christ. The despicable human body, as dwelling of the *pneuma*, receives no recognition. "As Gnostics, we who have been absorbed as *pneuma* particles in the Divine *Pneuma* Christ, no longer acknowledge the natural human being. Even though Paul introduced us to the crucified Jesus, he does not concern us at all."

Schmithals says that Bultmann did not find the explanation he gives in the manuscript of his thesis, that this verse is a gnostic comment, acceptable. Bultmann insisted that it be removed from the thesis, as it could influence the adjudication of the thesis. Schmithals complied and published it separately. Later on he included it as an addendum to his published thesis. Bultmann saw Paul's relationship to the historical Jesus as Paul's specific theological point of view. This verse served as support for his conclusion. Schmithals felt that the meaning of the verse was weakened in this way. Bultmann's attitude and criticism could not convince him that his explanation had no merit. With his newly found insight, Schmithals could not accept that Paul initiated or was alone in his relationship to the historical Jesus. Because Paul was not interested in the "how" of Jesus' life, but in "the fact that" he lived does not distinguish him from Peter and James. If the truth be told, at that stage Schmithals (1972b:49) thought that Paul had the same relationship to the historical Jesus as the whole of the New Testament, barring the Synoptic Gospels. We are not dealing with a specific theological point of view of Paul, but with a fundamental tradition, which can be seen in Paul's writings and which he shares.

Schmithals did not differ from Bultmann's basic views on the historical Jesus and the kerygmatic Christ. In reality he came to the conclusion that he could extend the basis on which it was founded, from Paul to the whole of early Christianity. The only material opposing Bultmann's fundamental point of view, were the Synoptic Gospels. They were interested in the details of the earthly Jesus. Schmithals (1972b:49) goes so far as to call the historical Jesus tradition as well as the Synoptic Gospels apocryphal. With his inaugural address on 9th May 1962 "Paulus und der historische Jesus" Schmithals accepts it as his life's work to reflect on the problem of the historical Jesus and the proclaimed Jesus. This is the ultimate theological question.

2.11 CLOSING REMARKS

Schmithals' remarks on the particular case of Corinth could later be expanded to form an historical concept that describes an era in the history of proto-Christianity. He reaches the conclusion that proto-Christianity theology cannot be depicted without taking the gnostic school of thought into consideration as motivation. The spiritual struggle between Christianity and Gnostic forms is an essential part of the history of early-Christianity.

Schmithals' finding on 2 Cor 5:16 was his first decisive step in the direction that he considered being the main problem of the theology of the New Testament. At first it looked like a windfall. He reaches the conclusion that Paul was not as alone in his theologizing as was generally accepted.

CHAPTER 3

POINTERS IN THE THEOLOGICAL UNDERSTANDING OF THE NEW TESTAMENT

3.1 INTRODUCTION

A serious need exists among students and other persons for a pointer in New Testament theology. The difficulty experienced in this area is clearly evident from Engelbrecht's (1982a:59) compassionate remark: "Blessed is also the exegete if he knows exactly what he is doing." Themes that are related to this accountability also form the basis of the lectures that Schmithals presented over the years. By these means the student is introduced to the history of the subject and the problems that have been experienced, as well as the solutions offered.

The main problem of New Testament Theology is the relationship between the proclaiming of Jesus and the proclaiming of the apostles. A whole chapter in this book (Chapter 5) is devoted to this problem. At this stage it is relevant only in so far as can be expected from a preliminary guideline. Other problems concerning the New Testament can be explained by means of the expression "New Testament theology." "New Testament" refers to historical documents that have to be interpreted through historical-critical exegesis. "Theology" refers to the fact that the New Testament is God's Word. The historical documents are proof of the divine truth. The problems of New Testament theology are interwoven with the fact that an historical method is applied in order to formulate a dogmatic truth. In what follows, an outline is presented and terminological interpretations are given of how Schmithals points the way to the theology of the New Testament. It is done with the conviction that these burning issues will force the reader to take part in the process. It is Schmithals' ideal to inspire theologizing.

3.2 THE GOSPEL

According to the oldest textual witnesses in 1 Cor 2:1, Paul describes his kerygma or proclamation as "the testimony about God": "And when I came to you, brothers, I did not come with eloquence or words of wisdom as I proclaimed the testimony about God to you." The description "testimony about God" for that which Paul proclaims was not fixed, but could vary. In the old Greek manuscripts the variation "God's mystery" appears. Schmithals (1982b:71) gains the impression that Paul did not, in fact, use a set expression to describe the "divine truth," "message of God," "religious testimony." It is as if the old scribes knew that other terms could be used to refer to the same issue. Paul's proclaimed "testimony about God" lays claim to the fact that it fulfills human expectations and provides the reason for existence. The "divine testimony" is able to lead us to a comprehensive self-understanding. In addition, it is in support of this claim, Paul continues, that he proclaims Jesus Christ, and him the crucified. A more common name for the declared Christian message than "testimony about God" is "gospel." It is the gospel that is proclaimed, and the gospel that is believed. Schmithals (1976b:145-146; 1979a:99; 1988a:376) points out that although the message may be unfolded in a variety of ways, the gospel is focused on the one unifying truth (Mark 1:14-15): After John was put in prison, Jesus went into Galilee, proclaiming the gospel of God. "The time has come," he said. "The kingdom of God is near. Repent and believe the gospel." "The time has come .... The kingdom of God is near," bears testimony to the sole content of the gospel.

From the above, it can be deduced that the New

Testament clearly focuses on a specific theme. This theme may be indicated by means of the words the "gospel," the "kerygma" or the "Biblical dogma," and shows that which is the truly Christian, or the subject of the Christian confession and preaching. Schmithals (1972g:188-189) regards the expression of this theme as the task of theology.

The first question to be raised with regard to this theme is how has this theme been empowered to be theme or dogma? On whose authority? How is the gospel revealed to bring one to the knowledge that this is the gospel? If the historical course is taken into account, it is evident that the New Testament does not have the authority to create the gospels for Proto-Christianity (Schmithals 1970a:44-45). When Paul writes his section of the New Testament, he already does so on the basis of the authority of the gospel. He himself received the fundamental confession (Schmithals 1972a:17; 1988a:261-262). The gospel precedes the New Testament; the theme comes before its unfolding.

Another possible source for the authority of the gospel is formulated as "he who speaks by the Spirit of God proclaims the gospel." According to this view endowment with the Spirit also lends authority to the message. Sin against the Spirit is a contradiction of the content of the message (cf. Mark 3:29). However, it soon became clear that the Spirit alone cannot serve as criterion for the gospel. Paul puts this experience into words: "Therefore I declare to you that no one who is speaking by the Spirit of God says: 'Jesus be cursed,' and no one can say: 'Jesus is Lord,' except by the Holy Spirit." (1 Cor 12:3) At the same time he states that the acknowledgement "Jesus is Lord" is the criterion used to distinguish between the Holy Spirit and other spirits. And in 1 John 4:1-2 the warning is also sounded that the spirits should be tested according to the criterion of the confession (Schmithals 1974b:105; 1979a:713; 1994a:295):

> Dear friends, do not believe every one who declares that he has the Spirit of God, but test the spirits to see whether they are from God, be-

> cause many false prophets have gone out into the world. This is how you recognize the Spirit of God: anyone who acknowledges that Jesus Christ has come in the flesh has the Spirit who comes from God.

The fact that Jesus in person, his message, his doctrine and his action makes a case for the gospel, is seen as another possible source for the authority of the gospel. The divine truth at issue is the divine truth as perceived by Jesus. In contrast to this view, it is noteworthy that Paul seldom quotes Jesus' words. In 1 Cor 7:10 he quotes the prohibition of divorce, "a wife must not separate from her husband," as a saying of Jesus. Yet it is quite clear that this citation revolves around a fringe phenomenon or question and not the determination of the essence of the gospel. An example containing all the possibilities of proving that Paul was indeed dependent upon Jesus' message, is the use of Jesus' words at the institution of the Lord's Supper (1 Cor 11:23-25; cf. Lichtenstein 1950/51:34):

> For I received from the Lord what I also passed on to you: The Lord Jesus, on the night he was betrayed, took bread, and when he had given thanks, he broke it and said: "This is my body, which is for you; do this in remembrance of me." In the same way, after supper he took the cup, saying: "This cup is the new covenant in my blood; do this, whenever you drink it, in remembrance of me."

Schmithals (1973b:222; cf. 1994a:206-207) notes that this is as far as quoting Jesus goes. In the very next verse it is not Jesus' sayings but Paul's words about Jesus that are quoted: "For whenever you eat this bread and drink this cup, you proclaim the Lord's death until he comes." Here Paul quotes the traditional, ecclesiastical interpretation of the Eucharist in which the church speaks of the "Lord's death" and of the fact that "he comes." The church that celebrates the Eucharist proclaims Jesus' death, that means that Jesus crucified is the basis of human beings' salvation. The "(received) from the Lord" is replaced by the more authoritative church tradition of an interpretation of Christ. It is Schmithals' (1972a:22) point of view that the preaching and the gospel of Jesus do not serve as the authority for the gospel of the church. The gospel is not based on the proclamation by Jesus himself, as he proclaimed it, but is to be found in the proclamation of Jesus, that is that Jesus himself is proclaimed by others. The criterion for the gospel is the church proclaiming "the Lord's death." The church does not believe as Jesus did, but believes in him.

If there is a difference between Jesus' proclaiming and the Jesus proclaimed by the church, we will have to know who the proclaimed Jesus is, the one proclaimed by the church. The church holds this proclaimed Jesus before us in its confessions of faith (Schmithals 1972a:12; 1994a:295). The best known description of the Jesus we believe in is to be found in the Apostles' Creed (*Apostolicum*) which dates back to the fifth century and reads as follows:

> I believe in Jesus Christ, his only Son, our Lord; who was conceived by the Holy Spirit, was born of the virgin Mary; suffered under Pontius Pilate, was crucified, dead and buried, he descended into hell; on the third day he rose again from the dead, ascended into heaven, and sits on the right hand of God, the Almighty Father, from thence he shall come to judge the living and the dead.

Although this is the best known description of the proclaimed Christ, it is by no means the oldest. If the ecclesiastical confession professes the Christ in whom we believe, the beginnings of the church will no doubt provide examples of such confessions. Faith means that one is in agreement with this confession. The confession was used to teach people before they were baptized and taken up in the church. The confession of faith serves as criterion for the message delivered during the church service, the yardstick of the gospel. In 1 Cor 15:3-5 Paul cites a confession of the church which is even older than the New Testament: "For what I received I passed on to you as of first importance: 'Christ died for our sins according to the Scriptures and was buried; he was raised on the third day according to the Scriptures, and appeared to Peter and then to the twelve.'"

Schmithals (1972b:17) indicates that the main thrust of this confession is not about what Jesus himself believed and proclaimed, but about the Jesus in whom the church believes and whom it proclaims. In this confession, the gospel of Christ's work of salvation is expressed: Christ died for our sins. To this we may add the general view of what the church proclaims, namely that it is concerned with the remission of sins. Remission of sins enables people to let go of the idea that they themselves are the basis and source of life and to live by the grace of God. Schmithals (1972b:20-21) explains that we should understand the term "sin" as people's attempt at justifying themselves before God, at realizing themselves without God. The formulae of the ecclesiastical confessions serve as criteria for the gospel in the sense that the act of salvation has become message and cannot reach people except through formularies (Schmithals 1988a:261-262). However, these Proto-Christian formulae were not regarded as final and eternal formulations of the Christian truth. This truth is to reach fulfillment through human existence and consequently the best words need to be chosen each time to express the dogma. If the expression of the Christian truth is not clear enough to be understood every time it will lose its character of being a message intended to achieve something with people. In order to illustrate this train of thought, Rom 3:25 can be used. A Proto-Christian formula appears, which Paul not only quotes and repeats, but also interprets to define the dogma more explicitly. Schmithals (1988a:121; 1994:100) reconstructs the formula as follows: "... which God openly presented as a symbol of atonement in his blood as a demonstration of his justice by the remission of sins." The formula is based upon the widely held opinion that there should be atonement for guilt and confesses that the death of Jesus creates the reality of remission of sins. According to the formula, human guilt results from the transgression of God's commandments, the individual sins of habit. Paul finds such a "moralistic" concept of sin too restrictive to serve as the answer of the catechumen or the church to the introduction by the catechist or liturgist: "We believe in Jesus Christ ...." From his own theological vocabulary Paul inserts "through the faith" between the phrases "as symbol of atonement" and "in his blood." Paul also adds his own words to the phrase "the remission of sins" to have it read as follows: "... the remission of sins committed beforehand during God's forbearance." The "sins committed beforehand" refer to all transgressions that took place before Christ's act of salvation. God's justice is linked to the remission of sins, yet it does not say enough about his justice as it is applied to the past. God patiently tolerated sin and now these sins have been forgiven. However, God's justice also applies to both the present and the future. Not only did God forgive, but he also bestowed his justification on those who believe. Therefore Paul continues: "he did it to demonstrate his justice in the present time, so as to be just and the one who justifies those who have faith in Jesus."

According to Paul's exposition, the remission of sins should, if it is to do justice to the gospel, break the powerful hold of such sin. Sin is not only forgiven but also stripped of its power. Thus the gospel, in turn, serves as criterion for the creedal statements. It provides the freedom to effect changes to creeds and the gospel is also the guarantee that it is the one message that will be preached. The gospel precedes the formularies, yet it is found again within the formularies; thus they form a circle. From Schmithals' exegetical activity it also becomes evident that the constants of the gospel form the basis of his exegesis. He continues to bear in mind that which is regarded as essential. The New Testament texts are evaluated in their relation to this central testimony. To Schmithals, his method in terms of which the New Testament has to be evaluated according to this criterion is in accordance with the purpose of the New Testament itself (cf. Bultmann 1975c:256). This is the interpretation given by Scripture. The New Testament seeks to introduce the gospel at the center. Seeking and finding of the confession and seeking and finding of the gospel is how the New Testament should be read. The church came into being as a result of the confession of faith and thus Christian theology cannot focus its attention on another investigative subject. Its subject was given to it, namely God's action in Christ (Schmithals 1971 a:24; 1972g:188; 1983h:139; cf. 1979a:66; 1972b:67; cf. Bultmann 1926:57).

If the scientific study of the Bible were to be employed by Marxism, for instance, to determine the place of the New Testament in the historical process, as Marxism understands it, it would lose its theological status because the historical process then becomes the canon according to which the New Testament is read. Christian theology is only worthy of its name if it is courageous enough to investigate and interpret the gospel as it applies to this day and age (Schmithals 1971a:24). The very choice of practicing theology implies adherence to the gospel. In this respect, it is therefore not incorrect to speak of a dogmatic truth as fundamental to Schmithals' exegesis, provided one does not take it to be a static dogmatism that imposes a strange dogma on the text when interpreting it. Dogma refers to a specific act of salvation performed by God; but an act done to people through which they see themselves anew and not as an act in itself. Dogma is an explanation. Dogma explains the state of affairs of humankind; what someone's life's truths are and expects someone to position himself or herself (cf. Schmithals 1980b:177). Schmithals wishes to do justice to both the dogma and the historically determined text testifying to it. To him it is important, in order fully to respect the meaning of the New Testament, that dogmatic core and historical exegesis should not be separated. The old texts express a dogmatic truth. Historical exegesis leads the exegete to the gospel. The historical dogma is revealed to the exegete who does justice to the text. It should be clearly understood that Schmithals applied historical exegesis and not some other form of exegesis pre-

Theological Understanding of the New Testament 41

scribed by dogma. The reading of the text gives rise to the theological meaning of the exegesis. Historical-critical exegesis acts in unison with the dogmatic claim made by the New Testament.

Put differently, Schmithals reads the New Testament as "a testifying document," in other words the document should be read together with the doctrine it hypothesizes and contains. The question is not only "What does it say?" but also, "What does it mean?" (cf. Bultmann 1975c:252, 257). With regard to a semi-moralistic concept such as conversion (more about this later) the case he puts forward should, for example, be investigated. The value of the New Testament can never be viewed independently from the content of its fundamental message. The New Testament is the product of the gospel. The dogmatic truth, the gospel, is the "text" which is revealed within the "texts" (Schmithals 1970a:45). The aim of New Testament theology is to interpret the "text" in such a manner that one can understand it today. The revelation of the human existence *coram Deo* through Biblical testimony forms the fundamental theme of exegesis and theology. Theology is dependent on the subject of investigation, namely the gospel. If the perspective of the gospel is disregarded, theology is sacrificed in advance. It should be kept in mind that it is the Biblical word that we wish to understand. This word should be understood so that on the basis of its authority and claim it leads its readers to a better understanding of themselves, namely that they are the recipients of God's grace.

3.3 THE WORD

Until now the concept "criterion" has been used in an objective sense. The gospel serves as the criterion for the confession of faith and this confession is the criterion for the gospel. The gospel and confession of faith can be described objectively, independent of faith or unbelief. However, this is not the end of the matter, because Schmithals maintains that the truth of the message can never be transmitted in a purely objective way. The listener also verifies the message. The truth of the message is fulfilled in the listener. The listener agrees with the gospel and it is thus legitimized.

The divine truth that precedes us and sustains us, is confirmed as divine truth by us. This confirmation consists of our yielding ourselves to God. Faith itself is the criterion for the truth of the gospel (Schmithals 1979a:219, 297; 1988a:260-261).

The subjective criterion of the confirmation by the listener indicates that the gospel is not about facts. Generally speaking, facts cannot be confirmed; facts are not legitimized because the listener assents to them. As an historical event Jesus' death by crucifixion is incidental and of no importance, as an historical fact his resurrection is implausible (Schmithals 1972a:19-20). Moreover, historical facts do not help us. Such facts do not influence us or involve us in anything, they mean nothing and serve no purpose. Schmithals (1967c:493) explains that by choosing to speak of "saving facts" and not "saving events" or "saving deeds", we already indicate that God's deed of salvation is seen as an object, which is like the other aspects of the reality of space and time at someone's disposal. Thus humankind can view saving facts from a distance, from a neutral position. Even unbelievers must be able to state that Jesus' cross is the ransom paid for the release of sinners by the physical Son of God. Schmithals (1967c:494) denies that this approach will do justice to the testimony of the New Testament regarding reality of salvation. This reality is not presented as saving facts from which the deduction can or cannot be made that a saving truth indeed exists. The confession that "Jesus is the Son of God" should, according to Schmithals, not be understood as a valid pronouncement regarding Jesus' nature. Jesus is not naturally divine. Neither does one need to find a correlation between "Jesus is the Son of God" and "Jesus is the Son of David." "Son of David" refers to the Jewish king in the fullness of time. These pronouncements are not meant to be about the being of Jesus, but indicate what he means to us; what he does for us: in him God comes to us, in him our sins are forgiven (Schmithals 1972f:170-171; 1981c:24-25). Lesser minds here tend to play off objectiveness against subjectiveness. They feel that the one should have precedence over the other. Usually the existential interpretation Schmithals strives to achieve is faulted for elevating the own subjective belief above the objective truth of the confessional content, with the result that the divine truth itself is also denied. However, Schmithals himself never states that a deed of faith confers truth upon the confession. He rather holds the view that the believer is convinced by the revelation. With reference to Jesus' word "your faith has healed you" (Mark 5:34), and although Jesus is the Savior, Schmithals wants to know who wishes to argue about which of the two is the more important: the savior or faith in the savior? It is the faith which saves, not as a result of inner events that have occurred, but because those who lose themselves before God, receive salvation (Schmithals 1979a:297).

Following on this, Schmithals also emphasized that faith, which saves, is an existential venture in which you dare to lose yourself before God. "Venture" here implies that there is not a gradual transition from unbelief to faith, no logical or psychological transition. Faith as obedience to the Word of God is not founded on human motivation but is a gift and wonder of God. Faith is not the incomprehensible presenting of something as the truth, which cannot be verified. The story of the hemorrhaging woman does not wish to report on the historical event of the woman's meeting with Jesus, but is a word which is directed to us in order to convince us to entrust our lives to God (Schmithals 1979a:296-297; cf. 1983:175; 1988a:52). In answering the question: "How does the meeting between the hemorrhaging woman and Jesus reflect the possibility of my meeting him?" Schmithals says that the help she received is proclaimed in such a way that I may also be a recipient. The proclamation spans the distance between the two of us, between the disciples of the first generation and those of later generations. The story has as its aim not to depict the faith of the woman, but to show the possibility of my believing (Schmithals 1979a:298). The story becomes a proclamation, which not only reports on faith, but should also be understood as a word that creates faith. Through the proclamation the meeting between Jesus and the woman is interpreted as Jesus meeting me. I am no longer expected to depend on my own strength but to expect life from God. This is the movement through which people's existence is completed so that they gain a new insight regarding them through God's act of salvation. Consequently the saving act of the past becomes part of the present. This existential movement of humankind concurs with the proclamation, which makes the "text" real. Through the proclamations of the church, the Gospel, the Christian dogma, reaches me. If it is not preached, or if such proclamation is not believed, sin remains my master. Without preaching, Christ cannot fulfill his work in me and I remain untouched by him (Schmithals 1988a:266). Where proclamation finds faith, Christ is present and at work.

According to Schmithals, preaching should not be regarded as a less important or second phase of the saving act. It is not salvation in the first place and a report on it in the second place. The proclamation is as original as salvation. The proclamation of salvation is also a saving act. The word is indeed a deed. Jesus tells the paralyzed man to get up (Mark 2:9). The word Jesus uses here is identical to the word that proclaims him. On hearing this word, the paralytic gets up. The word and salvation are identical. The paralytic, who cannot help himself, allows himself to be taken to that place where the grace of God has the word and he is helped (Schmithals 1979a:149-151). The listener is forced to see himself or herself as a believer or an unbeliever through the preaching, and grace is then bestowed upon him or her. The situation in which the listener finds himself or herself, only reaches a conclusion when such grace is bestowed. Now the preaching has attained its goal. Clearly, such a word, which is also a deed, cannot be verified by historical facts and indeed need not be verified. The so-called facts of the birth, cross, resurrection and ascension of Christ become meaningful because the preaching presents them as God's deed of salvation to the world.

Schmithals (1973b:221-222; 1979a:712) agrees with Bultmann's famous word, namely that Jesus has arisen in the word that preaches him. The cross means that God delivered Jesus into the hands of humankind and surrendered him to the power of sin and death. "Resurrection" is the raising of Jesus, through God's power, for the sake of our justification. "Ascension" means that God has given him the name Lord (Schmithals 1972a:20). He rules over his church through the word which proclaims him and which is identical to God's deed of salvation. However, the fact that the events of preaching are saving events does not mean that the Word of God has now been given over to human beings. It does not imply that people may now call their own word(s) divine or that people can be saved by the power of their language. Humankind's words do not carry weight. Provision has been made for events of the preaching to remain saving events and will not be placed at our disposal. Both preaching and saving events are protected. The preaching events are safeguarded because people will not of their own free will present themselves to become a "substitutionary messenger for Christ." The volunteer does not preach God's message but his own. The true preacher is under duress and this compulsion opens up the possibility that his or her words may become more than a human undertaking (Schmithals 1979a:325): "For if I preach the gospel, I have nothing to boast of. For I am compelled to preach. Woe to me if I do not preach the gospel!" (1 Cor 9:16). The saving events are safeguarded from human interference because the preacher himself/herself does not decide on the content of the preaching. The salvation preached by the church is God himself; his presence in this world, which will always remain a gift to humankind over which we have no say (Schmithals 1979a:123).

Schmithals does not see grace as this or that miraculous healing, but as a whole: a human being experiencing relationship with God. If grace is seen as a whole, it is also clear that grace is not merely one part of one's life, but is, in fact, a vital truth, that is part of one's whole existence. If this truth becomes part of, and is realized in preaching, preaching will never be able to formulate this grace as one generalized formula, which will apply for all time, it is expressed time and again as a specific and temporary grace. In view of this, one should not talk about a pure formulation of the gospel. The aim of preaching is not only to say: "This is how faith becomes substantial," but to create obedience, faith. The rich diversity of the formulations that were to be found in the formularies of the early church gives expression to the fact that the gospel will always remain *viva vox*.

3.4 THE CANON OF SCRIPTURE

When one asks about Christian dogma, the church refers one to Scripture. It gives voice to the Gospel. Dogmatically the gospel is not the same as the Bible text and cannot be identified with it. Dogmatic truth is underscored by the historical text. There is no other way to gain entry to the Gospel than in the form of the historically determined texts that proclaim it. In the church the Gospel took on the shape that was given to it by its proclamation at a specific time and in those specific circumstances. The Gospel articulates itself in the texts of the canon (Schmithals 1970a:45).

From the above it becomes clear that Schmithals regards the Gospel itself as criterion for the preaching of the church. The church, which established the canon, did not determine the truth to which it bears witness. For this very reason, the church is bound to the gospel by means of the canon. Schmithals avoids referring to a canon within a canon, as that would give the impression of a fixed rule of faith that would not do justice to the presentation. To him the conscious canon within the canon is the Gospel itself and from this point of departure it is necessary to distinguish within the canon. In his criticism he establishes that the letter to the Hebrews and James have not maintained the full range of the Christian faith (Schmithals 1979a:158; cf. 19831:173-174). In the implementation of this process of "inner criticism of the canon" the Gospel maintains itself (Schmithals 1970a:45). The biblical texts form the canon, as a result of a choice made by the early church from the kerymatic texts at their disposal. The fact that the Bible consists of a choice of the more suitable texts means that in principle the canon cannot be limited. This, according to Schmithals, does not mean that there is any reason for the church to change or have to change the canon of the New Testament writings. The other writings of the church are, in fact, based on the canon and wish to be judged accordingly. The canon remains their yardstick and one does not replace primary with secondary sources. The primary sources not included in the canon, are few and of little value. Although the canon is open, it is in fact irreplaceable when it comes to conveying the proto-Christian message. The open canon is given meaning by internal criticism of the canon (Schmithals 1970a).

Since the second century, the church has reverted to the canonical writings; Paul reverted to the kerygmatic formulae. Schmithals explains this reversion by the fact that a particular historical event is the subject of the gospel, this event being the historical experience of Jesus of Nazareth. The old formulae of Christian dogma concerns Jesus. In early Christian preaching, his experiences are unfolded and explained (Schmithals 1970a:45). The saving act of God in Christ must be proclaimed and made real in the present. Without preaching, the experiences of Christ have no greater significance than any other events of that time. Without the confession of the cross of Christ, interpreted as God's judgment on the sins of humankind, the cross will become part of a meaningless past. The cross must be confessed as the saving act of God, because this act is unique and unrepeatable. The uniqueness of this act does not encourage a search for the historical facts before the preaching. There can be no portrayal of Jesus, based on historical research that can be the foundation of the preaching of the church. That is exactly why the proclamation is not prompted by historical interest. Uniqueness should not be understood in the historical sense, but in connection with preaching. The Christian confession lays claim to the uniqueness of that which it proclaims. Proclamation presupposes the uniqueness of what is being proclaimed, while the uniqueness of the saving act necessitates its being proclaimed. Proclamation which is historically founded on the uniqueness of the saving act, does not require general truths or natural or historical facts, because all these things can be reproduced or imitated. That to which the Bible text bears witness cannot be imitated or repeated and for that very reason it is attested. The fact that Biblical evidence attests is further evidence that the act to which it bears witness is divine, because, in principle, human acts are repeatable; they are not only active in the testimony of tradition. Witness must be borne to the divine truth and it can only be believed. This is not the same as the insight obtained into general truths or the understanding of natural phenomena or historical facts (Schmithals 1970a:46).

The fact that the saving events have to be attested gave rise to the idea that a primary oral tradition of the Gospel exists. It is believed that the church upholds this oral tradition. Then it is presumed that this oral tradition is an independent authority over against the Gospel. The church was to conserve this tradition intact and by means of this tradition the church became an extension of Christ, *Christus prolongatus*. Schmithals (1970a:45) denies the existence of a primary oral tradition, extending into the present time. According to him, the importance of the church does not lie in the tradition it has at its disposal, but in being an instrument of Christ to bear witness to God's act of salvation. The saving events must be proclaimed and, in proclaiming them, the church forms part of the completion of the saving act of God. In this sense, the church can be called *Christus prolongatus*, according to Schmithals (1979a:325). The proclaiming church truly represents

Christ. To enable the church to do this, it has declared the Biblical tradition to be its irreplaceable foundation, because this tradition lays claim to being the decisive, eschatological word of the saving act of God in Christ. Along with the Biblical tradition, the church accepts the fact that the divine truth was revealed to us (from beyond ourselves) unsurpassable, in Christ once and for all. Seen in this light, Schmithals understands the restraint on the canon as an inner restraint because the canon is focused on the one gospel Jesus Christ. All other messages are excluded. The last, eschatological message is proclaimed: the gospel of God. The *sola Scriptura* of the Reformation is not merely a formal principle, but expresses the Biblical, reformational dogma that the final message is proclaimed God has acted, "once and for all," for the salvation of the world (Schmithals 1970a:46; 1989b:16). Just as Luther saw himself as a doctor of Holy Scripture who had to broach the subject of justification by faith, *solus Christus*, Schmithals must be seen as a theologian of Scripture. Proto-Christianity managed to testify to the divine truth in texts, and, as responsible theologian, he feels bound by them. His commitment to the essence of this matter is the unifying factor in all Schmithals' theological work. This is his point of departure and to that he returns. His commitment to the subject can explain his strong will even his obstinacy in comparison to the mainstream of scientific theological practice.

3.5 THE HISTORICAL CRITICAL METHOD

Schmithals is adamant that the church can only be church with a canon and a text. The church is a creation of the word and its sole purpose is to elucidate the message. In essence, theology is simply exegesis (Schmithals 1970a:51; cf. Bultmann 1975:272).

For the exegesis of the Bible text, Schmithals' point of view is that historical consciousness and historical thinking are part of the modern ideology. The modern historical school of thought must be taken into account. The message of the gospel must be discussed within and with the help of this way of thinking. This realization is a precondition when using historical method. When applied to the exegesis of Bible texts, historical method implies that the distance between the time in which the text was written and today must be understood. In the first place the text is the word of humans, determined by specific circumstances, and this word of humans must be understood by the people of today. "Historical" in the term "historical-critical" describes the historical discrepancy between that time and today. The "critical" in describing the method should be read as an accentuation of the "historical" (Schmithals 1971 b:55). Here "critical" does not entail criticism. "Critical" is used in the sense of distinguishing and it amounts to drawing a distinction between that time and today. Today's exegete is not the original receiver of the Bible text; consequently each text must be understood in its historical setting. It was only through historical thinking that people came to realize the hermeneutical problem, namely how past history can be understood in the present (Schmithals 1970a:53). What is the reality of history and how does it become real again today? The reality of the history of the New Testament is dogma. If understanding is to bridge the gap in time, the past reality must become real again. The potential for human existence in the past must become possible again. Hermeneutics as the science of translation takes on greater significance. The translation must be able to express my present understanding of the dogma, which the old text conveyed in the wording of its time (Schmithals 1972g:190).

    The task of exegesis, in other words theology, in other words hermeneutics, remains understanding nothing more. "Understanding" means the understanding of the dogma, of the message expressed in the old text. It is the dogma that claims authority and has to be understood. From the Christian point of view, people can only understand themselves from dogma. Understanding takes place in the present. I only understand here and now. Present understanding is the actual dogmatic understanding. This does not take place in two stages as is widely accepted namely an understanding of the past which is then transferred to the present reality. Present understanding of the historical exegesis must not be represented as if the exegete is entering the past darkness, where anything is to be expected and where he must react to anything that he comes across. In reality, the exegete is guided by his perspective. This perspective, which the exegete keeps in mind, is not another method in itself, but a hermeneutic guideline functioning within the framework of the historical-critical method (cf. Bultmann 1975c:267-268). The exegete knows what to expect from the text. The texts of the New Testament suggest that they will be interrogated with the understanding of human existence in mind. More than one directive can be used within the historical method. Should the Bible wish to teach us concerning political realities or society, a sociological interpretation would be a suitable guideline for the exegesis.

Schmithals takes the existential interpretation as hermeneutic principle, because he is convinced that the Bible text expresses itself on human existence. Christian dogma is a pronouncement concerning human existence. Therefore, people only understand the Bible text to the extent that they understand themselves anew in it. Although the existential interpretation is not a method in itself, merely a guideline within the historical method, the exegesis of a Bible text by means of the historical-critical method depends on the good use made of this guideline. Without this directive there is no bridging of the gap between then and now. The charge that the historical method remains locked in the past and is not theologically productive is justified unless the existential principle is applied. Existential interpretation does not prescribe to the text what it should say concerning its content; the text must be allowed to speak for itself. This is exactly what the historical critical method tries to ensure. The contribution made by the existential interpretation, is that it makes one receptive to the ideas of the text on human existence. The correct question to be asked of the text is what it has to say on human existence. On the one hand, people are moved, by their existence, to the question of the possibility of understanding human existence. Human existence is incomplete and problematical; consequently the exegete can approach the text with an openness of spirit to find clarity concerning his or her being (Bultmann 1975c:259; Schmithals 1967a:237). On the other hand, Christian dogma claims to be the expression of the theological truth of human existence. Dogma tells us what is happening between God and human beings. The readiness to listen, in other words the problem of human existence, corresponds to the authority of the text. Where human existence is unproblematic, the text has no appeal. People are in search of themselves when they seek happiness, salvation and meaning. In this search for themselves, they go beyond themselves and seek God, because God is their salvation (Schmithals 1967a:243; 1970c:178).

Thus, the exegete is in a living relationship with the "text" which is unfolded in the texts. The possibilities concerning human existence raised by the text are still possibilities for human existence today. The theologian is not interested in understanding the situation of those days or today as a situation in itself. Rather, he or she wishes to understand the subject matter of the text within the context of life (Schmithals 1970a:54). In addition, this context changes continually. The satisfied person will ask the ancient question concerning God differently from the dissatisfied one, and the student's question will differ from the professor's. Human understanding of self is variable and must constantly be acquired anew in order to obtain an answer to this ancient question in the present time (Schmithals 1970c:176). Existential interpretation is not only appropriate because it can be linked to the meaning of the Christian dogma, it is also motivated because the purpose of the search for meaning is that people must reach an understanding of themselves. Understanding oneself is a precondition for all other understanding. It is only on this condition that one can understand the world and history, as well as one's neighbor and society, nature and culture.

Now the question arises: How does Schmithals see the relationship between faith and understanding? Does the Bible speak only to the believer? The answer is both yes and no. Yes, in the sense that the message of the Bible only comes into its own where it is also believed and where I understand myself anew (Schmithals 1970a:25, 53; 1972g:188). Apart from the fact that understanding can coincide with faith (in the sense of understanding oneself), there is also the possibility of taking understanding to mean an effort to meditate on faith. Then it can be expressed in words and ideas, in other words formulated scientifically. Now faith and understanding are no longer the same, but they constitute the relationship between believing existence and theology (Schmithals 1970b:84). To Schmithals, theology implies being scientifically active and achieving scientific results. He expects theologians to be able to defend their point of view scientifically (Schmithals 1967b:100; cf. Bultmann 1975c:273). According to Schmithals, theology is science in the true sense of the word. It is possible for theology to formulate the subject of its research concisely: Jesus Christ. Theology is not a science of comprehension or the humanities, but the science of a subject, the subject being the Biblical evidence concerning Jesus Christ (Schmithals 1972g:188). This subject is examined scientifically by means of historical interpretation of the text. This requires critical rationality from exegetes in their elucidation of the text. It would not be incorrect to call theology an historical science, but Schmithals (1972g:190) prefers to describe it as a hermeneutical science. His reason is that in carrying through the process of understanding, the historically given Christ testimony, fulfills its empirical critical function in the present. This is expressed in John 9:39: "Jesus said, 'For judgement I have come into this world, so that the blind will see and those who see will become blind'" (cf. Schmithals 1972g:191). Furthermore, Schmithals (1972g: 192) understands theology as an ecclesiastical science, in other words it is a function that has to be fulfilled by the church which is faithful to its calling in constantly looking to its foundation and constantly being ready for its task. In the same way, technical society requires modern physics to maintain itself and keep on track. This implies that theological work must culminate in proclaiming, that historical critical exegesis must lead to sermons, because the church is created by the word.

The fact that theology should lead to proclamation does not mean that a sermon must be produced willy-nilly, but presumes that the texts lend themselves to sermons in order to do them justice. As far as the relationship between faith and understanding is concerned, for Schmithals preaching must be classified as scientific understanding. His pastoral compassion urges him to distinguish between understanding, on the one hand, and believing the content of the Christian message, on the other (cf. Schmithals 1970b:84-85). When preaching, he wishes to arouse faith by his sermon, but what he does in the concrete circumstances is, at best, to get an understanding going of what faith is and what it does. That this understanding eventually becomes faith is no longer the responsibility of the preacher, but is *donum Spiritus Sancti*. In the sermon itself we find existentials or objectifying understanding, but what the sermon achieves is existential or subjective understanding. Existential understanding is real understanding, where understanding has become agreement. Seen in this light, faith and understanding cannot be distinguished quantitatively, because the one who understands what faith is, and does not believe, knows what he or she is doing in rejecting faith. Faith and understanding are quantitatively equal. Both have the same amount of insight. Faith does not have more knowledge than understanding. As far as quality is concerned, one can distinguish between faith and understanding. The one who understands can repudiate faith while someone else accepts it. It can also happen that one who repudiates it at first, subsequently understands himself or herself better through faith. Paul is a good example of one who became familiar and developed a living relationship with that which he at first persecuted but later proclaimed (cf. Schmithals 1978e:391).

"Ecclesiastical" in the expression "theology as ecclesiastical science" does not mean that the church and theology do not serve the world. The service rendered to the world by the servant is to bear witness to the Christ event. However, this service can only be rendered for as long as theology remains ecclesiastical science and is constantly busy confirming the authority of the church. This must not be understood theoretically, but should be practiced in the true sense of the word. That is exactly what the historical method teaches: confirmation of the authority of the church only takes place when the message is proclaimed in understandable language to real people. The old text must be made understandable in the present (Schmithals 1967b:98). Understanding precedes faith. The unbeliever must be able to understand the contents of the Gospel. It is in the interest of the Gospel itself to be easily understood by unbelievers, because how can preaching change unbelievers into believers if it is not understood in the world of unbelief (Schmithals 1970b:84-85).

Schmithals (1967b:97) stresses the fact that the Gospel is proclaimed, not some or other theology. The preacher who tries to motivate the congregation to accept objective saving facts as the truth, or one who presents results of historical Biblical science, has not yet proclaimed the Gospel. A detailed historical analysis still contains no message. A congregation does not benefit from theological information. Even literary analysis does not mean anything. The proclamation of the Gospel must always be new, always different and yet the same. Making the theological tradition real by means of the historical-critical method does not mean that dogmatic themes are of no importance to the exegete. On the contrary, one could describe Schmithals as an authority on dogmatics and he himself says that he learned dogmatics from Bultmann (cf. Schmithals 1971 b:56). One realizes that Luther is the constant interlocutor of Schmithals. The large number of assenting references to

Luther typifies his commentary on Mark. As far as method is concerned, Schmithals did not learn from Luther, because the latter reached his conclusions by pre-historic thinking, in terms of which the past and the present coalesce. This unhistorical method does not distinguish between long ago and today. Despite using a different method, Luther was still occupied with the same subject matter, the same dogma: Jesus Christ; only faith. Luther tried to understand the dogma of the church by means of his methodical *modus operandi* and in his time he succeeded in a most exemplary manner.

The meaning of the text is not established beforehand by the teachings of dogmatics. The dogmatic expectation with which the exegete approaches the text serve as a preconception of what the text says and how the text should be questioned. Although it constitutes a preconceived idea, it is not unimportant. The exegete cannot approach the text without something specific in mind or with any kind of question; the question must be applicable and should be raised responsibly (Schmithals 1971a:38). One cannot afford to ignore Luther or any other worthy theologian in the dogmatic tradition, when it comes to understanding this tradition. The answers that they obtained regarding salvation, sin and happiness, form part of the methodical equipment of the historical exegete. The exegete is helped by the history of church, dogma and theology. It enables him to acquire his preconceived ideas responsibly (Schmithals 1971b:60).

The existential relationship to the substance of the text is necessary for understanding the text at all. Moreover, this existential understanding is explained in the preconception. Because of this preconception, the exegete can grasp what the text says concerning salvation. It is necessary to explain this preconception, in order for it to become clear at what the questioning of the text is aiming. The questioning must be done systematically so that the preconception can either be strengthened, corrected or abandoned. An example of one of Luther's ideas that Schmithals corrected by means of the text, was the reformer's *simul ius-*

tus, simul peccator both justified and sinner. Schmithals (1980b:119-120; cf 1988a:275) is of the opinion that Paul does not imply a duality in the redeemed. On no account does it mean growing sanctification, in which the redeemed struggles against himself or herself until the battle is won. The formula *totus iustus, totus peccator* is a better indication of Paul's intent. When seen as the "old human being" of the old dispensation, someone is still a complete sinner; but seen as the "new creation" of the new dispensation, someone is totally justified. Pelser (1984:109) also agrees that, according to Paul, the old and the new human being exclude one another in principle.

Preconception must not be confused with prejudice. Unlike a preconception, a prejudice is never put to the test, but is taken as final understanding. The understanding, obtained with the help of preconception by means of exegesis, becomes preconception for further understanding, because the exegete never reaches a point where he or she knows everything and becomes a spectator in relation to the saving act of God (cf. Schmithals 1967a:238-239). In preaching preachers presume their listeners to have a preconception of the subject matter of the text. They often encounter prejudice among their listeners. They tie in with ideas that the listeners may have. For example: the listeners might understand conversion in relation to their moralizing sense of sin, as being an improvement people can achieve in themselves. From the redemption in Christ, preachers tie in with this representation, so that they can contradict it in their explanation that the salvation of the human being begins with God and all human renown is excluded (cf. Schmithals 1953:534-536).

The generally held opinion is that dogmatics follows on exegesis. For example, Boers (1979:87) states: "after that, one could perform the dogmatic task of interpreting the subject matter of the New Testament discerned in this way in doctrines that are relevant for the present." Schmithals sees dogma and exegesis as moving in a circle. According to his view, the entrance to the circle is the expectation that the redemption of the sinner is the matter to be discussed in the text. If the text is approached from different angles, using other questions, it is a futile effort to try to reach the dogma after the exegesis has been done (cf. Bultmann 1975c:277). Rather, theological work consists of presupposing the dogma, understanding it as the subject matter of the text. In other words to allow the questioning of the text to be guided by the dogma and in the process to put it into words for today. The preconception of the dogma expresses the fact that the word has been given and salvation has come. The subject of theological research is both dogmatical and historical: the Biblical evidence concerning Christ (Schmithals 1971b:59). The advantage of the existential interpretation is that it unites the historical and dogmatical interpretations. Dogmatics becomes the methodical preconception of historical-critical theology and thus the unity of theology can be seen. The purpose of historical exegesis is not to compile points of doctrine, but to understand the text *in actu*. The process of understanding is still an adventure. The intrinsic value of Schmithals' work lies in the fact that he, in carrying out his theological task, has succeeded in unifying theology in an exemplary manner. This is no mean accomplishment, considering the fact that the historical and theological interpretations of most theologians diverge. Each professor is usually a specialist on his or her subject and the task of unifying theology is left to the student. In this way students are expected to achieve something professors have given up on a fact that is very conveniently disregarded (Schmithals 1971b:60-61;1996a:43-44).

Schmithals (1967b:101) also noticed that ministers were not using their training in historical method in practice. They use other methods when preparing the Sunday sermon. He compares these preachers to pilots who cannot cope with the complicated technical apparatus of their machines and then decide to earn their living as taxi drivers. This state of affairs can satisfy no one. So Schmithals asks whether the historical method is really so difficult. If this is so, ministers should be trained in other methods, so that the tremendous gap between training and practice can be overcome. Perhaps the problem is that the historical method is not taught correctly. This should receive serious attention. Even if other methods are introduced, the best use must still be made of the historical method (Schmithals 1967b:101). From this exposition it is also clear that Schmithals had a definite concept as to what should be studied in historical theology. This encyclopaedia should include an explanation of the present theological situation. From the history of historical exegesis, theology can account for the fact that the subjects Old Testament, New Testament, Church History and the History of Dogma, have become distinct from Dogmatic Theology. Together these subjects, always associated with practical theology, form the system of historical theology. This interdependence should be maintained (Schmithals 1971b:60). A thorough introduction to hermeneutics should be given. The old rules of hermeneutics are no longer adequate. The problem of historical-critical exegesis must be spelled out: "How can the reality of the past be made relevant in the present?" Responsibility must be taken for the hermeneutical principle: "What is our perspective regarding the Bible text?" The objective and subjective elements in interpretation must be clarified. "What is theology?" "What is preaching?" "What is preconception?" "What is existential understanding?" "What is scientific understanding?"

For historical theology to abandon the dogmatic work done through the ages would be wrong. The history of the church and dogma, especially with reference to the theology of the Reformation, is necessary for the preconception of the Biblical dogma. The fact that the word "history" is mentioned in theological, ecclesiastical and dogmatic history emphasizes the fact that the message is always proclaimed temporarily. With regard to method, these disciplines find themselves in the same situation as exegesis. They should all apply hermeneutics as the science of translation (Schmithals 1971b:60). Schmithals (1971b:

60) refers to so-called Practical Theology. It is called practical, although in reality it studies the many theories of service in the church. Practical Theology explains how the message can be made understandable in preaching, dogma and ministry. Although exegesis tries to penetrate to the heart of theology, where preaching becomes a possibility, the detail of preaching, dogma and ministry must not be underestimated. The manifold theories concerning ecclesiastical service include everything that has to be done: ethics, liturgiology, ecumenics and missionary work.

Schmithals (1974a:82) feels that there is no other subject in the arts which gives as wide and scientifically based training as a well-directed study of theology. It relates to the content of the study: Jesus Christ. To understand him does not mean merely to take note of a snippet of human history and experience. To understand him means to see history itself moving as a whole towards him and from him. The one subject of theology cannot therefore be understood without many other connections. Theologians need philology to understand the testimonies of faith; they need the historical sciences to express the old words as new today; they learn from philosophers, poets and authors which questions they should answer. Psychology and sociology teach them about people and the world. Because they have to deal with everyday occurrences, they take note of what the behavioral sciences have to say.

There is no room for dogmatic theology in the system of historical theology, because Schmithals feels that dogmatic theology works according to its own, unhistorical method. Both historical and unhistorical methods are occupied with Biblical dogma. Between them there is no possibility of division of labor. One reaches its goal in one way and the other the same goal in a different way. They are in competition (Schmithals 1971b:61; 1996a:52). Dogmatic theology must look after its own encyclopaedic arrangement of its subjects. In his essay, *Barth, Bultmann und wir,* Schmithals (1971b) pleads for the acknowledgement of the methodical distinction between dogmatic and historical theology. Revisions and adjustments to theological syllabuses will not bring the required clarity for students and lecturers. One or other way will make becoming a theologian possible for anyone. No one becomes a theologian in two ways. No one has yet been able to reconcile the historical with the dogmatic method of working. Anyone trying it is sure to fail. This does not mean that there is no commonality. Historian and dogmatist meet when they reach their final goal. Schmithals (1971b:52; 1996a:35) tells how Bultmann, after having read Barth's dogmatics painstakingly, sighed and remarked: "Yes, this is all very well, but one cannot express it in this way." This remark shows that Barth and Bultmann did not differ fundamentally only regarding the method used.

3.6 THE DOCTRINAL METHOD

In contrast with modern ministers, who find it difficult to prepare one sermon per week, their predecessors of three hundred years ago had fewer problems. What is more, they had to deliver sermons lasting two hours on Sunday mornings, another of one hour in the afternoon, and during the week as well. Schmithals (1967b:99) explains this contrast as resulting from a lack of historical consciousness at that time. The New Testament was read as if written for today. The Bible was not read according to the historical method, but the unhistorical, doctrinal method (cf. Schmithals 1996a:38). This made Scripture subordinate to the accepted dogma, whether it is the system of Thomas Aquinas, Luther's doctrine of justification or the early-Protestant dogmatics. The professed understanding of faith would determine the interpretation of the text. A hermeneutic circle also existed between the accepted dogma and the Bible text, because the dogma was developed from the text. In reality, dogmatics was exalted above Scripture (cf. Schmithals 1996a:50). In the doctrinal tradition it is easier for ministers to produce a sermon. They do not have to do thorough exegesis in order to find the historical meaning of the text and its significance for today; they simply consult their

Catechism (which they know by heart anyway). The catechism supplies them with all the answers, while their successors, who read historically, have far more to account for if they take their task seriously. At that time it was easy to write dogmatics and Catechisms; this has become virtually impossible today. The historical exegete has to interpret the catechism of the Reformation by means of historical criticism (Schmithals 1967b:99-100).

Schmithals (1971b:58) states that it is still possible to do theological work according to the unhistorical doctrinal method, as long as the principle of interpretation sets free the essence of Biblical dogma. Barth's principle that God is God and not a human being showed that he was able to verbalize the reforming power of the Bible anew. Schmithals also reminds us of the fact that the most Bible readers read the Bible unhistorically. It would be wrong to pretend that the doctrinal era is past. Everyone is not equally conscious of history. Doctrinalism still plays an important role in the modern world. Everyone should be taken into consideration, because the message concerns us all. Consequently the doctrinal method can still be considered necessary for the interpretation of the Bible. Theologians who feel attracted by the unhistorical method must use it to the best of their ability. Even in dogmatics there is confusion, because there is no clear distinction between historical and unhistorical theology. Doctrinalists try too hard to think historically (see Engelbrecht 1982c:65) and in doing so neglect their own method. It is quite unthinkable that Bultmann would send his students to Barth to round off their theological studies on a high level of dogmatics. It would be equally unthinkable for Barth to send his students to Bultmann in order to introduce them to theological work. Each does his own work from start to finish. Barth as doctrinalist is his own exegete and Bultmann as historian is his own doctrinalist (Schmithals 1971b:54). Barth (in Jaspert 1971:196; in Schmithals 1971b:51; 1996a:34) describes the unbridgeable gap between doctrinalist and historian, when he compares an encounter between them to a meeting between a whale and an elephant. Both would be filled with amazement. One would spout water in vain while the other would beckon or threaten with his trunk to no avail. Neither has a key to what the other is trying so eagerly to say from his/her element and in his/her language.

3.7 CLOSING REMARKS

The insight that theology must reflect on and explain its subject—the saving acts—is still no guarantee that it takes place satisfactorily. The assessment of whether the task of theology is being carried out properly must in itself be the subject of theological science. The subject will determine whether theological work has succeeded or not. This subject is active and present in the church in that it gives life to the church. The church always exists in its relationship to the truth of human existence and therefore the church itself must decide whether or not theological work is of any value. This controlling function of the life of the church is described by Pont (1991:44): "Without the space provided by the church and without the surrounding support of the church and directives from the church, training will not be possible." In practice, these "directives form the church," as far as theological work and the training of future ministers are concerned, can take place only in differences of opinion, refuting and supporting of arguments. The Word of God is not typified by a specific written form, but by its appeal to human hearts. In answer to the question whether the directives are given officially or spontaneously, the answer must be that they can only be given spontaneously. The type of decision made here is made in obedience to the Gospel obedience that is always received as a gift. In the church one could find an obedient individual and a disobedient multitude. To leave the control in the hands of the majority of the groups in the church would be unwise and furthermore it would amount to a particular official meeting deciding on the truth.

CHAPTER 4

Early Christianity

4.1 INTRODUCTION

Schmithals said that, as minister, he had to preach up to four times on a Sunday. He also had to conduct several Bible study groups per week This completely exhausted him and rendered him incapable of theological work. If he was to busy himself scientifically, he could only do so if he worked on the history of the New Testament. Historical work provided some relaxation, because he could turn his attention to a different field.

Meanwhile, to Schmithals, the theological and historical work never became separated. The exegesis of the New Testament must be combined with the reconstruction of the historical setting of early Christianity. The circumstances that led to the writing of the Scriptures produce their own particular commentary on these writings and the two must be read in conjunction. What is more, dogma can be retained through the critical examination of history and can benefit anew, because the dogmatics of the text is interwoven with the situation at the time of writing.

4.2 THE OFFICE OF THE APOSTLE

Schmithals (1961:104; cf. 1979a:737) finds it remarkable that the gnostic apostles are ignored by researchers in their deductions concerning the early Christian apostolate. Schmithals himself examines Gnosticism as the predecessor and challenger of the church's mission and apostleship. While the Jews had never had any organised missionary effort, the Gnostics were convinced that the Second Coming depended on the missionary activity of the community. The Gnostics did not expect the eschatological intervention of God, as did the early church in Jerusalem. To their way of thinking God had already done his decisive work. The saving gnosis had been sent. The scattered divine sparks had to be assembled into the cosmic body of Christ. To achieve this salvation, the Gnostic was obliged to do missionary work. In the Syrian region, the church adopted its mission and apostolate from the gnostic example (Schmithals 1961:187-188).

Not only the gnostic system, but also the concept "apostle" appears here and leads to this conclusion. Simon the Magician, also known as the "Great Power," was not considered to be the only great power by his followers. Other pneumatics were also busying them with redemption. The names of Dositeus, Cleobius, Apositos and Cerinthus are mentioned in this regard. The term "apostolos" is sometimes used in connection with these names. Cerinthus also laid claim to the title of "apostle." In that gnostic system the title of apostle was used for those pneumatics who endeavoured to find other pneuma particles and to assemble them by explaining their divine origin to them (Schmithals 1961: 149-153).

In the *Simonese Gnosis*, Celsus tells of gnostic prophets comparable to the apostolic figures. They could also illuminate their preaching with ecstatic speaking in tongues. These prophets were active in Phoenicia and Palestine. It is in this same region that we find Simon the Magician, and here Paul became a Christian and an apostle (Schmithals 1961:153-155). To Schmithals (1961:79-81) Jerusalem appears to be an unlikely place for the origin of the apostolate. Moreover, he points out that the well-known apostles, Andronicus, Junias and Barnabas were, like Paul, Greek speaking Jews of the Diaspora. The trail leads to Syria and Cilicia.

According to Schmithals (1961:177-179) the apostolate in gnostic circles was a multiple apostolate. The multiple apostolate is opposed to the singular apostolate, where redemption is the work of one celestial being. He has been sent to the world for the salvation of the fallen light particles: "I tell you the truth, I am the gate for the sheep. All who ever came before me were thieves and robbers" (Jn. 10:7b-8).

According to the multiple apostolate, there is not only one redeemer but in principle an unlimited number. It is the light particles themselves that act as redeemers of the pneuma as a whole. Paul adheres to the gnostic tradition of the multiple apostolate. He never applies the term apostle to Jesus Christ. In the Gospel of John, which is in the tradition of a singular apostolate, the disciples are never called apostles.

In Corinth, Paul came across gnostic opponents in the tradition of the multiple apostolate. He describes them aptly when he says that they are preaching themselves (2 Cor. 4:5). These apostles questioned Paul's apostleship and, according to Schmithals, (1961:163164) 2 Corinthians only becomes understandable when read with this controversy in mind.

Schmithals (1961:185) is not only convinced that there is a connection between the multiple apostolate of the Gnostics and the apostolate of the church but that the latter developed in emulation of the gnostic apostolate. Paul himself was not aware of this dependence. His theological concepts had already been shaped by the time he came into direct contact with Gnosticism.

Schmithals (1979a:738) asserts that the generally accepted idea of twelve apostles originated with Luke. To counter the pre-Marcionite threat, Luke combines the era of Jesus with the apostolic tradition. This school taught that Paul was the original and directly empowered apostle of Jesus Christ. In opposition to this idea, Luke portrays Jesus as witnessed by the twelve apostles (Schmithals 1980a:19, 77). Lohse (1962:140) calls this anti-Marcionite tendency that Schmithals ascribes to Luke a surprise to the reader. However, this should not be surprising because Strastman already noted in the Acts of the Apostles "een apologie van het door Marcion bedreigde kerkgeloof in den vorm eener geschieden is van Petrus en Paulus" (cf. Van Rhijn 1883:296, footnote 2).

4.3 COMPARATIVE EXEGESIS

Schmithals could succeed in giving a noteworthy example of comparative exegesis by describing the united front of Paul's gnostic opponents, together with a historic reconstruction of the events. Although differing from the dominant trend in modern research, Schmithals is of the opinion (as was F.C. Baur) that Paul had to do with a single group of opponents and not with different groups. He differed from Baur in identifying this group, not as Judaistic Christians, but as Gnostics. According to Schmithals (1965a:132; 1984a:87) the gnostic apostles did their missionary work in the footsteps of Paul in Galatia, Philippi, Thessalonica and Corinth. During his so-called third missionary journey, Paul joined issue with these false apostles, who were trying to hijack the churches he had established (Schmithals 1965d: 185).

Schmithals finds that Paul defends himself polemically against gnostic accusations in the first sentence of his letter to the Galatians: "Paul, an apostle, sent not from men, nor by man, but by Jesus Christ and God the Father, who raised him from the dead." The Gnostics tried to neutralise Paul's influence by querying his apostleship, by averring that he was no pneumatic and had not received his apostleship directly from God but from men. Paul refutes this accusation.

Exegetes immediately think of judaistic propaganda in Galatia because of the renewed interest in circumcision. Schmithals (1965b:23; 1980:51-52) does not accept that those behind this movement were Judaists, because they did not show a Judaistic interest in circumcision. They themselves do not maintain the law (Gal. 6:13) and Paul is the first one to point out the full implication of circumcision: "Again I declare to every man who lets himself be circumcised that he is required to maintain the whole law" (Gal 5:3). Schmithals (1965b:25-26; 1983o:48-49) refers to the fact that Gnostics also had themselves circumcised and that removal of the foreskin symbolized the liberation from the body. However, in the case of the Galatians, there were no theological reasons involved. Paul himself admits that it was a tactical measure. They would escape persecution by the synagogue if they had been circumcised (Schmithals 1984e:113): "Those who want to make a good impression outwardly are trying to compel you to be circumcised. The only reason they do this is to avoid being persecuted for the cross of Christ" (Gal 6:12).

Paul's remarks to the Galatians: "You are observing special days and months and seasons and years" (Gal 4:10) does not necessarily apply to Jewish feasts but is also aimed at Gnostics. They believed that the demonic powers, embodied in the stars, rule at certain times and then pose a threat to humans (Schmithals 1965b:31; 1983o:48-49).

In Galatians 6:1 Paul addresses them as "you who are spiritual" and complains about the fact that they received him like an angel on his first visit, but now he has become an enemy on account of physical weakness: "Even though my illness was a trial to you, you did not treat me with contempt or scorn. Instead, you welcomed me as if I were an angel of God, as if I were Christ Jesus himself" (Gal 4:14). Schmithals (1965b: 34-35) comes to the conclusion that with this accusation the pneumatics imply that Paul is not a spiritual, but merely a physical being. Paul himself took this accusation to apply to his health, not realizing that is was rather aimed at corporeality as such (cf. Schmithals 1983o:29).

In Philippi Paul also had to battle to retain the hearts of the congregation for his gospel. The heretical teachers are disposed of: "Watch out for those dogs, those men who do evil, those mutilators of the flesh" (Phil. 3:2). Schmithals (1965c:62) sees this as applying to the same heretical teachers as these described by Paul in 2 Corinthians 11:13: "For such men are false apostles, deceitful workmen, masquerading as apostles of Christ." These are early Christian missionaries described here. They are active as Christians, but Paul clearly does not approve of their work; they are "deceitful workmen."

Schmithals (1965c:6142) does not agree with the generally accepted view of researchers, that these "deceitful workmen" are Judaists. He bases his opinion (Schmithals 1965c:61-62) on the abusive word "dog." Impure and immoral people were called "dogs" by Jews and Gentiles. Moreover, Jews or Judaists were the most unlikely people to whom this abusive name would apply. Thus the contumely points to the libertarian gnostic movements in the Christian churches.

Schmithals (1965c:79) explains that gnostic libertarianism was not altogether dishonorable, but only as far as the corporeal substance, which is inimical to God, was concerned. The ordination in which one's corporeality is respected, is the means by which demonic powers keep the spiritual being captive in the prison of the body. For the sake of their salvation the Gnostics must reject this ordination, either by means of asceticism or libertarianism. The behavior of the gnostic libertarians offended in two ways: their sexual immorality and disregard of dietary laws. Schmithals sees a direct reference to this repulsive behavior in Philippians 3:19: "Their God is their stomach, and their glory is their shame." The Gnostics pride themselves on their sexual licentiousness, because to them everything is permissible (Schmithals 1965c:81). They despise the dietary laws because corporeal purity is of no importance to them that the body as such is unclean.

In the letter to the Ephesians, preserved in Romans 16:1-20 Schmithals (1965e: 168; 1988a:561) finds the nearest equivalent to the anti-libertarian controversy in Paul's letter to the Philippians: "For such people are not serving our Lord Christ but their own appetites. By smooth talk and flattery, they deceive the minds of naive people" (Rom 16:18). "Appetites" refers to eating and sexual drives and that means that this is a reference to the gnostics' flouting of the dietary laws and their sexual licentiousness.

In Thessalonica Paul had to defend himself against the same accusations as in Corinth (cf. 2 Cor 12), that his ministry was ineffectual. Because he was not spiritual, he could not emulate the many ecstatic demonstrations or wonders of the gnostic apostles. In defending himself, Paul uses the ecstatic formula of the gnostic apostles: "because our gospel came to you not simply with words, but also with power, with the Holy Spirit and with deep conviction" (1 Thes 1:5). The fact that Paul used the pneumatic formula without concrete presentation does not mean that he approved of ecstasy as confirmation of in the preaching of the gospel. He rather had in mind the miraculous work of the gospel that was preached (Schmithals 1965d: 102). To Paul the fact that the Thessalonians believed was proof enough that the preaching was not only done with words but also with power, as he said: "You became imitators of us and of the Lord when, in spite of severe suffering, you welcomed the message with the joy given by the Holy Spirit" (1 Thes 1:6).

In his struggle with the Gnostics Paul insisted that leadership in the church be respected. In 1 Corinthians 16:15-18, Philippians 2:29 and Galatians 6:6 he asks this and in the letter to the people of Thessalonica it reads: Now we ask you, brothers, to respect those who work hard among you, who have authority over you in the Lord and who admonish you. Hold them in the highest regard in love because of their work. Live in peace with each other (1 Thes. 5:12-13). Schmithals (1965d:122) points out that these admonishings had become typical in the later church in its anti-gnostic struggle. To the freedom of the pneumatics and the unrestricted revelation of the pneuma, the church opposes the teaching handed down and the minister. The apostolic tradition and the ecclesiastical office gave the church the victory over the Gnostics.

4.4 EARLY CHRISTIANITY

Schmithals (1961:247) says that three trends are

usually distinguished in early Christianity, namely Judaistic, Hellenistic and Gnostic Christianity. In the course of his investigations Schmithals reached his own conclusion as to the relationship between these trends. He also adapted some of his earlier conclusions (cf. Schmithals 1963:21-23; 1978e:400-401; 410 footnote 55). Therefore, our aim is to reproduce Schmithals' last depiction of early Christianity, as he outlined it and filled it out.

Schmithals (1978e:413; 1984b: 154-155; 1994a: 86) thinks that Palestinian Jewish Christianity (Judaistic) developed simultaneously in two directions, namely Hellenistic Jewish Christianity or Hellenistic synagogical Christianity (Hellenistic) and purely universalistic Christianity (gnostic). Hellenistic Jewish Christianity was based in Antioch and is the relative continuation of Palestinian early Christianity (Schmithals 1984b:154). Unlike universalistic Christianity, the Antiochene point of view did not represent a thoroughgoing universalism. Their interpretation of the law, however, was not judaistic either. Mark 7:24-30 can serve as an example where we clearly see the theology of Antioch:

> Jesus left that place and went to the vicinity of Tyre. He entered a house and did not want anyone to know it; yet he could not keep his presence secret. In fact, as soon as she heard about him, a woman whose little daughter was possessed by an evil spirit, came and fell at his feet. The woman was a Greek, born in Syrian Phoenicia. She begged Jesus to drive the demon out of her daughter. "First let the children eat all they want" he told her, "for it is not right to take the children's bread and toss it to their dogs." "Yes, Lord," she replied, "but even the dogs under the table eat the children's crumbs." Then he told her: "For such a reply, you may go; the demon has left your daughter." She went home and and found her child lying on the bed, and the demon gone.

The theme of this passage is "Jesus and the gentiles" salvation coming from the Jews to the world.

Schmithals (1979a:354) explains that the word "first" in the passage "first let the children eat all they want", promises a later time when the dogs will get their share. "Dog" is the Jewish abusive word for gentile. Jesus expects the woman to realize that the Jews have precedence and that the gentiles will follow after. The gentile has no claim to salvation; he receives it undeservedly. At the same time there is a warning to the gentile Christians against pride. Christians from the gentiles are not the only ones who can lay claim to God's grace. God has not rejected his people (Schmithals 1979a:351-356). This Antiochene point of view does not represent a thoroughgoing universalism, but rather concerns the admission of a few uncircumcised people into the church (Schmithals 1978e:401).

Schmithals (1978e:413) locates universalistic Christianity in Damascus. After his conversion, Paul became convinced that he had persecuted people so violently for what was in fact the truth. Christ is the end of the law. As a Jew, Paul now relinquishes his obedience to the law. Here we do not find a practical or theoretical mitigation of the law, as in the Antiochene tradition, but a basic antinomy, where the principle of Jewish privilege is denied. There is no longer any distinction between Jew and gentile, therefore a law drawing this distinction is no longer valid (Schmithals 1978e:400; 1982a:64; 1989c:239). In Galatians 3:28 Paul quotes a doctrinal formula from this theology: "There is neither Jew nor Greek, slave nor free, male nor female, for you are all one in Christ." This is clearly the language of gnostic dualism. To the dualistic way of thinking, earthly differences lie only in the corporeal. The divine pneuma is above the mundane and not affected by the difference between man and woman, slave or free man, or between nations, race or language. Universalism, a basic idea of Gnosticism, was adopted and incorporated into Christianity. As members of the church of grace, in faith, man and woman, slave and freeman, Jew and Gentile are equal, although the natural and sociological differences still exist

(Schmithals 1978e:401).

In reply to the question of how a universalistic Christendom could have developed so early (a fact that is accepted by other researchers cf. Cadbury 1933:70, footnote 1) Schmithals maintains (1984b:156; 1989c241; cf. 1978e:406; 1994a:84-85) that it could be explained in theological history by the meeting of the "Hellenists" (among whom Stephen played a leading role) and gnostic Jewry in Samaria, to which the name of Simon Magus is linked. In this meeting a branch of missionary Palestinian Jewish Christianity were able to Christianize gnostic dualism by translating the substantial dualism into decisive dualism. "Johannine theology," that is the theology of the fundamental gospel and the gospel, is rooted in universal Christianity (Schmithals 1992a:149).

In depicting the era of the Apostles, Schmithals is objective when it comes to the tendency of researchers to allow either the Jewish Christians or the Gentile Christians to play the preponderant role. This objective view is expressed in the term Hellenistic Jewish Christianity. Schmithals (1989c:244) imagines that the persecution of Christianity, freed from the law, led to victory for the synagogue. This victory must be understood in the sense that the Jewish Christians relinquished their radical freedom from the law and joined the gentile mission of the synagogue. Paul himself became integrated into this group during the more than ten years of his work in Syria and Cilicia. (Schmithals 1988a:39, 51; 1989c:244; 1994a:113-118; cf. Schmidt 1929:col 1695).

At this stage Schmithals revised his own interpretation of history. At first Schmithals (1963:21-22; cf. 1978e:410) saw a connection between the theology of Antioch and universalistic Christianity. In this group it was presumed that there would no longer be missionary work among the Jews. Schmithals placed the whole of Paul's ministry within the frame of Christianity, freed from the law. Now, however, he has Paul working in synagogical Christianity along with Barnabas for a time. This implies a continuation of missionary work among the Jews. Not until the Apostolic meeting where new arrangements were taken did Paul return to the Christianity freed of the law, the Christianity of his conversion (Schmithals 1988a:39, 1989c:244; 1997a: 16-18).

At the Apostolic meeting in Jerusalem (Gal 2:1-10) it was agreed that Paul and his assistants "should go to the Gentiles and they to the Jews" (Gal 2:9). By means of this arrangement, the problem of Jewish Christians on Palestinian soil, who could not dissociate themselves in principle from the Torah, was solved. The relinquishing of the law led to Jewish resistance. The church could not hope to succeed in its missionary work with this aggressive approach. The option of Antioch was more suited to mission among Jews. Within the framework of Hellenistic synagogical Jewish Christianity, Peter takes the initiative as far as missionary work among the Jews in the Diaspora is concerned. Paul, meanwhile, introduces Christianity, freed from the law, to the Gentiles (Schmithals 1963:34-36; 1988a:40 1989c:244; 1997a: 18-20).

Schmithals (1963:94; 1985a:378) finds this same arrangement mentioned with regard to the Jewish-Christian situation in Matthew 10:5-6 These twelve Jesus sent out with the following instructions: "Do not go among the Gentiles or enter any town of the Samaritans. Go rather to the lost sheep of Israel'."

Schmithals (1963:50;1988a:397;1989c:2491994a: 121-122;1997a:17) adds that there were parallel missions by Paul and Peter. Peter maintained ties with the synagogue through Jewish Christianity, while Paul organized the *ecclesia* among the god-fearing Gentiles, outside the synagogue. For this purpose Schmithals (1984:126-127; 1988a:43) sees Paul corresponding with the gentile Christian home congregations in Rome. Paul wants to organize a congregation, based on the universalistic gospel, outside the national association of the synagogue.

4.5 Q AND Q1

The symbol Q denotes the hypothetical collection of Jesus' sayings or *logia*. This is the second of the two sources regarded as common to Matthew and Luke. In addition, it furnishes the foundation for work on the Synoptic Gospels. Schmithals writes his own literary history of Q and in the process he clarifies historic relationships.

Schmithals (1979a:23; 1985a:384-404) invokes the scientific consensus that in Q an older tradition should be distinguished from a more recent edited version of the tradition. He identifies the older tradition, Q1 (Schmithals 1980a:51; 1982f:622; 1985a:399-400; 1994a:29, 47) as being a document of a prophetic-apocalyptic group, who were expecting the last days. Jesus and John were considered to be the prophets of the end-time. The turning point is John, and Jesus continues his work. With the advent of the Son of Man, God's kingdom will have reached its goal. Later on the Apostolic Fathers reported the continued existence of such a group, the Ebionites. According to the Fathers, they did not belong to the church, because they considered Jesus to be an ordinary human being. They denied his divinity and his status as Son of God. Schmithals (1979a:52) is convinced that these followers of Jesus lived in Galilee.

In this unkerygmatic prophetic tradition of Jesus of the Q1 Church, Jesus is placed on a par with John the Baptist:

> To what then can I compare the children of this generation? What are they like? They are like children sitting in die market place and calling out to each other: "We played the flute for you, and you did not dance; we sang a dirge and you did not cry." For when John the Baptist came neither eating bread nor drinking wine, you say "He has a demon." The Son of Man came eating and drinking, and you say, "here is a glutton and drinking, and you say "Here is a glutton and a drunkard, a friend of tax collectors and sinners."
>
> (Luke 7:31-34)

Schmithals (1980a:97-98) is of the opinion that the original Q document read "Jesus" instead of "Son of Man," thus placing Jesus on a par with John. The title "Son of Man" was not originally a kerygmatic title given to Jesus. It was the designation of the celestial being, who would be the judge when the Old World came to an end. Thus the quoted passage (Lk. 7:31-34) is a kerygmatic version of an unkerygmatic text. Here Jesus is identified as the eschatological judge, the Son of Man, because that is what he called himself. His messianic task of salvation is emphasized by the addition of "a friend of tax-collectors and sinners." After these adjustments, Jesus and John the Baptist were no longer parallel figures; now John is the predecessor of the Messiah.

The Little Apocalypse appearing in Mark 13 came as a separate document, probably from the same church (Schmithals 1979a:561, 583; 1985a:400). The apocalyptic tension in the group where Q1 circulated Schmithals (1979a:561-586) observes *inter alia* in Mark 13:24-27:

> In those days...the sun will be darkened and the moon will not give its light; the stars will fall from the sky, and the heavenly bodies will be shaken. At that time men will see the Son of Man coming in clouds with great power and glory. He will send his angels and gather his elect from the four winds, from the ends of the earth to the ends of the heavens.

Schmithals (1979a:582; 1994a:51) holds Mark, the evangelist, responsible for the Christianizing of a typically apocalyptic product ending with these verses. The way that Mark does it in this passage is by identifying the Son of Man with Jesus: "Jesus said to them: 'Watch out that no one deceives you. Many will come in my Name, claiming, 'I am he' and will deceive many" (Mk 13:5-6).

Mark indirectly criticizes the apocalyptic views of the group, warning them to be watchful as the time of the end was unknown (Schmithals 1979a:583): "No-one knows about that day or hour" (Mk13:32).

Especially in Chapter 13, Mark quotes from Q1. In this way he identifies the group to whom this tradition belongs and relativizes their apocalyptic tension (Schmithals 1979a:57, 585).

Another example of the history of the tradition of the Q-material can be illustrated by means of the different versions of the parable of the mustard seed: "Then Jesus asked: 'What is the kingdom of God like? What shall I compare it to? It is like a mustard seed, which a man took and planted in his garden. It grew and became a tree, and the birds of the air perched in its branches' " (Lk 13:18-19). This parable could have been part of the authentic preaching of Jesus. It must be seen against the background of the apocalyptic expectations of the Old World changing to the new. The sceptics, who doubted that this change would take place, were told that the reign of God would be established suddenly and that the world would change (Schmithals 1979a:251-252).

Within the Q1 church the function of the parable is altered to overcome the problem of the delayed of the Second Coming. The Q1 congregation are warned to be patient: As surely as a mustard seed will develop into a tree, just as surely the kingdom of God will come in his own time (Schmithals 1979a:252; 1980a:152-153). In the light of the delayed Second Coming the non-apocalyptic wisdom passages of Q1 can caution the church to love and tolerance (Schmithals 1975c:84). For example: "If someone strikes you on one cheek, turn to him the other also" (Lk 6:29; cf. Schmithals 1980a:83-84).

In his editing of the parable, Mark, the evangelist, accentuates the small seed and the large plant and with the word "grew" he achieves association with the "good soil" of the parable of the Sower (Mk. 4:8) and therefore the Christian church: "It is like a mustard seed, which is the smallest seed you plant in the ground. Yet when planted, it grows and becomes the largest of all garden plants, with such big branches that the birds of the air can perch in its shade" (Mk. 4:31-32).

Now the parable no longer has a bearing on the apocalyptic coming of the kingdom of God, but on the growing church. Mark wants to convince the Q1 community that Jesus was referring to the church. He sowed the church, so that a "large tree" could grow from a humble beginning. The one who understands the secret of the kingdom of God joins the church. The shady tree symbolizes the Christian church that offers the faithful, who had experienced the destruction of Jerusalem, the salvation of God (Schmithals 1979a:252-253).

Mark succeeded partly in his attempts at winning over the Q1 congregation for the church. Proof of his success Schmithals (1979a:57-58; 1985a:403) finds in the Christian adaptation of their document by Mark himself, or someone from his school. This document, called Q, was handed down and distributed along with his version of the Gospel. Later on Matthew and Luke could independently introduce Mark's gospel as well as Q to their congregations.

To summarize, it can be said that Schmithals succeeds in establishing an alternative to the form critical treatment of the subject matter. The originators of the form critical approach, Dibelius and Bultmann, were of the opinion, that from a broad stream of kerygmatic, oral tradition, a collection of paraenetic material had developed (Schmithals 1979a:24; 1980:153; 1985a:277, 396; cf. Bultmann 1913: 24). Schmithals no longer accepts one original Christianity as bearer of the material that was handed down, one broad stream of oral tradition. He adduces appropriate historical relationships in support of the literary history of the synoptic material.

Further evidence of the existence and views of the Q1 congregation, Schmithals (1982a:171-172; 1985a:404) finds in the remarks about Apollos in Acts 18:25-26. Apollos taught very accurately about Jesus but he was ignorant of baptism in the name of Jesus Christ. He only knew the baptism of John. That means that the cross and resurrection of Jesus had not yet become the essence of his creed. The preaching of Jesus was preached by Apollos, but not the preaching of the church of Jesus as Lord. He might have been one of the Q1 group and Priscilla and Aquilla had to instruct him in the confession of the church.

Apollos might have brought the Jesus tradition, Q1, of his group to Ephesus, where Paul, having seen it, referred to it: "In the same way, the Lord has commanded that those who preach the gospel should receive their living from the gospel" (1 Cor. 9:14). In Ephesus Apollos encountered Pauline theology and adopted the christological creed of the church.

4.6 THE *APOSUNAGOGOS*

The concept of *aposunagogos* can be found in John 9:22, where it describes a person excluded from the synagogue: "for already the Jews had decided that anyone who acknowledged that Jesus was the Christ would be put out of the synagogue." To Schmithals (1985a:358-359; 1987d: 371:374; 1993b; 1994a:231) the *aposunagogos* became the *terminus technicus* for describing the exclusion of the Jewish Christians from the synagogue in the period after the destruction of the temple in 70 A.D. Up to the time of the destruction of the temple, Jewish Christians enjoyed the protection given to a privileged religion in the Roman Empire. They were considered a part of Jewry. After the loss of the temple, the Pharisees reorganized Jewry, with the pharisaic interpretation of the Torah as its focal point. The Jewish-Christian church was now confronted with the law as the new focal point in the synagogue. Anyone disagreeing with this new approach had to leave the synagogue: *aposunagogos*. The Jewish Christians, as well as the Gentile Christians, who had been part of the synagogue as "God fearers," could no longer remain under the sheltering roof and still uphold their creed. Consequently they had to leave the synagogue.

The reorganization of Jewry was also in the interest of the Roman State, because the Pharisees took a stand against the Zealot revolt and were a stabilizing factor in the

Jewish Diaspora. From this point of view, Jewish Christians, who left the synagogue, were regarded as deserters and potential rebels. The synagogue opposed these rebels and reported them to the Roman authorities. This was also in the interest of the Pharisees for their own protection. By the end of the first century the curse of the heretics, *Birkat-ha-Minim* had been incorporated into the daily prayer of the Jews. This represented the acme of these measures. This was an overt demonstration of the rejection of the Christians, who could no longer be considered to be a group within Jewry.

Schmithals (1983c:27; 1985a:375; 1994a:235) sees signs of this division between synagogue and church, *inter alia*, in the Gospel of Matthew. The Jewish-Christian church is pressurized by the synagogue, and it is not yet clear to all the members of the congregation that they cannot go along with the reorganization of the Pharisees. Matthew takes a firm stand against "their" synagogue and insists that they follow the Christian way to the end. The church consists of Jewish Christians and non-Jewish Christians:

> Be on your guard against men; they will hand you over to the local councils and flog you in their synagogues. On my account you will be brought before governors and kings as witnesses to them and to the Gentiles. However, when they arrest you, do not worry about what to say or how to say it. At that time you will be given what to say, for it will not be you speaking, but the Spirit of your Father speaking through you.
>
> (Mt 10:17-20)

These verses depict the persecution of the Jewish-Christian congregation. In the Diaspora, the synagogue received legal empowerment to act against rebels, while the Roman law is also mentioned as the compass within which evidence could be given. Matthew comforts and encourages the church by pointing out that they would not have to do anything, the Spirit of God would say what was necessary. Neither the Christians nor their persecutors and judges, but God was in control of this situation. Through the witness of suffering Matthew establishes the fact that the church is the salt of the earth and the light of the world. The respect and recognition that the oppressed and helpless, "meek" church should command, causes "your" Father to be glorified, when the church overcomes the evil being done to them with the good that they do (Schmithals 1983c:34; 1985a:377; 1987d:376; 1994a:235).

To counteract the influence of the Pharisees, doctrinal discipline was imperative. Schmithals identifies the brother sinning against you with someone expounding a foreign doctrine:

> If your brother sins against you, go and show him his fault, just between the two of you. If he listens to you, you have won your brother over. If he will not listen, take one or two others along, so that every matter may be established by the testimony of two or three witnesses. If he refuses to listen to them, tell it to the church; and if he refuses to listen even to the church, treat him as you would a pagan or a tax collector.
>
> (Mt 18:15-17)

This discipline would have to be applied, but simultaneously there would always be the duty to forgive and to readmit the one who had been excluded to the church. (Schmithals 1985a:378; 1987d:376; 1994a:235-236).

Matthew found it important that members of the church be baptized. This act ensured that baptized members would dissociate themselves from the synagogue and join the church. The insistence of Jesus on being baptized served as an example to everyone. Thus all righteousness is fulfilled (Schmithals 1978f:77; 1985a:377; 1987d:376; 1994a:236): "John tried to deter him, saying, 'I need to be baptized by you, and do you come to me?' Jesus replied: 'Let it be so now; it is proper for us to do this to fulfill all righteousness' " (Mt 3:14-15).

With regard to the accusation of the synagogue that the Christian faith annulled the Law and the preaching of the prophets, Matthew contends that this is not the case; on the contrary the Law and the Prophets are fulfilled in Jesus, the Messiah. In opposition to Jewry, the church claims that its law is the true law (Schmithals 1985a:378; 1987d:376; 1994a:236): "For I tell you that unless your righteousness surpasses that of the Pharisees and the teachers of the law, you will certainly not enter the kingdom of heaven" (Mt 5:20).

Proceeding from the fulfilling of the law, Matthew aimed at bringing about a separation between the church and the synagogue. So he quotes his twelve realizations of prophecies to demonstrate that Jesus was the expected Messiah, for example: "All this took place to fulfill what the Lord had said through the prophet" (Mt 1:23; Schmithals 1994a:236).

Matthew was writing at the time of the *aposunagogos*. Luke, on the other hand, wrote when the division between church and synagogue had already taken place. He looked back on the persecution of Christians, which led to either martyrdom or apostasy (Schmithals 1985a:359; 1987d:377; 1994a:236-237): "I tell you my friends, do not be afraid of those who kill the body and after that can do no more. I will show you whom you should fear: Fear him who, after the killing of the body, has power to throw you into hell. Yes, I tell you, fear him"(Lk 12:4-5).

In view of possible martyrdom, Luke advises the church not to protest and to remain joyful. One should behave like Paul and Silas should one be imprisoned because of one's faith (Acts 16:23-25; Schmithals 1982a:151).

Luke also has a message for the Roman authorities. There was no truth in the accusation against the church that it was politically unreliable. Paul, the great missionary among the gentiles, was even a Roman citizen and the authorities had previously conceded the innocence of the Christians (Schmithals 1982a: 153-154):

> The jailer told Paul "The magistrates have ordered that you and Silas be released. Now you can leave. Go in peace." But Paul said to the officers: "They beat us publicly, without a trial, even though we are Roman citizens, and threw us into prison. Now do they want to get rid of us quietly? No! Let them come themselves and escort us out." The officers reported this to the magistrates, and when they heard that Paul and Silas were Roman citizens, they were alarmed. They came to appease them and escorted them from the prison, requesting them to leave the city.
>
> (Acts 16:36-39)

Schmithals (1987d:373-374; cf. 1994a:240-241) even maintains that the circumstances of the *aposunagogos* played an important role in determining the character of the writings of the New Testament that were written in the period after the destruction of the temple. These books comprise the whole of the New Testament, excepting the genuine Pauline letters. Apart from the tendency already discussed, the church had to cope with members who wanted to return to paganism under the pressure of persecution. Some rejected the authority of the government, while others tried to detach Christianity from its Old Testament roots. The persecution of the Jewish Christians brought them closer to the Pauline churches. For example, they lived under constant threat of persecution in Nero's time. All Christians now being outside the synagogue, the original working agreement between gentile Christians and Jewish Christians no longer made sense. So together the two groups could form the early catholic church.

Schmithals (1984a:18) places the collecting and editing of Paul's most important letters, those to the Corinthians, Galatians, Philippians, Thessalonians and Romans in the time of the *aposunagogos*. The aim of this collection was to put the heritage of Paul's writings at the disposal of the different groups within the church. These people now had to constitute themselves anew outside the synagogue. In the editing and publishing of the main collection, the well-known passage of Romans 13:1-7 found its way into the Pauline corpus, to serve as a political apology (Schmithals 1984a: 162-163; 1994a:242).

Apart from the main collection, Schmithals (1984a:165-188) also distinguishes a secondary collection of Pauline letters, namely Colossians, Philemon and Ephesians. Almost half of Colossians and the entire letter to the Ephesians Schmithals attributes to the work of an editor. Schmithals states the main theme of Ephesians as being the unification of Jewish and gentile Christians in the same church.

On the other hand, James, in his letter, again expresses the initial reservations concerning the amalgamation of the Jewish-Christian and Paulinian congregations (Schmithals 1989d:27-28).

4.7 THE EMPEROR CULT

Schmithals (1980c:125) gave the title "Bethlehem or Rome" to the history of the birth of Christ according to Luke. In this way he indicates the scope for the understanding of the narrative. The Hellenistic emperor cult as embodied in Caesar Augustus, it is Rome, gives rise to a profound theological stand being taken. In this the Savior in the city of David is placed in opposition to Caesar Augustus, the peacemaker. The emperor cult provides a religious and historical contour to the narrative of the birth of Christ.

Schmithals (1980a:41; 1980c: 129; cf. 1994a:93) also points out that Caesar Augustus was worshipped as a god for the peace and prosperity achieved during his reign. His praises were sung in all parts of the Roman Empire. In 9 B.C. an altar, *Ara pacis Augustae*, was consecrated, thus uniting Augustus and peace. In Asia (Minor) the Greek cities decided that 23 September, the birthday of Augustus, would mark the beginning of the year.

The Christmas narrative of Luke is enlivened by the contrast between the reign of Augustus and that of Jesus Christ (Schmithals 1980a:41-42; 1980c:128). On the one hand, Augustus issues a decree that a census is to be taken of the whole (Roman) world. This is enough to remind the readers of the oppressive imperial rule. To the people census registers meant tax, military service and pressure on minorities. On the other hand, the angel of the Lord questions the expectation of salvation through human, imperial powers and might. The emperor is not the Savior:

> The angel said to them: "Do not be afraid. I bring you good news of great joy that will be for all people. Today in the town of David a Saviour has been born to you; he is Christ the Lord. This will be a sign to you: You will find the baby wrapped in cloths and lying in a manger."
>
> (Lk 2:10-12)

Schmithals (1980a:42;1980c:133) finds more to the message of the angel than just criticism of the powers of this world, reminding them of their limitations. If the Savior of the world is born in a remote corner of the empire in a shepherd' village among simple folk who are under the power of the emperor nobody would expect salvation from the powers of this world. Thus salvation and human impotence belong together. The inspiring "do not be afraid" is heard by people who could not rely on their own strength. In this way the angel is proclaiming the "theology of the cross."

Schmithals (1980c:137-148) finds the same intention in the Christmas narrative of Matthew. Here Jesus is contrasted to Herod. Herod had identified himself with the idea behind Roman domination. He endeavoured to make the *pax Romana* as attractive as possible to his compatriots. Augustus is the Savior of the Roman Empire; Herod the Messiah of the Jews.

The homage paid to Jesus by the astrologers shows where man will find salvation in honoring the celestial Messiah (Schmithals 1980c:146): "On coming to the house, they saw the child with his mother Mary and they bowed down and worshipped him" (Mt 2:11). Schmithals sees the homage as worship and not as religious honor in a worldly sense as Lohmeyer (1967:25) does.

The well-known Christ hymn in Philippians 2:6-11 is seen by Schmithals (1981a:11-12; 1994a:93; 1997b:295-299) in the light of the worshipping of the emperor as a God. The title "Lord" is deliberately emphasized in the confession "Jesus Christ is Lord" at the end. The song aims at depriving the emperor of the salvific title of "Lord." He has a Lord above him. Jesus Christ is the "King of kings and Lord of lords" (Rev 19:16) Furthermore, Jesus humbled himself and became human, although he was in very nature, God. The emperor, on the other hand delighted in being equal to God.

The Christ hymn of Philippians 2:6-11 makes Schmithals (1978e:404-405, footnote 45; 1994a:91-93) think of the shaping of the theological tradition of Damascus. Paul became acquainted with it at the time of his conversion. In verse 8 Paul adds the *theologia crucis* of the tradition of Antioch. "The Jesus or Herod" of Matthew was written much later, in fact after the failed Jewish revolt of 66-70 A.D. (Schmithals 1980c:145). "Bethlehem or Rome" was written still later than Matthew's gospel and incorporated into his gospel by Luke (cf. Schmithals 1985a:366, 375). Thus emperor worship and the tendency to equate human sovereignty with divine sovereignty constantly led to theological concepts repudiating these ideas (cf. Schmithals 1979a:730).

4.8 FUNDAMENTAL GOSPEL (GRUNDEVANGELIUM) AND GOSPEL (EVANGELIUM)

True to his view of the historical-critical method, Schmithals keeps to his basic rule of interpretation by examining the situation of the dialogue. Does the writer have some other concept in mind, even if he does not refer to it directly? Is there another opinion that is dismissed? Although this *modus operandi* is not seriously questioned and is generally accepted, when it comes from the pen of Schmithals, it takes on a pregnant form. It is important to note that Schmithals improved his presentation of the matter as he progressed and modified his earlier opinions considerably in his latest publications (cf. Schmithals 1984b: 116-117; 1987d:378-380). Originally, he allowed for an insignificant editing of the Gospel of John, but now, by making a new disposition, it appears that approximately fifty percent of the material used in the Gospel can be attributed to editorial adaptation. Taking as example the well-known passage of the true vine (Jn 15:1-17), Schmithals (1984b: 115; 1987d:379) originally saw it against the background of the struggle between the synagogue and the church. The congregation is encouraged not to yield to the pressure of the synagogue, but to remain in the church. Lately Schmithals (1992a:395) sees this text as applying to another conflict: that between the true and the false church, the conflict between the church and gnostic heresy. The true church is the one remaining in Christ and thus remaining in love and keeping the commandments.

Schmithals finds that the fundamental gospel (*Grundevangelium*) was written on account of the *aposunagogos*. After the destruction of the temple in Jerusalem in 70 A.D., the Pharisees converted the Jewish religion from one that could accommodate various theological viewpoints quite comfortably, into a law-abiding synagogue. Jewish Christians could no longer have any connection with the synagogue and, outside the synagogue, they had no civil rights. In this situation the danger of apostasy among Christians was acute. In these circumstances of expulsion from the synagogue, *aposunagogos*, the author of the *Grundevangelium*, wrote approximately fifty per cent of the gospel of John during the last decade of the first century (Schmithals 1992a: 158-159, 421). This "fundamental" author wrote to remind the church anew of its confession and affirm it to them. At the same time he wishes to encourage those among the Jews who, like Nicodemus, sympathize with the Christians, but do not dare to be baptized. For fear of persecution they were reluctant to leave the synagogue outright and take this step (Schmithals 1992a:312, 315, 330, 331). Any true teacher of Israel ought to be baptized

(Jn 3:10).

In this way John the Baptist testified, when he was approached by an official delegation of the Jews, that he himself was not the Christ, but concerning Jesus he says: I would not have known him, except that the one who sent me to baptize with water told me, the man on whom you see the Spirit come down and remain is he who will baptize with the Holy Spirit. I have seen and I testify that this is the "Son of God" (Jn 1:33-34)

At the wedding in Cana, Jesus reveals his Messianic glory in the land of the Jews by means of a miracle: "And his disciples put their faith in him" (Jn 2:11; Schmithals 1992a:327). The author of the *Grundevangelium* changes the synoptic text concerning the healing of the centurion's servant (Lk 7:1-10). He calls the centurion a civil servant or Herodian, in other words a Jew. This Jew becomes convinced that Jesus is the Messiah (Jn 4:46-47, 50-54a; Schmithals 1992a:341). The conversation Jesus had with the Samaritan woman develops to the point where he himself professes that he is the Messiah, "I who speak to you am He." To the Jews he says, "You will die in your sin. Where I go you cannot come" (Jn 8:21). In his parting words to his disciples he assures them that he is going to prepare a place for them and he will return to take them to be with him (Jn 14:3). To this is added another "I am" formula in order to exclude the synagogue as a way of salvation outside Christianity. "I am the way and the truth and the life. No one comes to the Father except through me" (Jn 14:6; Schmithals 1992a:389-390). Even when it comes to the history of the Passion. the author of the *Grundevangelium* does not use the *theologia crucis*, but it was the Jews who denounced him to Pilate, because he claimed that he was the Son of God. Here again Jesus acts like the expected Messiah in that he has control of his own destiny as befits a king (Schmithals 1992a:404-405). In the last scene depicted in the *Grundevangelium* we have the congregation, threatened by the Jews, but nevertheless filled with joy because their exalted Lord is with them: "On the evening of that first day of the week, when the disciples were together, with the doors locked for fear of the Jews, Jesus came and stood among them and said Peace be with you!" (Jn 20:19; Schmithals 1992a:411-412).

Schmithals (1992a:219) reached the conclusion that the editor of the *Grundevangelium*, the evangelist makes use of the *Grundevangelium* in his conflict with Docetism. His hand can be seen in the Johannine letters. He uses the language of the *Grundevangelium*. Where as the point of departure in the *Grundevangelium* is: Jesus is the *Christ*, the editor could use this same statement, just giving it a different emphasis: *Jesus* is the Christ. In this way he could employ it to support his own struggle. Schmithals (1992a: 293-294) could dispense with a detailed analysis of Johannine grammar and linguistics, because the literary contents and data supplied sufficient grounds for his assertion.

Schmithals (1992a:287-288) identifies the evangelist as the *presbyter* or "elder" (the word he uses when referring to himself) as the sender of 2 and 3 John. He is the author of the Johannine letters and of half of the Gospel of John, which he published as a unit.

In connection with the testimony of John the Baptist, where John is awarded the task of establishing the fact that the Spirit came upon Jesus as the expected Messiah, the evangelist manipulates the content of the baptism, so that it becomes the incarnation of Jesus. Schmithals (1992a:322) avers that the account of what occurred at the time of the baptism of Jesus must be seen in the context of 1 John 5:1-13. In John 5:6 an anti-dualistic stand is taken that "this is the one who came by water and blood: Jesus Christ." The *Grundevangelium* makes John visualize Jesus differently from the way the evangelist does. *The Grundevangelium* states: "The man on whom you see the Spirit come down and remain is he who will baptize with the Holy Spirit. I have seen and I testify that this is the Son of God" (Jn 1:33-34).

However, John the evangelist sees Jesus differently more directly, historically: "The next day John saw Jesus coming towards him" (Jn 1:29). A further indication of the fact that the evangelist wishes to use the baptism of Jesus as a testimony to Jesus' incarnation is that John deliberately refers to a man. "A man who comes after me has surpassed me because he was before me." This is the man to whom the evangelist links his central theme "Look, the Lamb of God, who takes away the sin of the world!" (Jn 1:29). As Lamb, Christ dies in an anti-docetic way for the sins of the world. According to Schmithals (1992a:306), the evangelist also expresses his *theologia crucis* in this way and shows that he is familiar with the concepts and formulae of Hellenistic Jewish Christianity. The Antiochene soteriology uses expressions like "delivered" "for us" and "reconciliation."

Schmithals (1992a:429) thinks that the author of the *Grundevangelium* is following the soteriological model of the humiliation and exaltation of the Son of God a model, which could be older than the theology of the cross. He also uses the missionary and the pre-existential Christology. The fact that Jesus was sent by his Father accentuates the fact that he is the Messiah (Schmithals 1992a:296, 427, 430). Relating to this, the evangelist contends that Jesus came from heaven physically: "Jesus knew that the Father had put all things under his power, and that he had come from God and was returning to God" (Jn 13:3; Schmithals 1992a:298). Schmithals finds (1992a:282) a reference to the pre-existence of Jesus in the text: I write to you, fathers, because you have known him who is from the beginning"(1 Jn 2:13; cf. Jn 1:1).

In the conflict with docetism, the evangelist links Jesus to the Jewish festival calendar. Jesus participates in three Passovers, a Feast of Tabernacles, and Hanukkah. Besides participating in feasts, Jesus travels more than in the *Grundevangelium*. The motive behind this is to depict Jesus more clearly as a true human being who is part of his environment. For this purpose the evangelist adjusted the fundamental gospel in order to allow Jesus to travel to Jerusalem four times, instead of the one journey described by the *Grundevangelium* and the Synoptic Gospels (Schmithals

1992a:300-301; 417-420). The evangelist also alters the date of Jesus' death to tie in with his message. Whereas the Synoptic Gospels have Jesus eating the Passover meal on the Thursday, the evangelist omits the meal so that Jesus dies at the time as Passover lamb had to be slaughtered: He is the physical Passover lamb that suffers an actual death (Schmithals 1992a:306, 382, 407). Jesus does this for the remission of our sins (Schmithals 1992a:306) to gainsay the heretics who denied the existence of sin and the forgiveness of sins (Schmithals 1992a:413). He is resurrected physically and bodily returns to the Father (Schmithals 1992a:299, 412-413).

The so-called high Christology is ascribed by Schmithals (1992a:296, 344; cf. 298) to the author of the *Grundevangelium*. With him there is a unity between the Father and the Son. This unity is dynamic, in other words God acts in Christ. He is the Son of God. The so-called lower or subordinate Christology Schmithals (1992a:296, 384-385) finds in the formulations of the evangelist. According to this the Father makes the Son what he is he is not anything of himself. The Son of Man is glorified by the Father. He is also sent by God, he is sent physically (Schmithals 1992a:297). Anything like a pneumatic ascension to heaven does not exist. The only knowledge of heaven is brought by the earthly man, Jesus: "No-one has ever gone into heaven except the one who came from heaven the Son of Man" (Jn 3:13; Schmithals 1992a:332). Schmithals (1992a:297, 429) reached the conclusion that Bultmann's conviction of the sufficiency of "the fact that Jesus came" does justice to the theology of the evangelist to a certain extent but not to that of the compiler of the *Grundevangelium*.

The gnostic heretics were of the opinion that they were free from sin. There is no sin for the *pneuma*, captive in this alien world because the *pneuma* is essentially divine. When the gnostics say that they have "fellowship with God" (1 Jn 1:6) they mean that the *pneuma* is identical with God. From the point of view of the soul of the pneumatic that ascends to heaven and leaves the corporeal world, they can declare: "we claim to be without sin" (1 Jn 1:8, 10). In opposition to and against the dualistic concept of a divine sphere and one opposed to God, the evangelist states that human beings have no need to be like God they may be sinners. Their sins are forgiven. The evangelist distinguishes between forgiven sins and the sin that leads to death (1 Jn 5:16). This sin consists in going along with the apostasy of the heretics. For this he does not pray for forgiveness; it must be stopped immediately. There must be no association with the heretics; they must neither be received in their houses nor greeted (2 Jn 10). Gaius, on the contrary, is praised for his hospitality shown to those who were travelling for the sake of the Name of Jesus (3 Jn 5-8; Schmithals 1992a:289).

Schmithals (1992a:283-284) does not interpret the constant admonishing to brotherly love, as for example in 2 John 5: "I ask that we love one another," as being a call to specific social behavior of the congregation. In view of the polemic context it would rather point to an admonishing to be faithful to the congregation and the Christian tradition that had been handed down and not to break away from the church unlovingly.

Concerning the dualistic mode of expression in the *Grundevangelium:* "Flesh gives birth to flesh, but Spirit gives birth to spirit" (Jn 3:6), it would be grist to the mill to his adversaries, the Docetists. To the Docetists the main theme of their theology was the Spirit and so the evangelist also had to develop a doctrine of the Spirit. So he corrects his dualistic use of language by adding the remark: "The wind blows wherever it pleases. You hear its sound, but you cannot tell where it comes from or where it is going. So it is with everyone born of the Spirit" (Jn 3:8). The heretics, on the one hand, taught that the Spirit was something people themselves brought along it was humankind's own contribution. On the other hand, the gospel states that the Spirit is a gift from God. The Spirit blows wherever it pleases, in other words it does not become a possession of the pneumatic, it is given and received (Schmithals

1992a:281, 310-311, 393). Spirit is the indication and acknowledgement of the fact that Jesus was truly human. "Streams of living water" that is the Spirit, will flow from "within him," meaning his body (Jn 7:38-39; Schmithals 1992a:263). From the exalted body of Christ the Spirit comes. Consequently only the believers and not the docetic heretics receive the Spirit. After his exaltation Jesus can no longer be present in the flesh with his church and the Holy Spirit works in his stead. This theological concept the evangelist could have taken from Luke (Schmithals 1992a:311). As opposed to the yearning of the pneumatics to be set free from the world, the Spirit is sent to the church to be with them always: "And I will ask the Father, and he will give you another Counsellor to be with you for ever the Spirit of the truth (Jn 14:16-17; Schmithals 1992a:393). The Spirit is only the comforter, not the extension of the deity that the pneumatics can allow to emit from themselves. The Spirit is sent, "in my Name" (Jn 14:26). The prayer in the Name of Jesus is a prayer for the Holy Spirit. Schmithals (1992a:301, 393) explains that it can only refer to the specific name of the man, Jesus. In this Name the true church prays (Jn 14:14) and receives forgiveness of sins (1 Jn 2:12).

4.9 THE PROLOGUE

Schmithals thinks that the wisdom myth is the foundation on which the prologue is built. Nevertheless, he does not share the opinion that we are dealing with a pre-Christian hymn. Right from the beginning the poem moves towards the triumphant conclusion: "The one and only, who came from the Father full of grace and truth." In the first two verses the prologue proceeds from a general revelation, which however, is not believed. The Light is not accepted by the darkness. Universalism is brought to a head where "grace and truth" are placed in opposition to the "law." The contrast in verse 17 is even more radical than Paul's "justification by law-justification by faith." Paul can still make the law subservient to grace, but here the law has no positive function to fulfill. Schmithals (1992a:149, 273-274) places the author of the prologue as originating from the region where Paul and "John" (= the author of the *Grundevangelium* and the evangelist) learnt their universalistic Christianity, set free from the law. The principal theological ideas of the prologue, namely the pre-existential Christology, incarnation, theology of the Word and the eschatological knowledge of the church, all point in this direction.

4.10 THE BELOVED DISCIPLE EDITING

Schmithals believes that the figure of the beloved disciple is not part of the Grundevangelium or the gospel, but was added at the last editing of the Johannine writings. He calls this the beloved-disciple editing. The editorial additions are John 6:63; 13:20-26a, 36-38; 16:12-13; 18:15-18, 24-27; 19:24b-27; 20:2-11a; 21:1-25 (Schmithals 1992a:258).

The fact that Jesus loved this disciple (e.g. Jn 13:23) is an unemotional indication of his being considered worthy to be an authentic apostolic witness (Schmithals 1992a: 231). Peter enjoyed the same status and was possibly raised above the others because of his martyrdom, "more than these," so that he took the first place in the order of precedence of witnesses. When they had finished eating, Jesus said to Simon Peter, "Simon son of John, do you truly love me more than these?" "Yes, Lord", he said, you know that I love you." Jesus said, "Feed my lambs." Again Jesus said, "Simon son of John, do you truly love me?" He answered, "Yes, Lord, you know that I love you." Jesus said, "Take care of my sheep." The third time he said to him, "Simon son of John, do you love me?" Peter was hurt because Jesus asked him the third time, "Do you love me?" He said, "Lord, you know all things; you know that I love you." Jesus said, "Feed my sheep." (Jn 21:15-17.)

The intention of this passage is to create a parallel between Peter and the beloved disciple. Jesus loves the beloved disciple and Peter loves Jesus. By means of love the same relationship between the Lord and his two disciples is described (Schmithals 1992a:231).

To pinpoint the historical circumstances of this material more exactly, Schmithals points out that the threefold injunction, "Feed my lambs," "Take care of my sheep," "Feed my sheep," already presupposes the claim to primacy of the congregation in Rome. The shepherd feeding the sheep is the image of a leader of the congregation. This depiction of Peter as the great church leader is not appropriate for Peter in his lifetime. It was only after his martyrdom in Rome and in connection with the claim to primacy of the Roman church that Peter grew in stature to such an extent that he was depicted as leader of the church as a whole. His martyrdom was the foundation of Peter's empowerment as dignitary and the sealing of his authority as the ruler and bishop of the congregation of Rome. The texts in which the beloved disciple acts in such a way that he is placed on a par with Peter must be dated to a period when the claims of primacy had already been made (Schmithals 1992a:239).

Schmithals (1992a:241) reaches the conclusion that the purpose of the beloved disciple editing was to gain recognition from the church in Rome for the gospel of John. The ground for this would be that the writer of the gospel, the beloved disciple, could be equated with Peter in apostolic authority.

To determine who used the beloved-disciple editing to make the Gospel of John acceptable to the ecclesiastical authority of Rome, Schmithals analyzes John 21:20-23:

> Peter turned and saw that the disciple whom Jesus loved was following them. This is the one who had leaned back against Jesus at supper and said, "Lord, who is going to betray you?" When Peter saw him, he asked, "Lord what about him?" Jesus answered, "If I want him to remain alive until I return, what is that to you? You must follow me." Because of this, the rumor spread among the brothers that this disciple would not die; he only said "If I want him to remain alive until I return, what is that to you?" This is the disciple who testifies to these things

and who wrote them down. We know that his testimony is true.

Schmithals agrees with the assumption that the disciple who was to remain alive until Jesus came, also had to be the writer of Revelation. More than once Jesus says "I am coming soon" in Revelation (e.g. 3:11) and the deduction could have been made that this minister would not die before the Lord came. The disputants on Revelation took advantage of the miscalculation of the writer to bring the book into disfavor. This accusation is refuted by the explanation that Jesus did not say that he would not die. That is a misunderstanding. Jesus merely mentioned a possibility if he wished the beloved-disciple to remain until his Second Coming, it made no difference to the course of Peter's life (Schmithals 1992a:248, 253). According to Schmithals, this explanation saved both the Revelation of John and the apostolic authority of the author from losing credibility. At the same time it revealed that according to tradition, the beloved disciple was identical to this John, son of Zebedee. Prior to the editing of the Gospel of John, it was thought to be the work of an unknown author. By means of this editing it was now ascribed to the apostle John, who had long since been regarded as the author of Revelation.

Schmithals deals with this argument historically by means of the remark that the Montanists, in the time of the formation of the canon, invoked the divergence between the Gospel of John and Revelation. At this time they were active in Phrygia. Under threat of persecution from the authorities, they kept alive the Revelation of John and expected the coming of the New Jerusalem and the Millennium in Pepuza, in the near future. They never doubted that this prophetic claim of theirs was well founded, because the Paraclete had been promised to them:

> I will ask the Father, and he will give you another Counsellor to be with you forever the Spirit of truth. The world cannot accept him, because it neither sees nor knows him. However,

> you know him, for he lives with you and will
> be in you.
>
> (Jn 14:16-17)

In any case Montanus considered himself to be the Paraclete, so that the Montanists felt a relationship with the Gospel of John.

Schmithals (1992a:253) is convinced that Montanus and his apocalyptic movement were the first to invoke Revelation and the Paraclete of the Gospel of John and consequently he ascribes the adaptation of the Gospel by means of the beloved-disciple editing to the early Montanists. This was undertaken, on the one hand, to prove the apostolicity of Revelation and the apocalyptic expectations of the Montanists. On the other hand, the editing lends apostolic status to the Gospel and the included promises of the Paraclete, thus justifying Montanistic prophecy. This took place with the specific acknowledgement of and deference to the authority of the Roman church and it took place in direct or indirect association with the forming of the canon.

Presumably, the point of contact between the Gospel of John and the Montanists was the promise of the Holy Spirit made in the Gospel. The Montanists subscribed to these views and adapted them to suit themselves. Schmithals (1992a:25-46) has no doubt that the Montanist hand intervened in the last of the Paraclete passages:

> I have much more to say to you, more than you can now bear. However, when he, the Spirit of truth, comes, he will guide you into all truth. He will not speak on his own; he will speak only what he hears, and he will tell you what is yet to come.
>
> (Jn 16:12-13)

This remark directly contradicts John 15:15 where Jesus assures his disciples that he made "everything" known to them. Here, however, it is stated that only when the Spirit has come, will he guide them into all truth. This also contradicts John 14:26 where the Spirit is given the function of teaching, in other words, of reminding them of everything Jesus said. This is typical of Montanus and his prophecy revealing the apocryphal events (Schmithals 1 992a:257).

4.11 CLOSING REMARKS

In depicting the historical situation of early Christianity, Schmithals adopts the scheme of the school of religious history, namely: the early Palestinian church, the Hellenistic-Jewish Christian Christianity, gentile Christianity. His aim was to highlight the historical circumstances that led to as specific theological pattern. The heresy of the Gnostics and awakening Marcionism played their roles in the church. Traces of the attempt to evangelize the Galilean followers of Jesus are found in literature. The conflict with the synagogue and refutation of the claims of the human powers-that-be, leave their imprint on the text of the New Testament.

The observant reader will have noticed that the essence and validity of historical exegesis cannot escape the objection of circularity. Historical exegesis leads to a better understanding of the theological language as reaction to certain views and circumstances. In turn, this reaction helps the exegete to form a picture of the historical background. The objection of moving in circles applies to the historical method as much as to Schmithals. All historical exegesis moves in a circle. Real criticism of the results obtained by Schmithals would have to come from a better circle of exegesis or historical interpretation of the texts.

CHAPTER 5

The relationship between the "proclaimer and proclaimed" as the main problem in the theological understanding of the New Testament

5.1 INTRODUCTION

Rudolf Bultmann (1979:393) in his description of the history of the synoptic tradition, came to the conclusion that the need of the early Palestinian church to vindicate itself in theological discussions led to certain writings. It collected and produced discourses in which Jesus argued with his opponents or had discussions with his disciples. The need for subject matter for teaching, and the liveliness of the prophetic spirit in the church, led to the production and collection of the prophetic and apocalyptic pronouncements of Jesus. The need for subject matter that could be used for reprimanding stimulated collection still further. Bultmann says that it was natural that stories about Jesus would be told in the church. There might have been a direct motive for the telling of stories, such as propaganda, or apologetic proof that Jesus was the Messiah. Even without any direct cause, it would have happened. Spiritual assets have a way of objectivizing themselves, even without a given cause.

On the one hand, Bultmann assumes an intrinsic interest in the life and work of Jesus in the early church. On the other hand, he is well known for his opinion that Paul and John were not interested in the historical Jesus. These two points of view seem to contradict one another. The tension is produced by the fact that Paul and John do not go back to the historical Jesus, while the synoptic tradition does. How can one theologize with Paul and John and at the same time search for the historical Jesus? Or to put it differently, if there is a common source for the shaping of the theology of the church, how can both trends be accommodated within it; the one trend being interested in the historical Jesus, while the other is not? Schmithals (1980b:154; cf. 1972b:66) says that he took up this matter of discrepancy in the shaping of Christological theology with Bultmann, but that Bultmann repeatedly dismissed his objection, presumably because he would not, or could not, see any problem.

5.2 BULTMANN AND THE MAIN PROBLEM

Bultmann (in Jaspert 1971:63; 1972b:266; 1980:35; in Schmithals 1984f:74) maintains that the main problem in New Testament theology is the question: how did the Proclaimer become the Proclaimed? Why did the followers of Jesus, when they took up his teaching anew, replace Jesus, the Proclaimer, with Jesus the proclaimed Lord. The historical Jesus who taught people now becomes the eschatological Son of God, about whom they preach. The task that now lies ahead is to describe and justify a pertinent connection between the proclaimed Lord and the proclaiming Jesus.

Bultmann (in Jaspert 1971:63-64) alleges that the problem becomes clear when one compares the Gospel of John with the synoptic gospels. In John, Jesus is depicted as the revealer. As revealer Jesus does not reveal anything, but introduces God himself. The people do not come to him to receive anything, but simply for the sake of coming to him. As revealer, Jesus calls the people, and those who wish to receive life from him must believe in him, or, in terms of the mythical ideal "come to him" (Bultmann: 1968:168). People wanting anything from Jesus must realize that they will have to receive Jesus himself. As revealer he says: "I am the bread of life. People who come to me will never go hungry, and people who believe in me will never be thirsty"

(Jn 6:35). Bultmann proceeds that this revealer became human, and also stresses the fact of Jesus being someone who said something. In addition, the synoptic gospels give an account of this someone and something. Furthermore, it makes no difference that the synoptic gospels are heard in Christian preaching as Christological narratives about Jesus. The synoptics not only speak of Jesus as revealer, but also of the way in which he did it. John did not do this.

Bultmann (in Jaspert 1971:65; cf. Schmithals 1967a:201) agrees with Kierkegaard's point of view. The tradition regarding Jesus would have been sufficient if it had said: "We believed that in such and such a year God showed himself as a humble servant, lived among us, taught us and then died." Still the Synoptics handed down more than what Kierkegaard considered necessary. To Bultmann the main problem lies in the relationship between what is necessary and what is excessive in the tradition of Jesus. Why did they tell more than was necessary? Why were people interested in the extra information?

Leading up to, and as part of the pre-history of Schmithals' handling of the problem, it will be advisable to pause for a moment to interrogate Bultmann. Bultmann believed that we know nothing more about the life and personality of Jesus, in spite of the interest, past and present, in more than the necessary facts. Christian sources tell us nothing about it and what little there is, is fragmentary and legendary. What has been written in modern times about the life, personality and inner development of Jesus lacks credibility and is more suited to fiction than reliable historical fact. Researchers are unable to agree on the question as to whether or not Jesus considered himself to be the Messiah. If clarity on such an important issue cannot be reached, we will have to concede that we know nothing about his personality (Bultmann 1983:10-11). The greatest setback to efforts to forming a characterization of Jesus is that we do not know how he understood his own death. Whatever can be read about it in the gospels is already an interpretation of his death (Bultmann 1967a:452).

Bultmann was definitely interested in what Jesus taught, his preaching, because this would indicate what Jesus' aims were. The will of Jesus can be deduced from this. Here the position differs from that obtaining in regard to the life and personality of Jesus. We don't know anything about his life and personality, but we can form a coherent conception of his teaching, about which Bultmann wrote his book *Jesus*. To reconstruct the teaching of Jesus, Bultmann distinguishes three layers in the synoptic gospels, namely the oldest material containing the original teaching of Jesus; the adaptation of this material by the oldest Palestinian churches; and later on by the Greek-speaking churches (Bultmann 1983:13). Bultmann aims at presenting the train of thought of the original teaching of Jesus. He considered using the title *The Preaching of Jesus* for his *Jesus* book to show clearly that it concerned Jesus as the Proclaimer (Bultmann 1983:14).

Bultmann (in Schmithals 1984f:75) wrote a letter to one of the critics of his Jesus book, telling him that this book was to be considered the first volume with regard to the problem of the proclaiming Jesus who became the proclaimed Christ. To begin with, the Proclaimer is clearly shown to us by his teaching. The readers are introduced to the situation before they are informed of the death and resurrection of Jesus. When the cross of Jesus is proclaimed as the divine redemption, a new situation arises which is not discussed in this first volume.

In his *Jesus* book Bultmann succeeded in reconciling two sections of the preaching of Jesus: Jesus as the eschatological prophet, proclaiming the coming of the reign of God, and Jesus, the rabbi, teaching the will of God. This was done within the framework of Bultmann's (1983:91) existential interpretation. The sense of Jesus' eschatological proclamation was that humankind had reached his or her last hour. People are asked to make a decision against the world and for God. In this decision one relinquishes any claims of one's own. When Jesus explains the will of God in his ethical preaching and says that we must forgive seventy times seven times, he asks an attitude of complete self-renunciation (Bultmann 1983:82). For the sake of the argument, we can add that the people who have come to this decision, no longer consider their life to be something under their control, but as a gift from God. This is the very essence of Christian teaching.

What is remarkable, is that Bultmann himself does not rate his *Jesus* book very highly. Schmithals (1967a: 209), on the other hand, recommends it as a starting point for anyone interested in Bultmann's theological work. Scholars who study Bultmann's theology consider this first volume to be Bultmann's outstanding work.

This recommendation sounds strange in view of Bultmann's own reservations about his book. From his students' point of view Bultmann must have achieved more than he envisioned through his presentation of the teaching of Jesus. The difference between the first and what must be considered his second volume, where the gospel is propounded, is not as great as Bultmann would have liked us to believe. The first volume serves as a useful introduction to the rest of Bultmann's theological work.

Schmithals (1967a:214-216) explains this state of affairs by pointing out that there is no material difference between what Jesus taught, as expounded by Bultmann, and what Paul proclaimed. The preaching of Jesus corresponds to the Christianity of Paul, in which Jesus is proclaimed. Bultmann's *Jesus* book serves to describe his own theology just as much as does his expounding of that of Paul or John. As far as the concept of God is concerned, there is no difference between the preaching of Jesus and that of Paul and John. Neither is there any difference in their view of the nature of humankind, the sinner, faith, and God's act of redemption.

Bultmann never expected this development. To his way of thinking, the teaching of Jesus, as expounded in his book, was not yet gospel. Only the proclamation of the church, into which Jesus was incorporated, became gospel (in Schmithals 1984f:75). Schmithals (1967a:216) points out that Bultmann eventually in his last stand, conceded to his students on the issue that they had convincingly shown the unity between the message of the church and the teaching of Jesus (Bultmann 1967a:463-464). Jesus, like the kerygma itself, proclaimed the grace of God, through judgement. Bultmann's *Jesus* book is indeed a good introduction to the rest of his theological work.

Thus it appears that Bultmann's interpretation of the teaching of Jesus does not support his point of view that the theology of the New Testament originated from the kerygma of the church. For argument's sake, New Testament theology could have begun with the teaching of Jesus, because basically there is no difference in the essence of what Jesus as proclaimer preached and what the church preaches concerning him. The upshot of these arguments is that a discrepancy in Bultmann's description of the theology of the New Testament must be recorded. The unsolved problem of the relationship proclaimer-proclaimed would lead to many of Bultmann's students and adherents becoming intensely involved in the study of the historical Jesus and his significance in Christian theology, quite contrary to Bultmann's intention. Bultmann (in Protokolle 1953) still disapproved of any attempt to supplement the fact of the coming of Jesus with historical detail in order to use this vivid portrayal to make the historical Jesus theologically relevant.

Once more the question arises: Why did the Proclaimer, Jesus, have to become the Proclaimed, Christ? Bultmann alleged that the transition from Proclaimer to Proclaimed could not be demonstrated historically. No depiction of Jesus makes the transition from his message to the preaching of the church acceptable. The fact that the Proclaimer became the Proclaimed is not a question of historical continuity (Bultmann 1967a:465).

The question concerning the relationship of what Jesus taught and the proclamation of the church inevitably becomes the question of why the Proclaimer has to become the Proclaimed: If what Jesus taught is essentially the same as the teaching of Paul and John, why is their message still necessary? Couldn't the church just have repeated what Jesus had said? If Bultmann can lead his readers to a situation where they can make a decision as regards Jesus, then the Christ-message of the church becomes superfluous. Conversely, if the Christ-message says everything that needs to be proclaimed, the church can do without the teaching of Jesus. It becomes unnecessary as Paul and John make clear (Bultmann 1967a:465).

Concerning the problem of the intrinsic inevitability of the Proclaimer becoming the Proclaimed, Bultmann has an answer. The kerygma of the church changed the once of the historical Jesus into the once-and-for-allness. In the teaching of the church, the eschatological event of the history of Jesus remains and lays claim to us. The preaching of the church maintains the continuity between the once and the once-and-for-allness. The preaching actualizes the claim, imposed by the once. For the sake of making it actual, it is necessary to exalt the historical Jesus when spreading the gospel. Jesus, who is present in the teaching, is more than the historical Jesus, who promised salvation; the kerygmatic Christ brought salvation (Bultmann 1967a:467).

Bultmann maintains that the basic difference between the teaching of Jesus and the Christ kerygma must not be overlooked. Paul and John clearly taught more than Jesus did. The utterance: "Therefore, if anyone is in Christ, he or she is a new creation; the old has gone, the new has come!" (2 Cor 5:17) cannot be traced to the teaching of Jesus. Whenever something similar is found in the words or work of Jesus, this interpretation came from the kerygma (Bultmann 1967a:468). To prevent the historical Jesus from getting more than his share of meaning, Bultmann describes his relationship to the ecclesiastical dogma in terms of law and gospel. The historical Jesus proclaimed the law, while the church proclaimed the gospel. Only on condition that the distinction between law and gospel is clearly understood, and the historical Jesus is incorporated in the law, can the gospel of the church be treated on its merits (Bultmann 1975b:197; in Jaspert 1971:64-65). Bultmann (1980:

37) incorporates the preaching of the historical Jesus with the Old Testament. He also understands the Old Testament to be the expression of the pre-Christian existence under the law. Through the preaching of the church the existence under the law is superseded by the existence under the gospel.

If the teaching of the church claims that it preaches Christ as an eschatological event and that Christ is present in it, the kerygma replaces the historical Jesus. The preaching of the church not only refers to the saving acts; salvation takes place as proclamation. To believe in Christ one must, at the same time, believe in the church as the bearer of the message; or expressed in dogmatic language, believe in the Holy Spirit. Bultmann explains that in this sense the church must not be understood as being an institution, but as an eschatological event. The church itself must be believed and is no guarantee of faith. In addition, this faith in the church, which is faith in Jesus Christ at the same time, could not have been taught by the historical Jesus (Bultmann 1967a:458).

The fact that the historical Jesus taught as he did has no significance as far as salvation is concerned. It is just a coincidence that the historical Jesus really taught that which Bultmann expounded in his *Jesus* book. Bultmann (in Schmithals 1984:75) has no objection to putting the "Jesus" in inverted commas, if anyone wishes to use it for naming the phenomenon as described in his book. The purpose of the inverted commas is to distinguish between the historical "Jesus" and the proclaimed Christ. Bultmann (1983:14) himself did not doubt that Jesus really taught as he did, but the historical Jesus is not yet God's eschatological saving act by God. The decisive message of the early church is that this Jesus, who was crucified, will come as the Messiah. The church could understand the appearance and person of Jesus eschatological, but they could still look back and see him as a historical phenomenon. To Paul, the appearance and person of Jesus were purely eschatological phenomena, they never became historical again. The significance of the cross became evident in Paul's theology. That which was implicit in the message of the early church became explicit in Paul's message: Jesus is the eschatological saving act of God (Bultmann 1972a:204-205).

Although Bultmann based his *Jesus* book on the material concerning Jesus, which he had collected from the synoptic gospels, he is convinced that these narratives were not motivated by historical interest, but were already told with a view to the requirements of the faith (Bultmann 1975a:32). However, while the traces of the historical Jesus material from the synoptic gospels were still evident in the kerygma of the church, Paul and John took leave of it. Paul does not see Jesus as a teacher of eternal truths, teaching a new concept of God, a new philosophy of life, or a new morality. Where Paul does invoke Jesus as teacher, he does it, not referring to the human Jesus, but to the confessed Lord of the church. Paul does not consider Christ as an example, except when seen as the pre-existent one who is acknowledged as Lord: "Your attitude should be the same as that of Jesus Christ" (Phil. 2:5). Paul does not consider Jesus to be a hero. He does not present the life and death of Jesus as a feat of human courage. He is preached as the crucified one, to make it clear that God condemns human achievement and glory, and that the cross was the eschatological act of salvation. Paul does not admire the personality of Jesus, because that would only mean "knowing him as he existed historically" (Bultmann 1972a:206-207).

In order to explain the significance of the historical Jesus to the Christian message, Bultmann used a controversial expression. He spoke of "the fact" (the *Dass*) of his existence in contrast to the historical details of his life. That Jesus had come was sufficient; it is the eschatological event (Bultmann 1975b:196). The historical details of his life had no meaning for salvation and are eliminated from the eschatological event. As far as the message of the church was concerned, only the fact that he became human is important, not the type of person he was, or what he did. "The fact that" he came provides the link between the historical

Jesus and the kerygma of the church.

We must keep in mind that Bultmann includes Jesus, as a person and his teaching, in the "fact that" of the eschatological events (Bultmann 1972b:204-205). Jesus wished to be the bearer of the decisive word of God in the last hour. Neither what he said, nor how he said it, is important. The importance lies in the fact that he said it and that he says it now. As bearer of the word of God, the person of Jesus is important: "I tell you, whoever acknowledges me before humankind, the Son of Man will also acknowledge him or her before the angels of God. However, he or she who disowns me before men will be disowned before the angels of God" (Lk 12:8-9).

From this, Bultmann's well-known remark followed that the appearance and teaching of Jesus implied a Christology. Jesus asks that one should come to a decision regarding him as the repository of the word of God. This decision meant salvation or disaster. The kerygma of the church, in which the revelation of God in Jesus is acknowledged, must be understood as the proper response to this question. The kerygma explains the implicit Christology (Bultmann 1 967a:457).

Schmithals (1 975c:63) stresses that this only concerns Jesus' apocalyptic appearance and his apocalyptic preaching. Jesus has not yet breached the essence of Apocalyptic. Bultmann's idea was not to let the kerygma of the church begin with the historical Jesus. There is no continuity between the message of the historical Jesus and that of the church after his resurrection. It is the expectation of the coming of the Messiah, or the Kingdom of God that forms the link between Jesus and his disciples. The appearance and teaching of Jesus, in this respect, served as sufficient stimulus to bring the teaching of the church into being after Easter.

The fact that Jesus understood himself to be an eschatological manifestation and wished to be acknowledged as such does not guarantee the real continuity between the Proclaimer and Proclaimed. The claims and promises of Jesus do not reach later generations, and that is exactly what continuity demands. Later generations must hear these claims. This continuity is only achieved by the kerygma of the church (Bultmann 1 967a:458).

It is remarkable that Bultmann still takes the historical Jesus as point of departure, not of his theology, but when formulating this problem. His *Jesus* book was the first volume. Taking this as his point of departure, he formulated the main problem of New Testament theology: the relationship between the Proclaimer and the Proclaimed; the relationship between the teaching of Jesus and that which the church preaches. The message of Jesus is interpreted by the church in such a way that the Proclaimer becomes the Proclaimed. According to Bultmann's way of formulating the problem, it ends in the proclaimed Christ. The link between the point of departure and the final issue is the kerygma of the church. The preaching of the church has caused the historical Jesus to be replaced by the kerygmatic Jesus.

Bultmann formulated the problem in this way and provided his own solution. He thought that, to a considerable part of the early church Jesus became an historical phenomenon again. According to Bultmann, Jesus remained an eschatological phenomenon to Hellenistic Christianity, especially to Paul and also to John. To them, he never became an historical figure again. In the other group, Jewish Christianity, people became interested in the historical Jesus. Of the two sections of early Christianity, Jewish Christianity, in which the tradition of the historical Jesus was present, was the determining factor when it came to formulating this problem. The paradox of a historical event that is proclaimed as an eschatological event inevitably leads to interest in the historical Jesus tradition.

Schmithals succeeded in giving a new direction to the quest. He got rid of the initial, lively interest in the historical Jesus in formulating the problem. He pointed out that there was no great theological interest in the historical Jesus in the early church. In this respect the tradition of

Jewish Christianity did not differ from that of Hellenistic Christianity. The messianic tradition was accepted by the whole church. There are no historical grounds for assuming that there was within a section of the church the development of a return from Christ the Proclaimed to Jesus the Proclaimer. Where Jesus is understood to be an eschatological phenomenon within the church he is never regarded as a historical phenomenon again.

If the renewed interest in the historical Jesus is not to be found in the church, this tradition must have originated elsewhere. There must have been a group, isolated from the church, which kept this tradition alive. They considered it of great importance to keep the teaching of Jesus alive, because he was a prophet, preaching the coming salvation. This group who had heard and followed Jesus lived in the expectation raised by his preaching. Schmithals thinks that it is quite likely, considering the historical evidence of a sect propagating Judaism (Ebionites), that a Jesus-community, which was still pre-Easter, existed in the time of the early church.

The widening stream of the messianic tradition of the church eliminates the probability of a return to the tradition of the historical Jesus. Because of this the necessity of finding a theological motive for this return falls away. For the church, the line does not lead from the Proclaimer to the Proclaimed. The other remaining possibility is that the order must be reversed. Now the proclaimed Christ remains the point of departure within the church, and the historical Jesus, Jesus as prophet and teacher, is added later for practical considerations.

In his commentary on the Gospel of Mark, Schmithals (1979a:65-70) points out that the evangelist Mark brought the historical Jesus and the tradition of the church together. Mark's aim was to win over the Jesus sect to the church. The method that he used was to incorporate a part of the material of the Jesus tradition into his gospel. In this way he demonstrated the identity of the historical Jesus and the kerygmatic Christ Jesus. The argument Mark used for the Jesus sect was: This Jesus that you know as prophet, whose tradition you treasure, he is now the exalted Lord. In this way, the unkerygmatic Jesus tradition accidentally became part of the tradition of the church in the second or third generation of early Christianity.

Schmithals (1979a:70; 1997b:307-309) emphasizes the fact that the historical Jesus tradition was used for practical reasons. This must be kept in mind. The historical Jesus tradition was not meant to be an independent tradition of the church, but was part of the proclaiming of the kerygmatic Christ. The Jesus tradition was never fundamental to the church. The confession that Jesus is the Son of God is the foundation of Christian theology and this confession has always been the foundation of the church (Schmithals 1972c:67; 1979a:66).

The problem that Bultmann saw as being the great enigma of the New Testament, namely, the relation between the proclaiming Jesus and the proclaimed Lord of the church, Schmithals was able to explain historically. Schmithals (1972c:67; 1979a:66) does not regard it as an enigma. He establishes and confirms that whoever seeks the origin of the confession in Jesus Christ should not look to the very beginning or to the proclaiming Jesus, but must consider the present foundation of Christian theology, that is the proclaimed Christ.

Schmithals does not consider it to be the task of New Testament theology to find and establish the interdependence of the proclaiming and the proclaimed Jesus. New Testament theology does not begin with or revert to the proclaiming Jesus. The origin and the present foundation of Christian theology is the confession that Jesus is the Christ. The tradition of the church and the tradition of the historical Jesus do not belong together because of an inner inevitability. The confession regarding the exalted Lord does not require to be objectified in the historical Jesus; the two traditions met accidentally.

5.3 DISCONTINUITY

Schmithals' depiction of the circumstances surrounding the Jesus tradition determines his understanding and appreciation of this material. This tradition originated and belonged to a Jesus sect who, untouched by the events of Easter, remained independent of the preaching of the church. The New Testament does not indicate anywhere that it approved of the historical Jesus material. The Jesus material, which was used in the New Testament, had already been adapted by the preaching of the church. In this way, Schmithals could further guide ideas concerning the enigma of the historical Jesus by explaining that it is not a problem of New Testament theology. The province in which the adoption of the Jesus material by the church occurred, was not within the church, but it took place in the course of preaching to members of the Jesus sect. The meeting of the historical Jesus and the kerygma was not necessitated by anything within the church itself. New Testament theology is exempt from the task of finding and establishing a real link between historical Jesus material and the message of the church.

Schmithals (1972c:74) states unequivocally that the events of Easter did not activate the historical Jesus tradition, but eliminated it. The Easter events, which put an end to the tradition of the Jesus material, are the beginning of the kerygmatic tradition of the church. He describes the relation between the kerygma and the historical Jesus as a discontinuous one; the two traditions are opposed to each other. There is discontinuity between Jesus the Proclaimer and the proclaimed Christ (Schmithals 1975c:71).

Schmithals (1979a:67; 1994a:95) points out that, although the confessions of faith and the hymns of the early church mention the incarnation of Jesus, his true humanity, death, resurrection and exaltation, the historical Jesus is never referred to. All the details of the historical Jesus, are replaced in the Christ hymn in Philippians 2 by the mentioning of his humiliation as the Son of God. There is no christological interest in his life on earth, apart from his humiliation as a human being. Furthermore, the title, Son of Man, possibly the only title Jesus himself used, was omitted from the kerygmatic confessions.

The events of Easter brought about the separation between the church and the non-ecclesiastical traditions. This makes the idea of a double or gradual Christology unacceptable to Schmithals (1979a:479; 1988a:49-50; 1997b:303-304). Jesus could not be the Messiah in both traditions. In the period before Easter he was not yet the exalted Lord, leading the life of the Messiah. The title "Son of David" must not be associated with a preliminary exaltation of the human Jesus, which would then become the "Son of God" in the kerygmatic tradition. A text usually quoted in this connection and used to justify the "two-step Christology" exegetically is deliberately called antithetic parallelism by Schmithals (1988a:49-50; 1994a:95; cf. Käsemann 1974:8). The text is: "Who, as historical human being, was a descendant of David; who, as unique being, was declared to be the powerful Son of God, by the resurrection from the dead" (Rom 1:3b-4).

The fact that the two halves of the formula are unconnected indicates a contradiction. The induction to messianic dignity is contrasted with the natural birth of Jesus; the supreme title "Son of God" is contrasted with "descendant of David"; his human nature and existence in the flesh is opposed to his supernatural distinction "unique being." The stressed ending of the second half of the formula, "by the resurrection from the dead," surpasses "a descendant of David" in the first half.

Schmithals points out that the christological title "Son of David" is deliberately avoided and only his descent from David is mentioned. Jesus is descended from David, as was expected of the Messiah. The first half of the formula does not give the historical Jesus messianic status. Jesus is not a worldly ruler. He did not rule over Israel and the nations in Jerusalem. Jesus is not the "Son of David," he is the empowered "Son of God." In addition, he is not given this supreme title because of his descent, but "by the resurrection." The tradition of the church isolates itself from the historical Jesus tradition. Jesus did not live the life of the Messiah, and so the kerygmatic tradition could not make use of the historical material concerning Jesus. The kerygma does not need this material, as Jesus, the Lord, is present in his church.

Schmithals is of the opinion that the breach between the time before Easter and the time after Christ is the theme in Mark 2:18-19a: Now John's disciples and the Pharisees were fasting. Some people came and asked Jesus: "How is it that John's disciples and the disciples of the Pharisees are fasting, but yours are not?" Jesus answered: "How can the guests of the bridegroom fast while he is with them?"

In the historical Jesus tradition it was still presumed that the followers of Jesus would fast (Schmithals 1979a: 176):

> When you fast, do not look somber as the hypocrites do, for they disfigure their faces to show men they are fasting. I tell you the truth, they have received their reward in full. But when you fast, put oil on your head and wash your face, so that it will not be obvious to men that you are fasting, but only to your Father, who is unseen; and your Father, who sees what is done in secret, will reward you.
>
> (Mt 6:16-18)

The followers of John the Baptist also honored this custom in anticipation of the coming salvation (Schmithals 1979a:176). By fasting they abstained from the pleasures of the Old World in anticipation of the coming reign of God. In the early church, the custom of fasting was deliberately abandoned, as they believed that the time of salvation had already come. Christians no longer fasted, for the time of joy had come. The historical Jesus could still advise people on how to fast, but the exalted Lord asks: "How can the guests of the bridegroom fast while he is with them?" The exalted Lord brought the fulfillment of his own and John the Baptist's expectation to the church.

5.4 CONTINUITY

Schmithals denies that an attempt was made in the early church to incorporate the tradition of the historical Jesus into what the church preached. It is more likely that they definitely distinguished between the unmessianic earthly life of Jesus and his dignity as the Son of God, after his resurrection. It was done in such a manner, that the later ecclesiastical phase corrects the pre-ecclesiastical phase. They did this to prevent an interest in the historical Jesus from developing in the church. Questions concerning the historical Jesus were not encouraged. At first the church showed no interest in the pre-Easter Jesus sect.

Schmithals also thinks that the preaching of the church did not set great store by the idea of the proclaimed Christ being identical to Jesus, the Proclaimer. There was no theological motive for the church to elevate to a theme the real connection between the Proclaimer and Proclaimed. History does not show any such tendency in early Christian theology. The preaching of the church came into contact with the Jesus tradition by accident. Mark, the evangelist, told the members of the Jesus sect, that the Jesus whom they knew was actually the Son of God. Mark was able to stimulate an interest in the tradition of the church among this sect. From their point of view there was a movement away from the Proclaimer to the Proclaimed. They now confess with the church that the Jesus they had known was the Son of God. In this accidental way, the church moved from the Proclaimer in the direction of the Proclaimed.

Now the question arises: Did a breach develop between the church and Jesus? If the church did not absorb the teaching of Jesus of necessity, what is the connection between Jesus and the church? Schmithals (1975:70-71) replies that the discontinuity between the teaching of Jesus and the kerygma of the church does not mean a breach with Jesus. In spite of this discontinuity in the content of what the church preached, the fact that the Jesus who was being proclaimed had been part of history was never at issue. The person of Jesus remains the constant, amidst the discontinuity. The church confesses that God has revealed himself in an unsurpassable manner in Jesus, who still expected the revelation of the kingdom of God. Jesus, who lived an unmessianic life, is acknowledged as the Messiah. Jesus, the descendant of David, is confessed to be the Son of God.

According to Schmithals (1972a:23; 1975c:71; 1994a:20-21) the events of Easter not only show the discontinuity between the tradition of the church and that of the historical Jesus, but also, at the same time, there is the presumption of continuity between these two traditions. The message of Easter is tied to the teaching of Jesus. The kerygma proclaims the fulfillment of that which Jesus preached. Jesus expected the kingdom of God to be coming soon. The church goes even further in saying that the kingdom of God has already come. The expected Messiah is Jesus. Both the discontinuity and the continuity between the kerygma of Christ and the tradition of the historical Jesus are founded on the scheme of expectation and fulfillment. The fulfillment surpasses the expectation, but expectation and fulfillment are, at the same time, connected.

It is important to note that Schmithals does not find it necessary to depict the continuity between the historical Jesus and the Christ of faith in such a way that the same understanding of the human existence before God is necessarily present in both traditions. The church did not expound the teachings of Jesus. The common element is not that the church believes what Jesus believed. The personal faith of Jesus is never referred to in the New Testament (Schmithals 1979a:418).

Schmithals (1975c:71; 1994a:21) keeps to the scheme of expectation and fulfillment. Jesus expected and preached an overt intervention in the history of the world by God. The church preached that which Jesus expected, as a hidden deed of God. Jesus went to Jerusalem expecting the end of the world and the coming of the kingdom of God. The church preaches Jesus, his experience of death in the light of Isaiah 53 as this expected intervention of God.

5.5 THE HISTORICAL JESUS TRADITION

Schmithals concluded that the early church was unanimous in its opinion that the traditions of the historical Jesus were neither necessary nor useful as far as faith was concerned. The confessions of faith of the church brought about corrections and limitations, and so the post-Easter church opposed the tradition of the pre-Easter Jesus.

According to Schmithals, the early church depicted a messianic, rather than an ordinary, life for Jesus, in order to proclaim him as the Son of God. The life of Jesus is adapted to suit the kerygma and Christology, so that the kerygma of the church and the confession of the crucified and risen Christ could be proclaimed. Schmithals likes Martin Kähler's characterization of the Gospel of Mark as the history of Christ's passion with a detailed introduction. His understanding of it is that the introduction, comprising the words and deeds of Jesus, proclaims the work of the crucified and exalted Lord even before his crucifixion and resurrection. The crucified and exalted Lord is the point of departure of the whole narrative. The Latin term *evangelium* refers to the genre of the artistic, theological narrative about Jesus Christ and in the gospel according to Mark we have the first example of it (Schmithals 1979a:727-728; 1992c: 139).

Thus, the story of the boy suffering from epilepsy is told in this way: "The boy looked so much like a corpse that many said: 'He's dead.' But Jesus took him by the hand and lifted him to his feet, and he stood up" (Mk 9:26-27). Schmithals (1979a: 421-422) finds that the three verbs used in this passage concerning the epileptic boy, namely, "dead, raised, stood up" suggest the central ideas of the christological confession of the early church:

* Jesus Christ died for us (1 Cor 15:3; Rom 5:6; 8:34; 1 Thes 4:14);
* Jesus Christ was raised for our sake (Rom 4:25; 8:34; 1 Cor 15:4; 1 Thes 1:10; Mk 16:6).

* Jesus Christ arose and represents us (Rom 1:4; Phil 3:10; 1 Thes 4:14).

Schmithals sees the healing of the boy as an example of the meaning of Christian salvation. In the healing of the sick, the sinner receives salvation. The meaning of the healing is identical to the meaning of the "for us" in the dying, restoration to life and resurrection, that is the exaltation of Jesus Christ.

Schmithals says it in other words, namely, that these dogmatic utterances from the pre-Pauline tradition are developed in the form of a Jesus narrative: "We were, therefore, buried with him through baptism into death in order that, just as Christ was raised from the dead through the glory of the Father, we too may live a new life" (Rom 6:4). "We always carry around in our body the death of Jesus, so that the life of Jesus may also be revealed in our body" (2 Cor 4:10). "One died for all and therefore all died" (2 Cor 5:14). "Since, then you have been raised with Christ, set your hearts on things above, where Christ is seated at the right hand of God" (Col 3:1). The narrator of the gospel is at home in dogmatics expressed in the language of religious mysteries, he has the ability to clothe abstract formulae in the guise of vivid accounts.

This reconstruction by Schmithals, demonstrating that, on the whole, the early church showed no interest in the historical Jesus, compels him to identify another source of the tradition of the historical Jesus. He finds the construction by Dibelius and Bultmann that this tradition was later eliminated from the kerygmatic tradition, unconvincing (Schmithals 1980b:153). In post-Easter Christianity memories of Jesus would not be cherished. For Paul such memories were of as little interest as for Peter. If the early church had no interest in the historical Jesus tradition, who would have been interested?

Schmithals (1979a:52-53; 1985a:402-403; 1992c: 142) replied that the meaning of the Easter events had not reached all the followers of the human Jesus. He identifies such an uninformed group in Galilee. They saw Jesus, together with and like John the Baptist, as a prophet predicting the coming salvation. Jesus continues the work of John the Baptist. Schmithals finds his evidence in Matthew 11:18-19: "For John came neither eating nor drinking, and they say: 'He has a demon'. The Son of Man came eating and drinking, and they say: 'Here is a glutton and a drunkard, a friend of tax collectors and sinners'. However, wisdom is proved right by her actions."

According to these followers of Jesus, both he and John suffered the martyrdom of a messenger of God: "O Jerusalem, Jerusalem, you who kill the prophets and stone those sent to you, how often have I longed to gather your children together, as a hen gathers her chicks under her wings, but you were not willing" (Lk 13:34).

These followers of Jesus knew that Jesus had died, but not that he had risen. They did not hand down a messianic image of the work of Jesus; they stressed his prophetic and apocalyptic words. They had not yet acknowledged Jesus as the Messiah and they had not yet identified him as the Son of Man, who was to come. Schmithals (1979a:52-53; 1985a:402-403) identifies this group as the ones who had kept alive the tradition of the utterances of Jesus, namely, Q1.

He is of the opinion that, by proving the existence of a collection of the utterances of Jesus, Q1, he can also prove the existence of a Jesus group, which had no knowledge of the Easter events. Q1 does not contain any sign of Christology. The Jesus sect existed independently of the church in the period after Easter. Apart from the evidence in the New Testament, the existence of a group of Jewish Christians is confirmed by the Apostolic Fathers (cf. Graetz 1905:310-311; Goguel 1949:70-72). They spoke of a group (Ebionites) who denied that Jesus was the Son of God. He was an ordinary human being, who would only rise from the dead with the resurrection of all people.

Renan (1864:150-153), who may be considered the first person to undertake a biography of the historical Jesus, also came to the conclusion that the Jesus *logia* were formed in the Ebionite center of Batanea. Jesus taught the true Ebionism. This dogma taught that only the poor would survive and that their rule was at hand: "But woe to you who are rich, for you have already received your comfort. Woe to you who are well fed now, for you will go hungry. Woe to you who laugh now, for you will mourn and weep" (Lk 6:24-25).

It must be made clear that Schmithals does not consider the historical Jesus tradition as a second Christian tradition side by side with the kerygmatic tradition of the church. These are not two related traditions in which the one has no interest in what happened earlier on and the other records it all. These two traditions must be carefully distinguished from one another. The tradition of the historical Jesus is not authentic ecclesiastical tradition. It is pre-Christian. It has not benefited from the Easter kerygma (Schmithals 1972c:71).

5.6 PETER AND JESUS

In discussing the origin of the Christian credo, a distinction was made between Hellenistic Christianity outside Palestine and Palestinian Christianity. This division could also coincide with the difference between Paul and Jesus. Paul belongs in the Hellenistic tradition, while Jesus has a place in the Palestinian tradition. Hellenistic Christianity is usually associated with the idea that its confession of Easter represented the origin of the church. The origin of the Palestinian church, on the other hand, can be traced back to the historical Jesus; he himself laid the foundation for the teaching of the church. It can repeat what he said.

In this matter, Schmithals takes a unique stand. He makes an adjustment to the explanation of the testimony of the resurrection and still seeks the origin of the Christian confession in Jewish-Christian tradition, although its contents correspond to what is seen as inherent in Hellenistic Christianity. Schmithals (1979a:379-380; 1994a: 17, 23-24;

cf. Bultmann 1980:39) distinguishes between the confession of the resurrection and that concerning the Messiah, in other words that Jesus is the Son of God. The fact that Jesus rose from the dead is not the complete confession of the church. Only when Jesus is confessed to be the Son of God does it become the credo of the church. Easter is explained in an apocalyptic sense in the light of the confession of the resurrection as being the dawning of the last days (Schmithals 1979a:725). Jesus was the first to be raised from the dead. The state of blessedness has dawned. That is why Peter wants to build latter-day shelters when the eschatological figures of Moses and Elijah appear: "Peter said to Jesus: 'Rabbi, it is good for us to be here. Let us put up three shelters one for you, one for Moses, one for Elijah' " Mk 9:5). However, with these words Peter understood only partially: "He did not know what to say, he was so frightened" (Mk 9:6). The confession of the church is not just that Jesus is the first to be brought back to life; not only "He lives."

The apocalyptic explanation that the resurrection of Jesus was the beginning of the last days could not be maintained for long because the last days were not visibly dawning. The dead had not risen. A new and different interpretation of the events of Easter would have to be found to provide for the church's continuation. This new interpretation is given to Peter by the voice from heaven: "This is my Son, whom I love. Listen to him" (Mk 9:7). The resurrection of Jesus means his proclamation and enthronement as Messiah. The true acknowledgement of the events of Easter reads: "You are the Christ." Instead of "He lives" the church proclaims "He rules." The time of this confession is the church's hour of birth and the beginning of the shaping of Christian theology (Schmithals 1979a:735-736). Simon Peter played a major role here. Originally he was a disciple of Jesus; then the first witness of the Easter events; and then, by his confession that Jesus was the Messiah, he became the "rock" on which the church was built (Schmithals 1979a:738; cf.1994a:297).

Schmithals (1979a:380) adds that the use of the

Jewish "Messiah," that means Christ, as title, soon disappeared in Hellenistic Christianity, and was replaced by Son of God and Lord. None of the theological schemes showed any interest in the teaching of Jesus himself. They were involved in proclaiming him as Lord (Schmithals 1972b:79; 1979a:66-67).

Schmithals is able to redefine both the tension, purported to have been experienced in the early church, between Paul and the tradition of the historical Jesus in the synoptic gospels and the tension between Hellenistic Christianity and the Palestinian tradition. He redefines it by maintaining that Paul was not alone in ignoring the tradition of the historical Jesus. Paul joined the tradition of Hellenistic-Jewish Christianity in which Jesus was proclaimed to be the Son of God, already taught by Peter (Schmithals 1988a:51; 1994a:23).

Schmithals sees the theological history of the early church as an ever-widening stream on the side of the kerygmatic Jesus, that included virtually the whole of the early church. One can on these grounds hardly refer to tension between the kerygmatic tradition and the tradition of the historical Jesus. The support for the tradition of the historical Jesus cannot be compared to that for the kerygmatic tradition.

If Peter played a key role in the kerygmatizing of Jesus, both he and Jewish Christianity must be eliminated as the possible origin of the tradition of the historical Jesus, the reason being that it is inconceivable that the preaching in which the historical Jesus plays no part and that in which he plays a decisive part can be traced back to the same church or the same person, namely Peter. Pre-synoptic Christianity had not presumed a messianic life of Jesus. The insight they now gained was that Jesus, who had not been acknowledged as the Messiah, because he was not the Messiah, and did not want to be, is now confessed as the Messiah. This confession brings a correction and a delimitation of what was previously known about Jesus. This is how Schmithals (1988a:48-50) interprets the pre-Pauline formula in Romans 1:3b-4a: "who, as historical human, was a descendant of David; who, as unique being, was declared through the Holy Spirit to be the powerful Son of God, by the resurrection from the dead." Schmithals also points out that this formula contains the two aforementioned interpretations of the Easter experience, namely, the general resurrection of the dead and the exaltation of Jesus. This "adoptionist" presentation, in which Jesus becomes the exalted Son of God only after his resurrection, Schmithals (1988a:51; 1994a:95) presumes to be the oldest form of Christology.

At this stage there was no tradition of the historical Jesus in the pre-synoptic literature of Christianity, because the life of Jesus was not messianic. This did not present a quandary to the early church, because once the scandal of the cross was surmounted, the scandal of the unmessianic life of Jesus was overcome.

5.7 THE HISTORICAL JESUS

Schmithals (1972f:169) remarks that the fundamental utterance of the Christian faith, that Jesus was "truly human and truly God," has always been controversial. In early Christianity, especially, the true humanity of Jesus was called in question by all forms of Docetism. Nowadays the passage that says, "truly human" does not pose a problem. On the other hand, the utterance that Jesus is "truly God" does not achieve easy acceptance.

By means of a questionnaire Schmithals (1981c:24-25) illustrates the problems people have with the divinity of Christ. One question was: "Do you believe that Jesus Christ is the Son of God?" The other question was: "Do you believe that your sins are forgiven by Jesus Christ?" The result was that far more people replied "no" to the question of whether Jesus was the Son of God than to the question on the forgiveness of sins.

The one question concerns what Jesus is and the other what he does. It is easier to say what he does to us today, than to say who he is. Melanchthon already had this insight and formulated it in the classic way: To know Christ is to know his mercy.

In the early church, concerns who Jesus is, like "the only begotten Son of God," amount to utterances about his divine and human nature. Those people did not find it difficult to understand. Nevertheless, these utterances concerning the identity of Jesus do not differ from what we say today about what Jesus does. That Jesus is the Son of God is equivalent to "he forgives my sins."

Schmithals (1981c:25) concludes this train of thought with the comforting reassurance that whoever finds it difficult to say who Jesus is can give up these efforts. It is sufficient to be able to say what he does for us. If anyone confesses, "My sins are forgiven," he knows who Jesus is, because to know Christ means that you know what he does for you. The distinction that has been made so far between who Jesus is and what he does, still takes place on the dogmatic level where the person of Jesus and his work have been elevated to the dogmatic status of eschatological events. The answers to the questions "who is Jesus?" and "what does Jesus do?" are given, in both cases, by the confessions of the church. The utterances "Jesus Christ is the Son of God" and "Jesus Christ forgives me my sins" are equally part of the confessions of the church.

Where previous generations were indifferent to the details of the life of Jesus, through the growing consciousness of history, a need has developed for a historically accurate biography of Jesus. Jesus must be depicted as a man among man. Although Schmithals does not consider the "life of Christ" to be a theme of New Testament theology, it is historically possible and permissible to try to answer the questions regarding the historical Jesus (Schmithals 1975c:85; 1979a:70). The theologian should not avoid the issue of questions concerning the relation between the works of the human Jesus and the gospel (Schmithals 1979a:98).

Schmithals (1975c:59, 64; 1994a:11, 14) agrees with the general approval that the insight of Johannes Weiss has enjoyed, namely that Jesus should be regarded as being part of the apocalyptic movement.

The problem facing the biographer of Jesus, is that he is depicted in different ways. On the one hand, Jesus acts like an eschatological prophet. Schmithals (1979a: 251-252) illustrates the prophetic message of Jesus by means of a parable, which he considers to be part of the authentic preaching of Jesus:

> He also said "This is what the kingdom of God is like. A man scatters seed on the ground. Night and day, whether he sleeps or gets up, the seed sprouts and grows, though he does not know how. All by itself the soil produces corn first the stalk, then the ear, then the full grain in the ear. As soon as the grain is ripe, he puts the sickle to it, because the harvest has come."
> (Mk 4:26-29; cf. Joel 3:13)

This parable makes sense when seen against the background of the apocalyptic expectation of the sovereignty of God and the destruction of the power of Satan. The kingdom of God dawns surprisingly and infallibly.

Schmithals (1973a:116; 1975c:63) concedes that Jesus is not presented only as an apocalyptic prophet in the synoptic gospels. He is also shown as a rabbi and teacher of wisdom, who sets moral norms and discusses the interpretation of the law. Symbolic discourses were also known to the rabbis. They should be classified as wisdom, rather than apocalyptic literature (Schmithals 1980a:89):

> Why do you call me "Lord, Lord" and do not do what I say? I will show you what he is like who comes to me and hears my words and puts them into practice. He is like a man building a house, who dug down deep and laid the foundation on rock. When the flood came, the torrent struck that house but could not shake it, because it was well built. However, the one who hears my words and does not put them into practice is like a man who built a house on the ground without foundation. The moment the torrent

struck that house, it collapsed and its destruction was complete.
(Lk 6:46-49)

In the history of religion Jesus the eschatological prophet and Jesus as a rabbi teaching wisdom cannot be associated. Apocalyptic and ethical formulation belong to different religious traditions. The laying down of ethical norms is not appropriate to someone who is preaching that the end of the world is drawing near (Schmithals 1975a:65-66). From the point of view of apocalyptic, this world can no longer be improved; the sooner it comes to an end, the better. Schmithals (1975a:65-66) takes a more definite stand than before (Schmithals 1973a:117). Then he had his doubts as to whether the apocalyptic and non-apocalyptic material could be clearly distinguished in the Jesus tradition. This may be done by tracing the non-apocalyptic tradition to the church and the apocalyptic material to Jesus himself. Schmithals thought that the apocalyptic preaching of Jesus was combined with the ethical directions to the pious that listened and that sooner or later material from the wisdom tradition of the blessed rule of God in creation may have been added to this.

To make some progress in the forming of a concept of the life of Jesus, Schmithals (1975a:66) maintains that the teaching of Jesus in the synoptic tradition should be ignored, because of its conflicting apocalyptic and non-apocalyptic traditions. Evidence should be sought outside this tradition to form a clearer picture. The public activity of Jesus is even more obscure than the message that he delivered. Schmithals (1973a:118; 1975c:67; 1994a:16-18) thinks that no more than a few isolated remarks can be made on the nature of the life of Christ. Although these are separate remarks, they can be grouped under the image of Jesus the apocalyptic:

John the Baptist was the spiritual father of Jesus (see also Geyser 1951:139-141). Jesus was baptized by John. He used John's message as a point of departure and this message was tuned to apocalyptic. John called the people to repent, because the coming wrath of God was at hand. Those who repented and whose repentance was sealed by baptism would be safeguarded against the coming judgement of the world. They were assured of the coming salvation in the reign of God that was at hand (Schmithals 1973a:115; 1975c:67; 1979a:75-76). Jesus was also sealed by his baptism before the judgement and he joined the holy people of God.

* The confession of the resurrection of Jesus is the result of the work he had done. In addition, this confession of the resurrection is a basic utterance of apocalyptic. The earliest Easter faith indicates the rising of Jesus as the beginning of the universal resurrection of the dead: Jesus is the "firstborn from the dead" (Schmithals 1975c:67). The expression "firstborn from the dead" expresses the expectation that the last days are near. This expectation was an essential part of the hope entertained by the disciples, who had followed Jesus during his life on earth (Schmithals 1973a:115).

* The oldest original text (Rom 1:3-4) in which Christology is verbalized can only be understood by keeping in mind the decisive change as represented in Apocalyptic. The church confesses that the resurrection of Jesus was the turning point. Moreover, it confesses that he, as the firstborn, was raised and exalted to Son of God by the Holy Spirit (Schmithals 1994a:17).

* The fact that Jesus was crucified by the Romans, without doubt the death of a political criminal, always results in Jesus being classified as one of a group of political insurgents. Schmithals (1975c:67-77) cannot accept such a classification. It is contradicted by the early Christian tradition and the attitude of the oldest churches. Nevertheless, Jesus was actually put to death like a political opponent of the state. Moreover, even though this type of death could have been the result of a misunderstanding, what he did and the role that he played must have provoked it in some way. Schmithals seeks the cause in the apocalyptic expectations of Jesus. He expected and announced the end of all worldly sovereignty and that made the Roman authorities suspicious. They felt their authority being threatened. The Romans did not distinguish between the apocalyptic expectation of the coming of the kingdom of God and the revolutionary, Zealotlike expectations concerning the Son of David.

* Schmithals (1975c:68) explains the complex of traditions in the New Testament, in which the Spirit plays an important part, in terms of its apocalyptic origin. The spiritual gifts, which were from the Spirit of the last days, show the church to be the eschatological church of salvation (Schmithals 1974b:103). In the Jesus tradition there is also a warning not to resist the Spirit of the last days (Schmithals 1979a:223-224; 1980a:143): "And everyone who speaks a word against the Son of Man will be forgiven, but anyone who blasphemes against the Holy Spirit will not be forgiven" (Lk 12:10).

Schmithals (1973a:115) reaches the conclusion that the historical Jesus, as far as his conduct and his end were concerned, was enriched by two fundamental apocalyptic motives. These were the eschatological baptism of repentance and the Easter confession. To this can be added his crucifixion as a political criminal by the Romans and the preaching of the Spirit of the last days. This places the work of Jesus firmly within the framework of the Apocalyptic (Schmithals 1975c:68).

As far as the non-apocalyptic parts of the Jesus tradition are concerned, Schmithals (1975c:84) suggests two possibilities. Did the ethical admonitions originate from the delay of the expected end of the world, when the groups that took over the apocalyptic message of Christ had to cope with the continuation of the world? Alternatively, did two groups, each with its own tradition, unite, the one group being the bearer of the apocalyptic material and the other ethically oriented?

From within the framework of his own view of how matters developed, Schmithals (1973a:129; 1975c:72) comments on the finding of Käsemann the Apocalyptic is the mother of Christian theology. Schmithals concedes that this is tenable, as long as only the historical relation between Apocalyptic and Christianity is discussed. But as far as the essential relationship is concerned, this finding is untenable and should rather be reversed: The mother of Christian theology is the victory over Apocalyptic, in the fulfillment of apocalyptic expectations in terms of which God still has to act. The turning point expected by Apocalyptic has already come.

5.8 THE DECISIVE QUESTION

What Schmithals (1972c:67; 1979a:66) has ascertained in his search for the origin of the Christian confession must be considered in real earnest. This search is not for the early beginnings, but for the foundation of present-day theology. Saving events never belong to the past, as far as the church is concerned. Christ is not the founder of Christianity, but the present-day Lord of his church. The Christian theology and the church do not have a different origin from the christological confession of early Christianity, namely, the events of Easter. Schmithals (1972c:77) wishes to encourage the church to keep this origin in mind. They must realize that the events of Christ were not ones of promise, but of fulfillment. This is the crucial question confronting the church and the answer cannot be avoided: Does the church accept the message of the New Testament? Is the confession of Christ in the New Testament the foundation of theological work? It is a choice between the law and the gospel, between salvation based on human aid, and the salvation of God (Schmithals 1972a:30).

The church confesses and proclaims the crucified and exalted Christ as fulfillment of its own expectations. The early church experienced the Easter events as the sovereign redemption by God. Through Jesus, who expected salvation, God carried out his deed of redemption for the sake of the church. This is the origin of faith in Christ. Therefore, the church and theology ought not to revert to the preceding phase. This was the stage of expectation and the church should not fixate on this earlier stage of the tradition of the church. The promise, the hope of salvation is replaced by fulfillment; salvation in hope (Schmithals 1972c:75).

Schmithals (1979a:217) is of the opinion that this fundamental theological problem was intense right from the beginning of the Christian confession. It is not true that the contrast between the historical Jesus and the biblical Christ or the contrast between the prophet and the Christ of faith was forced on to the texts of the New Testament. This contrast is the theme in Mark 3:20-21; 31b-35 for example:

> Then Jesus entered a house and again a crowd gathered, so that he and his disciples were not even able to eat. When his family heard about this, they went to take charge of him, for they said "He is out of his mind." Then Jesus' mother and brothers arrived. Standing outside, they sent someone in to call him. A crowd was sitting around him, and they told him "Your mother and brothers are outside, looking for you." "Who are my mother and my brothers?" he asked. Then he looked at those seated in a circle around him and said, "Here are my mother and my brothers. Whoever does God's will is my brother and sister and mother."

Schmithals (1979:209-220) explains that in this passage we have to do with different assessments of Jesus. Christology is the theme. Who is right—those who think that he is out of his mind or those who congregate around him as his eschatological church? Who is Jesus really?

The schism between church and synagogue is implied. The Christians leave the synagogue and gather in houses. They know that the risen Christ is in their midst. In their hunger to hear the words of the Lord the people forget their hunger for bread (Amos 8:11-12). The parting of the ways and the time for decision came in Capernaum: church or synagogue?

Jesus' family does not want to enter the house. They deliberately wait outside and have him called. They want to possess him. From two sides people want to lay claim to him, on the one hand, his family and, on the other, his followers. Which of the two claims is justified? With whom does Jesus belong? Who belongs to him? Who really understands him?

The followers of Jesus understand him to be the "Son of God," the one who would bring God's redemption. When his family hear that his followers think him to be the "Son of God," they think that he has lost his mind and, to prove their point, they dissociate themselves from his followers. His family wants him brought back to their circle and back to normal. They think that he will be himself again, if he is the "son of Mary" once more and not the "Son of God."

The family of Jesus is trying to bring him back to his historical existence: He is the carpenter, the son of Mary, brother to James, Joses, Jude and Simon, the Jewish compatriot. They deny his paradoxical claim that God acted in him for the salvation of the world. They are not mistaken in considering him to be a relative; but they find it unacceptable that this relative of theirs is the "Son of God."

Schmithals points out that it was not antagonism towards Jesus that influenced their conduct. Including him in their circle meant that there was the possibility of honoring him in the highest way that is humanly possible. Jesus did not only have to return as an obedient son or hardworking tradesman. His return held the possibility of making an example of him; as an exemplary ethical personality; as a great prophet; as the most important son of the Jewish people; as an exemplary believer; as a teacher of the freedom of the human spirit; as a social revolutionary; as a helper of the poor and the oppressed; as the political leader against the Roman occupation; as a fascinating preacher of repentance; as the religious genius; as the model fellow human being; in short, the bearer of some of the thoughts necessary for our time. In the course of history these and many other highly admirable aspects have been found in Jesus.

In this and many similar ways, Jesus is again included in the historical circle and it becomes possible for humanity to follow him, to take up his work and to complete it. Schmithals (1979a:217) quotes Luther's judgement on this *imitatio* Christology: to understand Jesus in this way does not constitute the gospel. In this way the life of Jesus is limited to himself and is of no greater help to you than the life of any other saint. No one becomes a Christian in this way.

Jesus himself intervenes in this controversy around his person: "Here are my mother and my brothers." Jesus belongs to the church. The church understands him correctly. He is not the historical Jesus, but the Christ of faith. He came to overcome sin and death. That is why he does not go outside, but stays with his church. They do the will of God, by acknowledging him as the "Son of God."

Schmithals appreciates the fact that the contrast between the congregation within the house and those who remain outside is maintained. The relationship does not include a brittle peace. Those outside do not enter the church in order to make the church adapt to their expectations. The difference is respected. In this way the question concerning the person and the truth about Jesus is clearly formulated. Schmithals is of the opinion that the narrator of this passage knew that the family of Jesus later became active members of the church. The narrative indicates that a clear "no" is nearer to a clear "yes" than a tolerance which regards truth as opposed to love.

By means of this explanation, Schmithals clearly shows that he considers it to be a burning question. He explains that the existence and the appearance of the historical Jesus tradition in the New Testament, together with the awakening of a historical consciousness, made the Easter events appear dubious as the foundation of the confession of the church (Schmithals 1972c:76). In the past 200 years the time came to form a historical image of Jesus. The material was available to accomplish this.

Schmithals (1972a:28-29) accepts that there was an ecclesiastical and theological interest in the historical Jesus in the liberal "life of Jesus theology." With the aid of the personality concept of Liberalism, it was possible to depict Jesus as an example of an absolute personality that was to be emulated by the Christian individual. Thus the kingdom of God expands as the kingdom of perfect morality. The idea of an absolute personality of Jesus which expresses the fact that this religious ideal is humanly unattainable could uphold the theological character of this image of Jesus and thus save it from becoming totally moralistic. Although this was an effort to place Jesus in the center and to represent him as sophisticated, realistic and compelling, the "historical Jesus" of liberal theology was too modern to be the historical Jesus of Nazareth. Jesus as presented by the "life of Jesus theology" had very little in common with the Christ of the Bible (Schmithals 1971 a:12).

"Dialectical" theology, the theology of the Word, replaced liberal theology, when it became clear, during the First World War, that optimism with regard to human personality was misguided. Barth and Bultmann no longer sought the historical Jesus behind the texts, but rather the Christ witnessed by the Bible. Schmithals (1972c:76) blames dialectical theology for not solving the problem of the historical question concerning the origin of the tradition of the historical Jesus, satisfactorily. As a result, there was renewed interest in the historical Jesus.

In establishing a date for the renewed interest in the historical Jesus, Schmithals (1971a:13; 1990:494-495) refers to a lecture "The Problem of the Historical Jesus" by Ernst Käsemann in 1953. This lecture signalled the reversion to the liberal theological way of thinking. Käsemann tried to explain the biblical Christian testimony as a progressive unfolding of the message of the historical Jesus. Although this had not been Käsemann's intention, his scheme made the kerygma of the cross and the resurrection superfluous, because in this enlightened twentieth century, the biblical Christ is replaced by the historical Jesus, when the essential continuity between the two Jesuses is propounded.

In Herbert Braun's case, according to Schmithals (1971a:14), it is clear that only the historical Jesus remains. In principle, Jesus, as a historical entity, can be replaced and in consequence, must be replaced by the modern human being. Braun summarizes the historical Jesus, as "simple co-humanity," and to follow Jesus, means to become, like Jesus, a humble fellow human being, in this way encouraging others along the way of life.

Schmithals continues that he does not wish to pronounce a value judgment on such a sublime depiction of Jesus as the one Braun has given, but, as a theologian he must state that the Christ proclaimed in Scripture is irreplaceable and cannot be exchanged for anyone else. This is in contrast to the Jesus of Braun. The very basic theme of theology is: God cannot be replaced by humankind; grace cannot be replaced by works and the gospel cannot be replaced by the law.

Liberal theology had at least a theological reservation concerning the concept of the "absolute" personality of Jesus. Braun does not maintain this reservation and he reverts, according to Schmithals (1971a:14), to the stage of thinking of the Enlightenment. For the Enlightenment, the truth of human existence is realized by human beings as such, not as a gift of God. In this scheme of things, Jesus can no longer be Lord, but is at best a colleague, in the sense that he is the teacher of enlightened morality. Theology is absorbed into ethics. The liberating grace of God is no longer mentioned; sophisticated modern man has usurped the throne (Schmithals 1971:10).

Schmithals (1972a:29-30) points out two real causes of the renewed interest in the historical Jesus, both in theology and in the life of the church. Firstly it is said that the historical Jesus is necessary for a theology aimed at changes in the world. The Jesus of biblical testimony is too unworldly. Arising from what is deemed necessary, Jesus is depicted as revolutionary, reformer, apostle of love, pacifist, socialist, et cetera. Secondly, the historical Jesus is used to justify ecclesiastically the struggle against the preaching of the gospel. With the help of the historical Jesus, humankind brings about his or her own salvation and God becomes unnecessary. The historical Jesus must make his contribution to the de-theologizing of the church.

According to Schmithals (1972a:30; 1994b:14-15), it is impossible for the church to preach both the historical Jesus and the biblically proclaimed Jesus. A decision must be made. The crux of the matter is not active as against passive; open to the world as against personal, inward Christianity; but rather whether salvation is from God or from humankind.

5.9 JESUS IS GOD

To Schmithals christo-logy is also theo-logy. In Jesus Christ, God himself deals comprehensively with humankind. The question of understanding God is identical to the question of understanding Jesus. Theo-logy is christo-logy and christo-logy is theo-logy. Christology is not a subsection of theology; nor is it a more exact definition of a more general discussion about God. Actually, no theological conclusions can be drawn from the concept "God," because there is no presupposition of what or who is meant by the word "GOD." It is not a specifically Christian word, but has characteristics of all possible religions, philosophies and views of life. Only the confession "Jesus is God" determines the word "God" on the basis of his self-revelation. This confession is the enduring source of Christian theology (Schmithals 1972f:183).

Although Jesus is specifically called God only once in the New Testament, "My Lord and my God" (Jn 20:28), there is no doubt about the fact that Jesus was on the side of God in a special way in the New Testament. The titles given him, such as: Christ, Son of David, Son of God, Lord,

Word, et cetera, show him to be on God's side, even though subordinate to God. By means of these titles it is indicated that God comes to meet the world in Jesus (Schmithals 1972f:169-171).

The New Testament also tells us of the origin of the divinity of Jesus. Paul (Rom 1:3b4a) quotes the confession, that he was declared to be the Son of God by his resurrection from the dead. In the Gospel of Mark, the divinity of Jesus is fixed at an earlier date, that of his calling as Messiah, when he was baptized by John. Matthew and Luke adopted the history of his birth, in which the divinity of Jesus is fixed at an earlier date, namely the process of his incarnation. Paul and John locate the origin of the divinity of Jesus in his existence prior to the creation of the world (Schmithals 1972f: 172-174; cf. 1980a:47).

Schmithals (1972f:174-175) explains that these conclusions are not about the natural divine origin or divine nature of Jesus. The pre-existential Christology, does not presuppose a divine substance; the virgin birth a physical phenomenon; the baptism in the Jordan a metaphysical adoption. The divine origin of Jesus is shown in different ways because he is proclaimed as the one through whom God acts for the salvation of the world.

When the controversy concerning the Trinity was at its height, with the participation of Arius and Athanasius in the fourth century, the divine origin of Jesus was not under discussion. The problem was how to represent the divinity of Jesus in its relationship to that of the Father. Schmithals (1972f:177) explains that Arius made good use of the presentation of the divinity of Jesus in the New Testament, that is as subordinate to that of the Father. According to Arius the only eternal God the God without beginning created the Logos, his Son, as his first and perfect creation. As creature, this Logos, who became human as Jesus, was not of the same nature as the Father, although his glory was far above that of the rest of creation. Through him everything was created. Next to him and subordinate to him is the Holy Spirit. The Christian honors three different beings, a

Trinity, with a descending divinity.

As against Arius, Athanasius maintained that the Son is a being on the same level as the Father. The Son is as eternal as the Father. Athanasius avoids the doctrine of two or three gods and stands by the unity of God. At the same time he stands by the independent existence of the Son with the Father. The Trinitarian formulae express this concept, namely one being, but three persons.

Athanasius accused Arius of idolizing creatures with his difficult formulae. Christ is considered to be a created being and obtains divine glory in this way. Schmithals (1972f:178) agrees with Athanasius. Greek cosmology and metaphysics are behind Arianism. They do not know the qualitative difference between Creator and creature. To the Greeks the whole cosmos consisted of equal beings. Everything that God created is equal to him. That fallen creation is re-absorbed into the community of God is only natural. In this scheme, salvation is of no great importance, because people themselves are capable of the divine. They are not really sinners, subject to death.

Arius succeeds in formally doing justice to the New Testament with his subordinate Christology, but he ignores the qualitative difference between the Holy God and the human sinner (Schmithals 1972f:179). Schmithals is of the opinion that, although Athanasius cannot in reality prove "of equal being with the Father" from Scripture, he has biblical tradition on his side. Like the Bible, he maintains the infinite difference between God and humankind. People have no divinity within themselves. People must be saved from their estrangement from God. In the theology of Athanasius, the central idea is salvation and, in this way, he keeps firmly to the fundamentals of the New Testament.

By emphatically calling Jesus "true God," Athanasius held on to the divinity of God. Grace is the grace of God and humans are sinners in the eyes of God. People must be saved from their sin, their estrangement from God, their self-justification and estrangement from themselves. God must meet humankind halfway if he or she is to be helped. That God acts in favor of humankind, Athanasius expressed with the words that God himself became a human being in Jesus (Schmithals 1972f:180).

Schmithals (1972f:181) allows for the fact that the Trinitarian formulae are no longer a suitable means of communicating to people that sinners are brought back to life through the gracious intervention of God. The Christological honorifics are no longer an understandable way of saying that it is God who comes to our rescue through Christ. If we can no longer express the true meaning of "Jesus is God," it will be useless to repeat the utterance "Jesus is God." What we say about Jesus today must be intelligible.

However, speaking intelligibly today does not necessarily mean that the church must renounce formulations that need to be explained (Schmithals 1972f:181). In this way the church will renounce not only its history but also its enduring origin, the New Testament. Theology still has the task of interpreting traditional formulae. In this way, the testimony of the Bible remains the foundation of present-day church and theology. The claim that "Jesus is God" must be made meaningful in every age.

Schmithals (1972f:181) points out that the statement "Jesus is God" can be interpreted in two ways. Is it the question, "Who is Jesus?" that is answered with: "He is God?" Alternatively, is it the question, "Who is God?" that is answered: "He is Jesus?" Schmithals (1972f:182) feels that these two questions do not exclude each other. When Jesus asked "Who do you say I am?", Peter answered "You are the Christ." Here we have to do with the question concerning Jesus. Nevertheless, the question is also aimed at eliciting the latent question: Who is God, if I am the Christ, the Son of God? The true meaning of the utterance "Jesus is God" is that it wishes to answer the question: Who is God? In John 1:18, this becomes clear: "No one has ever seen God; God's only Son, he who is nearest to the Father's heart, has made him known." Here the inquiry is about God, whom no one has seen. And Jesus is the answer to the question concerning God.

The confession: "Jesus is God" does not, however, mean that the church sees the revelation of Christ as a new revelation, in the sense that a new God is making himself known. It is still one God, who is showing himself anew; the Lord has not left himself without witness.

The revelation in Christ is the declaration that is now valid. This valid revelation leads Paul to discover Abraham as an exemplary believer (Schmithals 1988a: 141). Each question concerning God, which is not concerned with Jesus Christ, is wide off the mark. In addition, each answer, not given from the point of view of the Christ event is a wrong answer (Schmithals 1970c:179-180).

Conversely, the confession that "Jesus is God" supposes that to ask about Jesus without asking about God is wide off the mark. The answer that Jesus was the founder of a religion or an outstanding religious personality has nothing to do with the New Testament's testimony concerning Christ (Schmithals 1970c:180). The concept "send" in the Gospel of John was not meant to make clear that Jesus represented the best of human possibilities, but that he revealed the God whom no one had ever seen, because he is the source of all life (Schmithals 1970c:181). The one sent by God stands in God's place (Schmithals 1976a:37).

5.10 CLOSING REMARKS

By way of summary we can say that Bultmann classifies the preaching of the historical Jesus with the Old Testament. The Old Testament as well as Jesus, expresses human existence under the law. This must be overcome by the teaching of the church, as it is pre-Christian. Schmithals classifies the historical Jesus with apocalyptic. Here, too, Jesus also represents a pre-Christian position that can only be fulfilled by the Christian kerygma. Schmithals' combination of Jesus and apocalyptic is a more consistently pre-Christian understanding of the historical Jesus than Bultmann's combination of Jesus and the Old Testament. Bultmann is surprised that the historical Jesus is so Christian.

Has he modelled his historical Jesus too extensively on the Old Testament and does he do justice to the Old Testament when he describes it in terms of law and "Scheitern?" Does the Old Testament not express the existence under the gospel and is it not more Christian than Bultmann is willing to concede?

As far as Schmithals' classification of the historical Jesus with apocalyptic is concerned, one must admit that he is more logical in his description of the relationship between Jesus and the preaching of the church. He succeeds in clearly distinguishing the two messages. In this sense, Schmithals is more Bultmannian than Bultmann himself. Schmithals spells out more clearly than Bultmann why the historical Jesus is not the subject of Christian theology.

CHAPTER 6

The Theological History of the New Testament

6.1 INTRODUCTION

In using the heading "The Theological History of the New Testament," we are not referring to the vicissitudes of the New Testament in the history of theology. Rather, there is a differentiation between different theologies in the New Testament. As far as the relationship between the New Testament and the Old Testament and apocalyptic is concerned, the point of departure is the unity of the Gospel amid the variety of theologies. Beyond that, the unity is set aside, as it were, and the variety comes to the fore.

The historical method necessitated the separation of the subjects "Old Testament" and "New Testament." Along with this separation came the question of the relationship between the New Testament and the Old Testament. On its own, the Old Testament cannot be regarded as a Christian book. What relationship can there be between the New Testament and the Old Testament?

Apart from the Old Testament, the early Christian movement also had to deal with Apocalyptic, Gnosticism and, broadly speaking, with Jewry. How did the Christian message distinguish itself from these movements and vindicate itself against their claims?

The historical method has made it clear that the Gospel cannot be proclaimed independently of the times, but must ever anew find correct understanding and expression. The one Gospel has a history in different theologies. The one Gospel is elaborated as different theologies in the canon. In tracing the different theological designs, Schmithals sketches the stages of Paul's theological development. In this process, he distinguishes an Antiochene theology, which was taught by Peter and forms the underlying principle of the Gospel of Mark. The contribution by the editors of the Pauline letters is briefly touched upon. The theology of the New Testament is broadly based and has an interesting development.

6.2 THE RELATIONSHIP BETWEEN THE NEW TESTAMENT AND THE OLD TESTAMENT

In a previous chapter we pointed out that Schmithals stressed the fact that the Christ testimony of the New Testament forms the foundation of the theology and practice of the church. The confession of the church that Jesus is the Lord is still the origin of church and theology today. A particular aspect of what "origin" means has become evident namely that an interaction between past and present, between the original and the modern, is presumed, in such a way that the modern still carries the stamp of its derivation. As far as the relationship between the New Testament and the Old Testament is concerned, attention is transferred to the other aspect of origin, namely what is not taken or derived from any preceding material. The Christ testimony is not dependent on the Old Testament, but stands on its own. The salvation of God can be revealed sufficiently in the testimony of Christ (Schmithals 1988a:343-344). The canon of the New Testament clearly shows the commitment of the church to the confession of Christ (Schmithals 1989b:16; 1994a:295; 1996b:252). The Old Testament is also read as testimony to faith in Jesus Christ (Schmithals 1970a:45-47)

The Christian confession has priority, even over the passion narrative of Jesus. The confession was proclaimed and taught long before the Passion of Christ was described in the Gospel of Mark (Schmithals 1979a:681). For that reason the many verbal and also indirect allusions to texts from the Old Testament are not meant to prove the reality and the truth concerning reports on the Passion of Christ.

Only a Christian congregation would, in general, acknowledge such allusions. Thus, references from the Old Testament make sense to the church only after the confessions of faith have been formulated (Schmithals 1979a:486).

Isaiah 53 is used as a key text in the Passion of Christ (Schmithals 1979a:475-476), not only for the narrative in the Gospel according to Mark, but also for the Palestinian early Christianity and the Hellenistic Jewish Christianity in the region of Antioch in Syria (Schmithals 1985a:373; 1994a:97; 1996b:251). If one studies Schmithals' commentary on Mark, it becomes clear that it is not a question of a particular interpretation of Isaiah 53. Rather the Old Testament text provides the material for the narrative. The Septuagint uses the word "hand over" in Isaiah 53:6 and 12, and concerning Jesus, we are told that the Son of Man is betrayed into the hands of sinners (Mk 14:41), the chief priests and others "turned him over to Pilate" (Mk 15:1) and Pilate "handed him over to be crucified" (Mk 15:15; see Schmithals 1979a:646, 676). As was said of the servant of the Lord in Isaiah 53:7, "yet he did not open his mouth." Jesus is silent from the time of his arrest up to his death. The believing reader accepts the fact that Jesus could not vindicate himself; he had to fulfill the will of God and die on the cross (Schmithals 1979a:673). Jesus is arrested like a criminal; Pilate offers to release him, but the people prefer Barabbas; Jesus is crucified between two criminals, just as the servant of the Lord, "was numbered with the transgressors" (Is 53:12; see Schmithals 1979a:675-676). Like the servant, he is buried in the grave of a rich man "with the rich in his death" (Is 53:9; Schmithals 1979a: 704).

Schmithals (1979a:673) maintains that the author of the history of the Passion of Christ does not give a direct interpretation of these events. Isaiah 53 is used as an example of the experiences that Jesus had and not of the work he did. The closest the author gets to the work of Jesus or the soteriology, is that he refers readers to the explanatory text in Isaiah 53 where Jesus "took up our infirmities and carried our sorrows" (Is 53:12). The writer does not use a theory of atonement to explain events. As commentator, Schmithals cannot resist a direct interpretation. He uses the Christ confession of the church, the *theologia crucis et resurrectionis*, as a hermeneutic key to the interpretation of the Passion of Christ. To believe in Christ, you have to take up your cross, die with him and be united with him in his resurrection, as Paul explained in Romans 6:2-11. Schmithals (1994a:104-106) is not sure where the idea of dying and rising with Christ originated. Neither Antioch nor Damascus seems to be clearly indicated. The figure of Simon of Cyrene, who carried the cross of Jesus, gives expression to this faith in a narrative form. Anyone who admits that he deserves to be judged by God and surrenders himself to death, hoping only in the grace of God, humbly receives the grace of God. In this way we are reconciled to God by the crucified one (Schmithals 1979a:686-687; 1988a:187; 1994a:105).

To take the idea of a redemption theory still further, Schmithals (1979a:67) interprets the "vicarious" death of the "Son of God" for all people as "exemplary." Simon must also carry the cross of Jesus. The Son of God identifies with the wretched, so that they can identify with him. The act of God to Jesus, in that he is crucified, is enacted between Jesus and us. It is not God that is reconciled through Christ. The narrative expresses the confession as given by Paul: "that God was reconciling the world to himself in Christ, not counting people's sins against them. In addition, he has committed to us the message of reconciliation" (2 Cor 5:19; Schmithals 1979a:673).

It is possible, in principle, to convey the Christian message without the Old Testament. Paul does not use quotations from the Old Testament as scriptural substantiation. In 1 Thessalonians for example, Paul never quotes specifically from the Old Testament, because he could not presuppose that those receiving the correspondence had any knowledge of the Old Testament (Schmithals 1982a:156; 1988a:343; 1996b:254-255). In addition, in Romans 11:11-

24 Paul omits references to the Old Testament because of the antagonism of gentile Christians towards Israel (Schmithals 1988a:394). To the apostle, revelation in the Old Testament is veiled, unless the hermeneutic key of the Christ events is used to unlock the Scriptures. "But their minds were made dull, for to this day the same veil remains when the old covenant is read. It has not been removed, because only in Christ is it taken away" (2 Cor 3:14).

The hermeneutic key used by the Pharisaic synagogue when reading the Scriptures, is the Torah, which was given exclusively to Israel (Schmithals 1988a:343-344). This key keeps them bound under the law and makes them seek self-justification (cf. Rom 10:3; Schmithals 1988a:368-369). Faith in Christ has superseded the law and the particular righteousness has given place to righteousness for all who believe (Schmithals 1988a:369-370). For the sake of the existential understanding that life is inseparable from the experience of death, judgment and human transience, there cannot be two ways to salvation, the Old Testament as law and the New Testament as gospel. Salvation through judgment can be understood only as *justificatio impli* and this salvation is universal for all people, and not only those who received the Torah.

The fact that the Christian message can be conveyed without the help of the Old Testament does not mean that this message is only brought home by means of christological formulations. Christian preaching seeks to find an answer to the question that is raised by the very fact of human existence, and that is the question concerning the truth of existence (Schmithals 1970c:178; 1979a:79; 1982a:161). In the cult of sacrifice, philosophy, apocalyptic and mystic religions, for example, inadequate and false answers are given to the real and necessary question of humankind (Schmithals 1989a:39-40). In a non-Christological way, Paul formulates the reality of salvation, which is founded Christologically, in this way (Schmithals 1988a:432):

> Therefore, I urge you, brothers, in view of God's mercy, to offer your bodies as living sac-

> rifices (cult of sacrifice), holy and pleasing to God this is your reasoning worship (philosophy). Do not conform any longer to the pattern of this world (apocalyptic), but be transformed by the renewing of your mind (mystic religion). Then you will be able to test and approve what God's will is, his good, pleasing and perfect will.
>
> (Rom 12:1-2)

Here Paul not only uses words familiar to his readers, he also addresses the question, "What is the truth?", asked in these systems and then answers it by means of his own message (Schmithals 1989a:39-40).

The adequacy of the Christ testimony as a message of the church, is not meant to impugn the authority of the Old Testament or to subvert it (Schmithals 1988a:343). Luke, particularly, retains unity with the Old Testament by addressing his writings to the rising pre-Marcionism. Marcion rejected the Old Testament as a legal document and as a book concerning judgmental righteousness and only accepted the Gospel of love of the New Testament (Schmithals 1980a:14-15). Schmithals (1979a:486) prefers describing the relationship between the Old Testament and the New by means of the scheme of "promise-fulfillment," but with a reservation (Schmithals 1995a:189). Jesus Christ is God's confirmation of all his promises: "For no matter how many promises God has made, they are 'Yes' in Christ" 2 Corinthians 1:20 (see Schmithals 1988a:105-106; 343). The Passion of Christ is the fulfillment of the promise of the Old Testament. In Christ we see the promised advent of God's salvation.

To do justice to Schmithals' point of view, the scheme of "promise-fulfillment" must not be considered as history, involving one dimension only. "Fulfillment" does not only mean "prediction come true." This does not imply that the promise was merely a foreshadowing of events that became a reality only after Christ. Paul can speak of an eschatological turning point in the course of world history, even as far back as Abraham. Taking the Christ events as point of departure, Paul recognizes the redeeming work of God in the Old Testament, leading human beings through judgment to life. God's salvation is offered, both in the Old and in the New Testament, as a present possibility of human life. The Old Testament fully reflects Christian existence. In this sense Abraham is an example to the Christian and identical to him. Paul would not have understood the question how Abraham could believe in Christ to be a problem, because for him the times and ages coalesce. He does not distinguish between the time of Abraham and the time of Christ (Schmithals 1988a:139; 1992b:22-23).

Characteristic of understanding God's salvation in this way, is that Christ did not bring a new revelation, but with his coming, salvation which had been possible from the time of creation, was renewed. Up to that time the Word could be heard but now the Word became flesh. Man is taken back to the essence and origin of his life. As a result of the opening verses of the letter to the Hebrews, "In the past God spoke to our forefathers through the prophets at many times and in various ways, but in these last days he has spoken to us by his Son" (Heb 1:1), he can now stand in the light that has always shone on earth.

Schmithals (1981c:22-24) takes the argument still further. He says that in the light of the testimony of Christ concerning religion, wisdom and nature, early Christianity discovered that God is never silent. The early Christians showed people outside Christianity what remnants and traces of Divine truth were in them, and that they might love it, when associated with the one unique and enduring spoken word of God, Jesus Christ. Christ does not reveal a new God, but the one God manifests himself anew (Schmithals 1970c:179; 1979a:447).

Salvation has no history, in the sense that it is slowly revealed or prepared by history. This would reduce the Old Testament to a preliminary revelation. According to the categories of the linear school of thought, the Old Testament, being a book before Christ, must also be one without Christ. This historical approach must not be applied to the perception of the Old Testament in the New Testament. The Old Testament must not be regarded as being in a preliminary relationship to the New Testament, but rather as being in a simultaneous relationship to the Christian faith.

In the Old Testament, both the law and the gospel are present in the full sense of the word. This view represents a more logical application of the existential interpretation of the Old Testament, than that provided by Bultmann. He portrays the Old Testament as unsuccessful ("*scheitert*"), because it proclaims human existence under the law (cf. Gunneweg 1984:322-347).

Looking back to the previous chapter, Bultmann's point of view can be summarized in this way: he classified the historical Jesus with the Old Testament. Moreover he considers the teaching of Jesus, as well as the Old Testament, as descriptions of human existence under the law. Schmithals classifies the historical Jesus with apocalyptic; consequently, he does not link the historical Jesus to the Old Testament and existence under the law as directly as Bultmann does. The Old Testament can also describe human existence under the gospel. Revelation does not consist of the introduction of various ideas; God himself is revealed. Revelation also means redemption and salvation as it breaches estrangement and brings reconciliation between God and man. In understanding God and salvation in the New Testament, the unity of God in the Old and New Testaments corresponds to the uniformity in the understanding of salvation in the Old and New Testaments (Schmithals 1979a:522-523): "The Lord is my light and my salvation whom shall I fear? The Lord is the stronghold of my life of whom shall I be afraid?" (Ps 27:1).

Thus it was described in the Old Testament and in the same way Christologically founded and eschatologically defined, we have it in the New Testament: "For I am convinced that ... nothing else in all creation, will be able to separate us from the love of God that is in Christ Jesus our Lord" (Rom 8:38-39).

Schmithals accepts the Christ events as an expression of the relationship between God and humankind; a specific explanation of human existence is provided. This Christological image of humankind amounts to the fact that all human possibilities are thoroughly transcended by God and that his human image is already present when the exegete examines the texts of the Old Testament with a view to finding the perception of life there. A text in the Old Testament, like the one quoted from Psalm 27, can verbalize a perception of life corresponding to that of the Christian testimony. A text like this could be used in church for a sermon without any christological change of direction. The text is to all intents and purposes implicitly Christological or the Old Testament is a "Christian" book. The fact that there are such texts in the Old Testament is not mentioned for the sake of giving credit to the Old Testament, but to illustrate the adequacy and the completeness of the Christ testimony. The "Christian" is the deciding factor.

It is important to note that the "once and for all" of the history of salvation, is also interpreted existentially by Schmithals. To explain this, the question "How does the history of salvation really function?" can be our point of departure. One suggested way of answering this question was the scholastic doctrine of satisfaction, developed by Anselm of Canterbury (Schmithals 19881:127-128). We can summarize this juridical representation, which has always fascinated theologians, as follows: God's righteousness demands reparation for the harm done to him by the sins of humankind. This reparation needs not necessarily be provided by sinners themselves. God punishes human sins by the substitutionary death of Jesus, who is without sin. In this way the injured majesty of God is appeased and at the same time he forgives the sins of believers. The doctrine of juridical satisfaction forms a logical, closed system that professes to describe and explain the historical events of salvation. These events are then understood to be unique historical facts that happened at a specific time. This satisfaction took place between God and his Son for the sake of humankind. The fact that it took place historically, makes it revelation. Everything that occurred between God and humankind previously, about which we read in the Old Testament, is downgraded to preliminary revelation, because the satisfaction had not yet taken place.

Schmithals does not accept the salvation which came in Christ as something new in the sense of a moment in an historical development. In Christ a full revelation is not reached, marking everything that happened before as preliminary. There is no new revelation in Christ, but the one God, who has always been the light of humankind, reveals himself anew. The Christ event means renewal of the salvation that was always possible for humankind. The word that was there in the beginning and the word that became flesh are identical. The word that is now preached presents people with the newness of the Word, but it could be heard from the beginning (Schmithals 1970c:179-180; 1979a:477).

In response to the question as to the functioning of the events of salvation Schmithals (1973a:221-222; 1989b:15), says that the proclaimed word makes the events of salvation present. The word is the only element in which these events can be found, because they are nonrecurrent and unrepeatable. If these events were repeatable, the evidentiary word would not be necessary. The uniqueness of these events also gives the proclaiming word the status of full validity, as an affirmation of salvation. The word makes present the truth of salvation as a reality, which does not come from man; and because of this function, the word is to be respected. The confession ensures that the original events are made present, with the result that people of all ages have the same relationship to the truth of these events (Schmithals 1979a:701). For Schmithals the "once" and "once and for all" of the Christ event are a description of the sufficiency and completeness of God's salvation encountering people in the church's proclamation. The "once and for all" of the Christ event is usually understood as being historically non-recurrent, as though Christian tradition is a matter of historical interest. One often reads the statement that the fact that Pontius Pilate is mentioned in the creed, means that the church wishes to mark the death of Jesus Christ as an event in time, which might have been the case if the historicity of the events were in doubt. Schmithals (1979a:681) makes the point that the historicity of the events as such was not stressed or regarded as an issue. Christians did not doubt the historicity of the events referred to in the words "was crucified, dead and buried." Schmithals speaks of the creed being anchored in unique, historical, empirical events (1 Jn 1:14). Such an anchoring of the events of salvation in time and space must be seen in connection with the changed behavior, which it brings about in believers. The new relationship of the redeemed to the world and the service of love are also events in time and space (Schmithals 1979a:682). The obedience of faith is not a result of our living in harmony with our nature but rather of our appropriate response to the proclamation with its claims on us in our daily lives. God's entrance into history makes every present moment an eternal presence, *nunc aeternum* (Schmithals 1982e:121; 1987c:12).

It is noteworthy that Schmithals' point of view regarding the relationship of the New Testament to the Old is determined by the Christian kerygma. It serves as criterion for both the New and the Old Testament. In this way the door is opened for a Biblical theology. One of the books Schmithals published in Cupertino with the late Gunneweg, an authority on the Old Testament from Bonn, was called *Herrschaff* (1989). It is dedicated to "den Freunden Biblischer Theologie" (cf. Schmithals 1996b:262).

Saying that the authors of the New Testament wrote what they wrote and saw it as commentary on what was written in the Old Testament (cf. Van Selms 1936:12) turns Christianity into a continuation of Judaism as though the New Testament is deduced from the Old. Schmithals insists that the act of God in Christ should be the criterion when reading the texts of the Old Testament. Using this criterion, he looks back on the Old Testament and recognizes the consistent act of God as it becomes clear in Christ. The

Gospel, that is the theology of the New Testament, is the principle by which the scientific study of the Old Testament has obtained theological status. Put differently, the New Testament is read as the forging of the Christian dogma and the Old Testament can be used to explain this same dogma. Thus the dogmatic nature of the Gospel comes into its own.

In my opinion, the greatest advantage of the approach of Schmithals and Gunneweg (cf. Boshoff 1987), as regards the relationship between the Old Testament and the New is that the decisive question is answered: can the text of the Old Testament be used profitably in sermons? The Christian faith becomes a perception of life that need not necessarily be expressed christologically. The basic structure of Christianity can also be found in the Old Testament, which can be used in preaching faith and the kerygma and still be fully Christian. The Christ events give an unambiguous directive for the highlighting of the "Christian" substance of the Old Testament. Instead of the multiplicity of meanings in the Old Testament, the Christ event brings coherence.

6.3 ESCHATOLOGY AND APOCALYPTIC

For a description of the theological history of the New Testament, from Schmithals' point of view, it is necessary to discuss the actual relationship between apocalyptic and Christianity. We have seen that he conceded that apocalyptic can be called the mother of Christian theology. To quote Schmithals' own words, he would prefer to make the historical relationships comprehensible by way of the relationship between expectation and fulfillment (Schmithals 1973a:119). Apocalyptic stands on the threshold of expectation of the act of salvation, while Christianity testifies to this act of salvation.

To make this matter abundantly clear, we are reproducing Schmithals' view on the essence of apocalyptic. It is not merely a literary genre, but a specific perception of the world, history and life. This system of reflection underlines apocalyptic literature as well as other texts (Schmithals 1973a:22). The first characteristic of apocalyptic is its orientation to history. God has planned history and it will run its course as revealed to the apocalyptic writer (Schmithals 1973a:23). Apocalyptic writers know that their hour is the last hour of the old dispensation: the time of the great upheaval (Schmithals 1973a:25). Humankind has a role to play in these great events, because a human being has the ability to come to a decision, in the midst of history, as far as his or her own life is concerned. A call to repentance and conversion is therefore typical of apocalyptic approach. People make their own decision whether or not to participate in the New World. Everything takes place now and it depends on every individual how things will turn out (Schmithals 1973a:29). This is the background for the interpretation Schmithals gives to the parable of the dishonest steward:

> Therefore, he called in each one of his master's debtors. He asked the first, "How much do you owe my master?" "One hundred gallons of olive oil," he replied. The manager told him, "Take your bill, sit down quickly, and make it fifty." Then he asked the second, "And how much do you owe?" "A thousand bushels of wheat," he replied. He told him, "Take your bill and make it eight hundred."
>
> (Lk 16:1-7)

The manager uses the short time remaining to him. The listeners to this parable are called upon to make use of the opportunity to ensure their entrance to the Kingdom of God before the end of the world. Conversion is necessary and it is still possible. No one would treat matters concerning eternal life with less ingenuity than the dishonest steward did in the case of secular affairs (Schmithals 1987c:9).

Apocalyptic sees human beings as confronted with a grave responsibility, yet, Schmithals suspects that pessimism with regard to reality as it is experienced and can be experienced is the original impulse of apocalyptic, giving rise to the attempt to deal with this experience in a positive way (Schmithals 1973a:32). Apocalyptists are freed of responsibility for the world and history, because the world has been wicked from its foundation. In mythological terms, Satan and God are opposed as being in control of the present and future worlds. Faith in angels and demons gives expression to the separation between God and this world. Salvation cannot be realized in this day and age. People can only await it (Schmithals 1973a:30-32).

The apocalyptic regards radical pessimism concerning this age is justified, but confronts absolute despondency by offering to the righteous the great hope of the new creation that is to come (Schmithals 1973a:33-34). The result of apocalyptic faith is that history becomes completely profane. No theological significance can be seen in any historical events. Even God is no longer able to perform an act of salvation in this world. He himself must wait for the fulfillment of predetermined times. The devil becomes the god of this age. There is no judgment within history; history itself is judged. The Old World will come to an end in fire and brimstone, to make way for the new (Schmithals 1973a:61; 1979a:100; cf. Heim: 1955:104). This apocalyptic conception can be presented schematically in the following way:

Turning point

Old World	New World
Kingdom of Satan	Kingdom of God

It may be mentioned in passing that Schmithals (1973a:60-61) opposed the Old Testament to apocalyptic faith and thought. The Old Testament does not expect deliverance from history, but salvation in history. God offers his salvation to his people as a possibility, which exists in every present time. God's judgment is executed in history and consequently sin and righteousness are not to be found on either side of the great turning point, but are humanly possible within history. As far as the New Testament is concerned, the following scheme becomes evident:

Turning point/Jesus Christ

Old World	Kingdom of Christ
—————————————	------------> Kingdom of God
Kingdom of Satan	

Old World

In all the variations of early Christian theology, Schmithals finds that the historical event "Jesus Christ" is understood to be an eschatological event; the turning point has been reached. Divine salvation meets people in the Christian kerygma as a possibility in history; and it becomes an historical reality when this possibility is accepted. The congregation which confesses that Jesus reigns, understands itself to be an eschatological congregation (Schmithals 1973a:119).

In the formula: "so that, just as sin reigned in death, so also grace might reign through righteousness to bring eternal life through Jesus Christ, our Lord" (Rom 5:21). Schmithals (1988a:180; cf. also 1979a:105) sees a breaching of the apocalyptic way of thinking. The scheme of two worlds is applied and the characteristics of both described: the reign of sin leading to death and the reign of grace leading to life. Instead of the old and new worlds, it is a matter of the old and the new human being, because the formula knows of the turning point that came in Christ. This turning point is reached in the lives of those who have received life in the midst of the world of death. Schmithals (1988b:65) finds it advisable to distinguish clearly between the terms "eschatology" and "apocalyptic." He shows the difference clearly by pointing out the concept of life informing in each structure. In each case the significance derives from its contrast to the other. Schmithals understands "eschatology" to be the notion of time and life, where believing in Jesus Christ causes one to see each present time as the time of salvation open to the future. On the other hand "apocalyptic" does not see the present time as a time of salvation, but as a profane time (Schmithals 1973a:61), even though these are the last days of the Old World. The Easter faith confesses that the Christ events are eschatological saving events: "But Christ has indeed been raised from the dead, the first fruits of those who have fallen asleep" (1 Cor 15:20).

The resurrection of Christ signals the end of the Old World order. Judgement has been passed on the Old World. People must not expect their life from the world or from their own possibilities, because these offer no future. In the midst of this world the Easter faith perceives God's salvation and confesses: the world is passing away, life has begun (Schmithals1978c:2).

The representation of the New Testament accords with apocalyptic dualism in that salvation cannot be expected from humans or from history, but only from God. People are the receivers of salvation in their actual history. They are not delivered from history, but from their own iniquity within history. Apocalyptic dualism becomes decisive dualism. The Old World and the new do not exclude each other; rather, they overlap. For the faithful the Old World has ended in this time, but for the unbeliever damnation has come (Schmithals 1973a:121). Schmithals (1973a:120) explains that early Christian preaching made use of dramatic representations of the apocalyptic last days. This was done especially to warn against the gnostic misunderstanding that salvation was a possession of the church. Furthermore it was used to emphasize the dialectic understanding of salvation as a gift of grace. The apocalyptic representations express the "not yet" character of salvation in relation to its "already" aspect. Schmithals keeps stressing the dialectic connection between the "already" and "not yet" of salvation. The truth lies in the tension between these two poles and not in either of them on its own. This tension should not be relaxed. Salvation is already fully present and at the same time fully outstanding. The higher unity between the inner contrast of "already" and "not yet" is possible, the reason being that it is God's salvation which can only be fully realized where people associate their lives with the advent of God in Christ. At the same time, salvation never becomes the possession of people, for they can only expect it again and again.

The faithful will definitely appear before Christ in the last judgment: "For we must all appear before the judgment seat of Christ, that each one may receive what is due to him for the things done while in the body, whether good or bad" (2 Cor 5:10).

These words underline the responsibility of a believer for the transient world. Nevertheless, believers are withdrawn from the judgment of God. They will judge the world along with God (1 Cor 2:2). This is only possible because the faithful have already accepted the judgment on themselves (Schmithals 1984c).

Schmithals (1980a:226) describes the words of Jesus when he spoke to the criminal on the cross: Jesus answered him, "I tell you the truth, today you will be with me in paradise" (Lk 23:43) as being "vertical" Hellenistic eschatology. Another example of Hellenistic eschatology (Schmithals 1979a:537) was written by Paul: "I am torn between the two: I desire to depart and be with Christ which is better by far" (Phil 1:23).

The idea in this representation is that communion with Christ does not cease, but continues. As opposed to the vertical, Hellenistic eschatology, we have the horizontal apocalyptic depiction of the resurrection. In this school of thought the resurrection is still outstanding. Apart from the fact that this representation maintains in the face of all certainty of salvation its eschatological reservation that the new life remains life bestowed, it directs hope to God the Creator. Resurrection directs man to the creative power of God, if he wishes to live (Schmithals 1984c).

The fact that there is no unanimity in the New Testament depiction of the future, Schmithals (1979a:537-538; 1983g:120-122) considers as an expression of the radical nature of Christian hope: "But hope that is seen is no hope at all" (Rom 8:24). Conditions are not described. It would be utopian. Utopias exclude hope, put an end to it. On the other hand, genuine hope has neither end nor results. Christian hope is the eternal openness to the new and unknown given by God. The one who believes does not set his or her hopes on a condition; "on something," but on Someone: God himself. The utopian descriptions in the Book of Revelation are enclosed by the confession: I am the Alpha and the Omega, the First and the Last, the Beginning and the End (Rev 22:13; cf. 1:17-18)

The way the Second Coming of Christ is depicted expresses the continuity of Christian salvation (Schmithals 1978d:163). The coming Christ is the one who came. Nothing more can come than that which has already come. The One who is coming has conquered death and brought life by means of the Gospel.

In 1978 Schmithals (1978e:390-391) still read Pauline literature as being pervaded by apocalyptic representations, concepts and formulae, for example 1 Thessalonians 4:13-18. At a later stage he thought that the passage from verse 15 onwards was an addition by the editor of the main collection of Pauline letters (Schmithals 1984a:160-161; 1988b:74-77). This statement intensifies and strengthens Schmithals' point of view that Paul was no apocalyptist. Rather he had an eschatological concept of time and life in view of the Christ event. The eschatological point of view was the foundation of his gospel from the beginning. Consequently, no development concerning Paul's representations and expectations of the future can be reconstructed. To this Schmithals adds (1988b:80-81) that, in this respect,

Paul is representative of the whole of early Christianity with regard to the relationship between eschatology and apocalyptic.

6.4 PAUL'S THEOLOGY OF CONVERSION (DAMASCUS)

One of the well known problems concerning the chronology of Paul's life, is a contradiction that he himself caused. On the one hand, he urges people to honor traditions and, on the other he emphasizes his own authority. Paul calls to witness what he has received from tradition: "For what I received, I passed on to you as of first importance" (1 Cor 1:5-13a). He continues by giving an Antiochene confession. He stresses the fact that he received the Gospel from men. On the other hand, in an autobiographical remark, he states that he is not dependent on tradition:

> I want you to know, brothers, that the gospel I preached is not something that man made up. I did not receive it from any man, nor was I taught it; rather, I received it by revelation from Jesus Christ.
> (Gal 1:11-12)

Thus Paul claims to have received the Gospel directly from Christ and that his calling as apostle is linked to this revelation.

In his historical interpretation of theology, Schmithals (1978e:398-399) finds that Paul plays a part in two different theological structures. On the one hand, he calls attention to the tradition of the Antiochene church, on which he based his theology. On the other hand, Paul has been accused of being dependent on people instead of on the Spirit of God, so we see another theological structure coming to the fore. This structure is older than the Antiochene theology, because Paul uses it in connection with his conversion and calling as an apostle.

Schmithals (1978e:397; 1994a:78-89) explains that Paul uses gnostic language when describing his conversion and vocation: "But when God ... was pleased to reveal his

Son in me" (Gal 1:15-16). "In me" refers to the "*pneuma* Christ," who was raised from the dead as seen from the point of view of the history of religion.

An important indication of the theological direction in which Paul started in the church, Schmithals (1978e: 400-401; 1989c:239; 1994a:80-81, 110-111; 1997:18-19) finds in the situation of the persecution of the church. When Paul speaks of his persecution of the *ecclesia* (of God) (1 Cor 15:9; Gal 1:13; Phil 3:6), he is not referring to the church of Jerusalem or any other Jewish-Christian church. Originally *ecclesia* was the concept with which the Damascus theology identified the body of Christ to outsiders. Soon the church described itself in this way. Christianity, in association with the synagogue, was not persecuted. Persecution was specifically aimed at Jewish Christians who disputed the synagogue's right of existence, in other words, Christians who were so impressed with the fact that salvation was universal that they became involved in fundamental criticism of the Jewish law and particularism. These Jewish Christians were persecuted by Paul because of their freedom from and opposition to the law. After his conversion, Paul, himself, a Jew, gave up his obedience to the law. The basic formula of the doctrine in which this universalism is expressed was often repeated by him and in various forms: "There is neither Jew nor Greek, slave nor free, male nor female, for you are all one in Christ Jesus" (Gal 3:28; cf. 1 Cor 12:13; Col 3:10-11, 1 Cor 1:8-20).

What is important is that the language used to express this universalism unmistakably shows the dualistic perception of Gnosticism. A Gnostic does not acknowledge the earthly difference between man and woman, because the divine pneuma is freed from the earthly prison of the flesh. Gnosticism is basically universalistic because all earthly particularism has been conquered. Although Paul was not himself a Gnostic, gnostic language is typical of the theology with which he came into contact after his conversion. Universalistic Christian theology itself did not deny the natural and social differences, but such differences can be overcome through faith.

When identifying the theology with which Paul came into contact at the time of his conversion, it is important to differentiate between different terminologies (Schmithals 1978e:387-388). Paul at first used gnostic-like terminology, but used different terminology when engaged in controversy with the Gnostics. According to Schmithals, Paul came into direct contact with Gnosticism only during his so-called third missionary journey. By that time, his theology had long since taken shape. Apart from his chance contact with Gnosticism, Schmithals sees a deep-seated theology inclined to Gnosticism in Paul. This he traces back to the time of the apostle's conversion. The basic structure of this original theology, to which Paul always remained faithful, Schmithals (1989c:250; cf.1997b:306) sums up as being preexistence Christology, incarnational soteriology, dualistic use of language and presentist eschatology.

Schmithals (1978e:404-405 and note 45; 1989c: 240; 1994a:73-74) ascribes the confession of the pre-existence of Christ in the hymn in Philippians 2:6-11 to a theology already existing in the church at the time of Paul's conversion. The development of this christological representation he explains in the history of religion, as resulting from a combination of the gnostic representation of salvation and the redeemer figure in the church. The Gnostic is convinced that humankind cannot be left to its own devices and cannot depend on the world for salvation from alienation. Salvation must come from an external source, not from the world, because people must be saved from their world. When this idea of salvation is linked to Jesus Christ, we have the resulting pre-existential Christology.

At first Schmithals (1978e:403-404; 1988a:51) saw the texts of Galatians 4:45 and Romans 8:3-4 as falling under the viewpoint of pre-existence Christology. The idea that God sent his Son, which occurs in these texts, is usually associated with the pre-existence. Later on Schmithals (1989c:240; 1994a:91; 1997b:299-301, 306) classified these texts under the heading: incarnational soteriology. It seems as if Schmithals sees the theme of these formulae, quoted by Paul, as being transferred from Christology to soteriology; from "sent" to "born of a woman" and " in the likeness of sinful man." It is not necessary to consider it contradictory; because the soteriology is developed within the framework of incarnational Christology. The Son of God is in solidarity with humankind in estrangement. People are entitled to know that there is no height or depth in their existence, where God is not with them (Schmithals 1988a:262).

The expression used in Romans 8:4: "who do not live according to the sinful nature but according to the spirit" is an example of the dualistic use of language (Schmithals 1989c:240; 1994a:70-71). In Christian theology the flesh and the spirit lose their substantial character, as found in Hellenistic dualism. Flesh and spirit become the description of two ways of existence, namely belonging to God or belonging to oneself (Schmithals 1988a:259, 275). The words in 2 Corinthians 5:17 express present eschatology: "Therefore, if anyone is in Christ, he is a new creation; the old has gone, the new has come!" The "new creation" is not something that lies in the distant future, but has already become a reality (Schmithals 1978e:407; 1979a: 178; 1988a: 288; 1989c:242).

To be more definite about the development and localizing of the Christianity to which Paul was converted, Schmithals (1978e:407-410; 1982a:64; 1989c:241; 1994a: 70) frames a hypothesis that an enthusiastic dualistic trend developed among the Jews of Palestine. The name of Simon Magus can be mentioned in this connection. In this gnostic Judaism the natural and the nationalistic were sacrificed to the pneumatic. Palestinian Christianity came into contact with this Jewish Gnosticism in its missionary work. The result of this contact was that Christian theology adopted the universalism and the accompanying freedom from the law without the dualism of the gnostic system. Substantial dualism was translated into decisive dualism. Stephen, about whom no biographical information is given in Acts, must have played a decisive role in this development. Schmithals (1994a:90) presumes that Damascus was the source of this theology. The carefully formulated ideas were typical. The prologue to the Gospel of John is a further example of the thinking and *modus operandi* of Damascene theology (Schmithals 1994a:93-94).

6.5 THE THEOLOGY OF ANTIOCH

Originally, in Antioch, Christianity was a Jewish doctrine proclaimed in the synagogue (Schmithals 1982a:109). This doctrine was sustained by the specific idea of the universality of the Gospel, for both Jew and Gentile: "First for the Jew, then for the Gentile" (Rom 1: 16).

Barnabas played a leading role in Antioch and the Syrian church. For more than ten years, Paul and he, formed the famous missionary partnership. To link the theology of Antioch to another personality, Schmithals (1979a:48) makes use of the sparse information concerning John, also called Mark, to be found in the New Testament. Although Schmithals states unequivocally that we know nothing about the author of the basic text of the Gospel according to Mark, the church traditionally ascribed it to Mark. This could not be anyone but John, also called Mark. He accompanied Paul and Barnabas on the so-called first missionary journey (Acts 12:25; 13:5) and worked with them in the Syrian region of Antioch. Mark, together with his cousin Barnabas, left Paul on account of a difference of opinion concerning the tradition of the synagogue. Later on, he again became one of Paul's collaborators (cf. Col 4:10). Mark was at home not only in Pauline circles, but is also referred to as Peter's "son" in 1 Peter 5:13. Bishop Papias of Hierapolis noted that he was the *hemeneute* to Peter and wrote down the narratives of Peter from his recollections.

Mark's contact with the Jewish Christianity of Peter and the Gentile Christianity of Paul gives one to suppose that he concentrated his missionary activity on the God-fearing gentiles in the synagogue. The basic text of the Gospel according to Mark is theologically speaking within the sphere of this early Hellenistic Christianity of which Peter was also a representative (Schmithals 1988a:51). The author of the *Grundschrift* must have been a theologian of the stature of Mark. It is possible that he himself was the author. By linking the theology of Antioch and the *Markus-Grundschrift* to the person of Mark, Schmithals departs from the supposition that the material used in the Gospel came from early oral versions. The *Grundschrift* came into being as a theological writing.

The earliest stage of the theology of Antioch is found, for example, in 1 Peter and in Paul's Antiochene formulae. The synoptic tradition represents the more recent stage of this theology (Schmithals 1984b: 154).

Schmithals (1989c:242-243; 1994a:95; 1997b:303-304) describes the Christology of Antiochene Christianity as adoptionist. According to this tradition Jesus was exalted to "Son of God" through his resurrection. The heavenly voice saying to Jesus: You are my Son, whom l love (Mk 1: 9-11) speaks from the same Christological framework (Schmithals 1979:48, 85). The representation of the conception by the Holy Spirit and the virgin birth could be linked to this matter and might even replace it (Schmithals 1994a:95).

In the explanation that the crucified and risen Jesus is adopted as the Son of God, the question of the significance of his death arises. Schmithals (1994a:97) reaches the conclusion that the early church in Palestine interpreted it with the help of Isaiah 53. They concluded that soteriologically he died "for us" "for our sins." Several expressions indicate that this explanation became part of Antiochene soteriology (Schmithals 1994a:96-99). Romans 4:24b-25 serves as an example: "for us who believe in him who raised Jesus our Lord from the dead. He was delivered over to death for our sins and was raised to life for our justification." Add to this: "Christ died for our sins according to the Scriptures" (1 Cor 15:3; Schmithals 1994a:102-103). The church celebrating the Eucharist, "proclaims the Lord's death" (1 Cor 11:26; Schmithals 1994a:103-104).

A further example of Antiochene soteriology Schmithals (1988a:120; 1994a:99-102) finds in Romans 3:25: "God presented him as a sacrifice of atonement through faith in his blood. He did this to demonstrate his justice, because in his forbearance he had left the sins committed beforehand unpunished." Schmithals (1979a:159-160; 1988a:122-123; 1994a:101-102) thinks that the word "sins" or "transgressions" is used here in the narrower sense of the word, namely in the sense of manifestations of being a comprehensive sinner; in other words rejecting or breaking the commandments of God. Sins, as immoral or indecent behavior, can be judged by moral standards. In the course of the history of the church, the narrower Antiochene concept of sin and the accompanying soteriology gained the upper hand over that of Damascus. From the context within which Paul's formula is found, Schmithals shows that Paul brought this formula up to date from his theology of conversion. Paul does not consider the act of salvation merely as God leaving the sins of the past unpunished, but, far more, as the dawning of the new creation.

According to Schmithals (1989c:250), Paul considered the Antiochene view of the death atoning of Jesus as most important. On this he based his characteristic theology of the cross. The soteriological formula of Antiochene theology (Rom 3:25-26a) of "in his blood," implies that God presented Jesus as an atoning sacrifice. The death of Jesus is explained as the act of salvation without mentioning his "death" or his "cross" as Paul was fond of doing (Schmithals 1988a:121). Earlier on Schmithals (1973b:221) thought that the pre-Pauline formulation, was moving along the traditional lines of the sacrifice of atonement. Later on Schmithals corrected himself (Schmithals 1988a:121-122). The formula does not link it to cultic representations deliberately and no theory of atonement is offered, especially not one that stated that Jesus was a sin offering. The formula makes use of the usual representation that there must be atonement for guilt and implies that God carried into effect this atonement by means of the death of Christ. Thus, the necessary atonement is achieved by means of his substitutionary sacrifice. During the time of Paul's ministry in Syria and Cilicia, he finalized his theology of the cross (Schmithals 1989:245). Paul speaks of it: "As for me, however, 1 will boast only about the cross of our Lord Jesus Christ; for by means of his cross the world is dead to me, and I am dead to the world" (Gal 6:14). In this way Paul expands the Antiochene concept of the saving death of Jesus, in order to preclude Israel from still having precedence in salvation. "It does not matter at all whether or not one is circumcised; what does matter is being a new creature" (Gal 6:15).

On examining it linguistically and from the point of view of the history of religion, Schmithals (1994a:10) concludes that the ecclesiological baptism of the Damascene theology "into Christ" was developed soteriologically to "into the name of Christ" (e.g. 1 Cor 13:5). At a later date it became "in the name of the Father and of the Son and of the Holy Spirit" (Mt 28:19). In accordance with the Antiochene point of view concerning sin and salvation, Christians are freed from their previously besmirched lives as Gentiles.

> Some of you were like that. However, you have been purified from sin; you have been dedicated to God; you have been put right with God through the name of the Lord Jesus Christ and through the Spirit of our God.
> (1 Cor 6:11)

As far as the Eucharist is concerned, the idea of Christ's death "for us" is used and expressed by means of the cup which symbolizes the blood that was shed "for us" and the bread that is broken (Schmithals 1994a:219-220).

The concept of church in the theology of Antioch is that of a holy *remnant* and the eschatological people of God (Schmithals 1994a:158-160). The transition of representing the church as a building or a crop poses no problem when seen against the background of the Old Testament (Schmithals 1994a:163-165). The church not only expects the coming of the Lord, but also is used by him and knows that he is always with them In the allegory of the weeds amongst the wheat (Mt 13:24-30; 36-43) it is presumed that the church has become a *corpus permixtum* and can no longer be isolated in holiness (Schmithals 1994a:167).

6.6 PAUL'S ORIGINAL THEOLOGICAL IDEAS

The Reformation has led us to assume that the doctrine of justification is central to Paul's theology. According to Schmithals (1978e:392; 1989c:251; 1994a:76) this complex, in reality, constitutes Paul's original theological ideas. This doctrine does not appear in all of Paul's letters, but only where he is involved in a controversy with the Jews, in the letters to the Galatians and the Romans. The doctrine comes into operation when Paul wants to organize the *ecclesia* apart from the synagogue (Schmithals 1988a:66; 1989c:245; 1994a:76, 118). What is remarkable in Schmithals' explanation of Paul's doctrine of justification, is that it does not have a juridical character. Consequently, the "doctrine of justification" can be placed in inverted commas. It is also noteworthy that Schmithals succeeds in incorporating the doctrine of justification into the whole of his theology.

The doctrine of justification was not an *ad hoc* development, but was a formulated teaching material for the instruction of members of the congregation who were active in missionary work (Schmithals 1988a:43). Paul quotes from this material, to explain his theology also in other contexts as being opposition to the synagogue, for example Philippians 3:9 (Schmithals 1984a:108): "not having a righteousness of my own that comes from the law, but that which is through faith in Christ the righteousness that comes from God and is by faith."

Schmithals (1986f:383; 1988a:62-63) warns us that the theological concept of righteousness must not be understood in the obvious sense that a jurist would understand it. The Pharisaic way of thinking can be considered as being that of a jurist: If someone can keep the commandments, he or she will be declared righteous by God in the last judgment. God acts like a judge who weighs guilt and merit against each other. When merit is greater than guilt, sins are forgiven and the sinner declared righteous. God's grace is limited to the wiping out of the guilt of the righteous, and for this he is praised (Schmithals 1988a:63-64).

As opposed to declaring people righteous in the manner of a jurist on account of their good deeds, Paul formulates: "justification by faith." To understand this expression, Schmithals returns to the non-juristic "original meaning" of the word righteousness. According to this meaning, humankind comes to the appropriate relationship with itself and all existing things. Humankind is put right. Human life reaches its destination in its truth. We are put right in relation to God, our neighbor and ourselves (Schmithals 1986f:383-384; 1988a:63). According to Paul, God is the one who puts people right. He is the author and creator of human's righteousness. God not only declares people to be righteous; from a linguistic point of view righteousness has a causative meaning: God causes people to reach the true way, God justifies humankind (Schmithals 1988a:127).

Schmithals (1989c:251) points out that the doctrine of justification by faith, which was later taught by the apostle, does not contradict the universalist formulae of the theology within which Paul was converted. With the help of the doctrine of justification, Paul unfolded universalism in his struggle against the synagogues. Thus, he tried to persuade the God-fearing to join the congregation of those freed from the law. Justification by faith replaces justification by the law and therefore there is no longer any real difference between Jew and Gentile (Schmithals 1984a:34, 141).

This period, in which Paul developed the doctrine of justification, Schmithals (1982a:111; cf. 244; 1989c:245; 1994a:76; cf. 1997a:16-18) indicates as being after the meeting of the apostles where it was agreed that Paul and Barnabas would go to the gentiles and James, Peter and John would bring the Gospel to the Jews (Gal 2:1-10; Acts 11:27-30; 5:1-34).

6.7 THEOLOGICAL ADDITIONS TO PAUL'S LETTERS BY EDITORS

The editor who placed Paul's most important letters at the disposal of all the churches at the time of the *aposunagogos* dissociated the church from the turbulent Jews (1 Thes 2:14-16). Unlike them, the church remained loyal to the Roman authorities (Rom 13:1-7). Persecution encouraged the apocalyptic expectation of the end of the Old World and the dramatic dawning of the new. So the editor had to allay the fears of the people that it would be prejudicial to those who were still going to die (Schmithals 1984a:31, 456-470).

The editor of the secondary collection of Pauline letters (Colossians, Ephesians and Philemon) also worked against the background of the *aposunagogos*. He did his best to urge the gentile Christians of the Pauline churches to welcome in their midst Jewish Christians who had dissociated themselves from the synagogue at the same time the moral rules of the synagogue were impressed upon them. The fact that synagogical piety is stressed more strongly also functions as a barrier against Christian Gnosticism, represented as part of Pauline Christianity. The church gets to know the love of Christ which surpasses all *gnosis* (Eph 3:19; cf. Schmithals 1984a:173).

6.8 CLOSING REMARKS

Ideas coming to the fore in this chapter serve as the greatest challenge to think with and differ from Schmithals. If one wants to set about really discussing theology from a historical point of view, the history of the theology of the New Testament must also be described. The Christian view of life is subject to history in the sense that the kerygma of the church must always be formulated anew.

CHAPTER 7

Theory and Practice of Preaching the New Testament

7.1 INTRODUCTION

According to the list of lectures given at the University of Marburg during the winter semester 1964/65, Walter Schmithals took it upon himself to lecture on the exegesis of certain prescribed pericopes for sermons. This was his way of replying to the normal complaints and questions and implied criticism of theological students. They wanted to know "Of what practical use are all the exercises in historical critical method to us in the church?" In the next semester he was joined by his Old Testament colleague, Gunneweg, for a study group on exegesis and preaching. After leaving Marburg, Schmithals to Berlin and Gunneweg to Bonn, they continued with this process, meeting regularly with students to carry into effect what may be called the way from exegesis to preaching. The forty-seventh and last meeting took place in Bonn from 8 to 10 July 1988. Usually four texts were taken, two from the Old and two from the New Testament. These texts were explained and then either Schmithals or Gunneweg delivered a sermon in a church service. In the final discussion the group could mull over the "way" which had been followed (cf. Schmithals 1992b:10).

The method used by Schmithals and Gunneweg was to lead the students into a process of understanding in which the text is really understood and could lead to an understandable sermon. There is no better way of demonstrating that historical critical exegesis is useful and necessary in the task of preaching the gospel.

What students ask of their professors is whether they can preach the way they think theologically. Is there a natural transition from theology to preaching? What makes the question urgent is the impression that there is a vast gap between the results of historical exegesis and the preaching on Sundays. Sermons come from elsewhere, not from exegesis. Schmithals committed himself to historical exegesis as the only method in keeping with modern perceptions. It is worth walking a mile with Schmithals, because he concentrates on showing that exegesis must be done with a view to preaching and it leads to the very doorstep of the sermon.

The method that we use is to study what Schmithals considered to be the task of preaching and then to discuss examples of how he and others carried out their task.

7.2 THEORY OF PREACHING

There is general discontent with the results of historical-critical exegesis and the apparent impossibility of this method bridging the gap between Scripture and the preaching of the message of the Bible. This has caused the traditional theory of preaching to be pushed aside; the theory being that preaching is explanation and application of Scripture. Dreyer (1989:359-360) formulated some of the reasons that led to this: On the one hand it is pointed out that there are different theologies in the Bible and that authors of the Bible worked with different concepts of God. Consequently, it would not be a simple matter to call upon God to speak in the sermon, because he is depicted in so many different ways. On the other hand, conveying the message of the text is impeded by the historical distance between the listeners of today and the circumstances in which the text originally spoke to people.

The diversity of theologies in the Bible is no cause for embarrassment to Schmithals, nor is it a reason for the church to be mute in the world. Schmithals does not solve the problem by recommending a unitarian exegesis of

Scripture. He fully admits that there is a difference between, for example, the theology of Paul and the theology of John and even further between Luther and Barth. Each has his own concept within which salvation is preached. Each has his own view of God. This does not mean that they are mutually exclusive. What they are speaking of is one and the same divine act and it expresses the same basic attitude of humans towards their own times and circumstances. The canon of the Bible does not contain only one theology, but it simply teaches the Gospel by means of different theological structures (Schmithals 1967c:494; 1970a:60; 1970c:181). This does not mean that the one message of Scripture is the point of departure for biblical research. It is rather its result (Schmithals 1967d:204).

As a whole, the theological work of Schmithals can be understood only on the pre-supposition of historical consciousness. When the present-day church wishes to speak responsibly, an essential condition of such discourse is that it must be scientific. In other words, the historical critical examination of Scripture. Scripture was written by humans and must be understood by humanity in a human way. This means that its meaning must be made clear in the here and now. In reality there is no gap between historical-critical exegesis and the conveying of it in existential interpretation. Exegesis is satisfying because it causes the text to speak to us in modern times. From the start, the text is understood in the present, here and now. Although this is a difficult way of working, there is no justification for abandoning it. No other method of working is scientifically accountable under the requirements of historical consciousness (cf. Schmithals 1970a:52-54; 1970b:84).

Although Scripture was written by people and understood by people, it does not mean that faith can be made a prerequisite to the understanding of the Bible
Understanding ought not to be equated with faith as the gift of the Holy Spirit. This would limit the practice of theology and exegesis to believers, thus endangering the scientific character of theology. A common consequence of

equating understanding and faith is that scientific endeavor is rendered superfluous (cf. Schmithals 1979a:60; 1970b: 84-85).

In his reflections on homiletics, Schmithals remains within the traditional purview of homiletics, which expected exegesis and meditation from the preacher. The preacher studies the text by means of exegesis and, by means of meditation, reflects on his or her audience. As far as Schmithals is concerned, meditation or the application of Scripture does not mean that listeners receive instruction on how to live their lives as believers. Rather, listeners are confronted with themselves, as a result of the text. The listener must be guided from self-understanding, within which he lives, and called to faith. A sermon must not be a lecture remote from life. The text must be propounded to lend content and authority to the sermon. As far as method is concerned, there is a difference between exegesis and meditation, but in practice it does not involve two separate steps. The possibility of actualizing a text emerges from the specific situation of the preacher and the congregation. Exegesis reveals thoughts that beg to be preached. The text is approached as called for by the situation and the situation is approached from the text.

In understanding a situation, Schmithals (1967b:96-97; 1972g:194) feels that a preacher can learn a great deal from sociology and psychology. However, a minister's special responsibility is to get to know the people to whom he or she preaches. In order to experience the reality of their lives, pastoral visiting is essential. The minister must get to know the circumstances in which people work, their way of thinking and the sins that beset them. The idea is not that their problems and needs should be discussed to such an extent that the congregation see themselves objectively as people with problems, but rather that their own understanding of themselves in their need is questioned (Schmithals 1970 a:56; 1973c:125).

According to Schmithals (1970 a:56; 1973c:125), biblical texts are the only foundation for preaching. Therein lies the evidence of divine revelation. Scripture ties the church to the original matter, that is, Jesus Christ. The matter to which the old texts bear witness, remains unaffected even though the latest scientific approach lays claim to greater historical objectivity. Schmithals (cf. Dreyer 1989: 359) cannot make a concession that in any way impugns the authority of Scripture. Scripture announces to the church that God's eschatological act of salvation is the deed through which he brought the church into being and to this act the church is linked. The *sola Scriptura* preserves the *solus Christus* and preserves the church (cf. Schmithals 1980a:18).

The canon is of the utmost importance to the church and theology as a form of authority (Schmithals 1970a:45). Usually, the organization of the church and the doctrine of the Holy Spirit are also quoted as authoritative. However, Scripture claims priority over the organization of the church and the Holy Spirit. With the development of the canon the church reverted to the first confessions of the basic Christ events and in this way the church is preserved for the future by this fundamental insight. Van Selms, however, is of the opinion that the Holy Spirit must have priority, preceding the canon and the church. The Holy Spirit makes people contemporaries of the time of salvation without the help of historical expedients. "*Door de werking van de Heilige Geest word men bij het lezen van het Evangelie tot discipel-tijdgenoot*" (Van Selms 1951:273). "In the reading of the Gospel through the work of the Holy Spirit, men are brought to contemporary discipleship!" However, this formulation actually supports Schmithals' viewpoint, because "*bij het lezen van het Evangelie*" stresses the necessity and the priority of the historical means, the canon. Association with the first bearers of the tradition is unnecessary, but the tradition itself cannot be abandoned.

The essence of preaching, as described and practiced by Schmithals, can be reduced to a formula: Preaching is presenting a text as an actuality (cf. Schmithals 1967b:96). The purpose of the text is to root the church in its enduring origin, the Christ confession. The purpose of the text is to edify the reader, leading him or her to faith; and this urges the reader on to preaching.

One can accept that theologians are unanimous that preaching must formally be based on Scripture. However, this does not mean that there is unanimity concerning the relationship between text and sermon. What sets the progression from text to sermon in motion is determined by each individual's concept of preaching. What is the essential content of the sermon? What is the aim of the sermon? Schmithals answers these questions by saying (1981 c:26) that public worship is concerned with the promise of the forgiveness of sins. That is the one necessity. Therefore the preacher examines the texts to find what is said concerning humankind as sinner and God's acceptance of the sinner. If one understands the sermon as guiding people who have already received forgiveness of their sins and who must now move beyond this (cf. Oberholzer 1990:654), one will search for similar people in the texts and supply a code of conduct for people finding themselves in this position. There is a reciprocal influence between the understanding of what the sermon is about and the understanding of the text.

Oberholzer (1990:654) contends that there should be two different types of sermon, one with content for the non-Christian world and one for the Christian world. In other words, one for prior to the meeting with God and one for after this meeting. Schmithals (1953:535; 1979a:99, 322, 711) is of the opinion that in principle the content of the sermon will always remain the same. All sermons are a definition of God's act of salvation in Christ. All sermons proclaim the one Gospel: "the time has come," he said. "The Kingdom of God is near" (Mk 1:15). "Do not be afraid, for I am with you" (Is 43:5). "My grace is sufficient for you, for my power is made perfect in weakness" (2 Cor 12:9).

Only those hear the sermon, who, while listening, no longer expect salvation from themselves. The Gospel is heard by those who know their own iniquity and are prepared to be receivers, beggars. God comes to the meek.

Schmithals (1980b:102-103) does not understand faith as a secure possession. Faith does not describe a condition in which humankind exists. When John, the evangelist, uses the expression "hold" as in: "If you hold to my teaching" (Jn 8:31), he does not wish to indicate a static condition, but accentuates the temporary aspect and that it really has to do with faithfulness. Faith is more of a command than a possession. Paul expresses the same idea in Romans 8:4: "We do not live according to the sinful nature but according to the spirit."

As far as faith is concerned, it is clear that we are sinners and the power of sin must never be underestimated. The life of man is described *coram Deo* by the words of Christ on the cross: "My God, my God, why have you forsaken me?" (Mk 15:34; Schmithals 1979a:698). God's judgment is passed on people as sinners, ("Why have you forsaken me") and God meets those halfway who accept this judgment ("My God, my God"). Judgment is not followed by grace, but judgment and grace occur simultaneously. Judgment and grace form a dynamic solidarity and remain in that solidarity. Judgment and grace are not contradictory but qualify one another. People reach their true humanity when judgment becomes grace. The grace which people receive is not something that they possess permanently. They can indeed fall from grace. The New Testament phenomenon of "sin" remains an "impossible possibility" to people, as long as grace, in the word of the cross, is proclaimed to them. As non-believers humankind receive faith (Schmithals 1979a: 173; 1980b:102). In the dynamic unity of judgment and faith Schmithals places *theologia crucis* over against *theologia gloriae*. According to the latter, once grace has been received, one cannot again fall under the judgment of God. Schmithals (1975a:14; 1979a:474; 1988a:374) is convinced that the canonical message of the church is articulated *inter alia* by the *theologia crucis*.

In preaching, judgment and grace are presented (Schmithals 1979a: 123, 712-713). People hear that their own possibilities cannot give them life; God offers them life as a gift. The essence of preaching is interwoven with the *theologia crucis*, because the might of sin is broken by a personal word taking effect in the life of a specific person. The bleakness of human potential is not revealed by a theory, but by the present word that promises God's grace to humankind. Preaching is an act of salvation. Word and salvation concur. Salvation is only present in the preaching of the word (Schmithals 1970b:83; 1988a:264). Faith originates as obedience to the word that is preached, proclaiming the Christ-event as God's saving act (Schmithals 1979a: 119; 1988a:382).

Schmithals keeps to the text. In other words, he is deliberately oriented by the witness of the Bible. According to the Christian faith, the only revelation of God is in the Christ-event. These events show clearly that the salvation of humankind lies with God. Schmithals' intention of allowing the biblical text to speak for itself preserves the theological character of the sermon. In no other way can a sermon be the word of God. When the preaching abandons exegesis, for instance because the exposition of the text would lend a formal scientific character to the sermon (cf. Dreyer 1989:365), it endangers its theological quality. If this movement away from theological emphasis occurs, because the exegesis and explanation have not been done properly, and as a result the sermon becomes a lecture, this moving away is quite unnecessary. What is required is not to move away from text, but rather to carry through its exegesis responsibly, because then it begins to speak to the present.

Schmithals is not in a hurry to introduce the Holy Spirit. Making a sermon is the work of humans and it is as greatly blessed as anything else humans do. The Holy Spirit does not mysteriously influence the historical exegesis. The preacher is expected to do his or her work diligently and to understand the text by using sound methodology. If exegesis does not elucidate the meaning of the text for the present time, prayer is not going to do it either. The theological character of the preacher's work is given by the text with which he or she is working. The personal faith of the preacher does not add to it. For the sermon to be effective and for it to inspire faith, is not the work of the preacher; it is God's work. He gives us faith when preaching is in accordance with what has been said in the text. Within the framework of Reformational and Biblical theology, the Holy Spirit only begins to act as illuminator at this stage (Schmithals 1967c:495; 1970a:60; 1970b:83). Schmithals is not trying to establish the authority of preaching. This authority is to be respected rather than established.

From the generally accepted fact that faith is a gift of the Holy Spirit, Dreyer (1989:361-365) made the wrong deduction, that "pneumatic exegesis" is the correct way of understanding Scripture.

Schmithals considers the application of a text to be a reality, as being down-to-earth scientific labor, which the preacher must be able to justify. Dreyer, on the other hand, ascribes it to the mysterious working of the Holy Spirit. Horizons of understanding merge when the inspiration of the Bible text has enlightened the preacher and his or her audience. One could call Dreyer's pneumatic exegesis a cautious one, because he warns that "exegesis is still the norm for ideas emerging in this process" (Dreyer 1989:362). For the sake of greater clarity on the matters being discussed, we must mention that Dreyer did not distinguish between the understanding of the text and believing in the message. To put it differently, he did not distinguish between what the preacher says and what God says. From Schmithals' point of view, this is exactly where that honor is given to God when we make this distinction. Humans can understand, but faith comes from God. The preacher preaches but never achieves the earnestness of God himself (cf. Bultmann 1926:44-45). Dreyer introduces great earnestness at the stage of exegesis and meditation. The Holy Spirit is already the inspiration and illuminator during this process (Dreyer 1989:363). According to this argument there is direct continuity between what the preacher says and what God says. The preacher has direct authority over the word of God. *Theologia gloriae* is not the framework for Schmithals' theology. As preacher, he has no authority over the word of God; the Holy Spirit makes the miracle take place; the miracle of people hearing the sermon as the word of God.

Dreyer's point of view was adopted by Oberholzer (1990:654) who defined preaching as "a pneumatic word event in which persons who are themselves believers lead people to a meeting with and a life before the living God. This occurs via an experience of communication with a text from Scripture." This definition loses sight of the Biblical tradition and replaces it with a so-called pneumatic experience. According to this view, preaching is primarily an appeal by the converted to the unconverted and secondly a devotional word from a pious man to other pious people to confirm their mutual inspiration. This is no new view of preaching; in French it is called "*sermons desanctification et d'appèl*" (cf. Vinet 1875:11).

According to Schmithals (1984c), the Holy Spirit distinguishes between the human and divine potential. The Spirit exposes the self-righteousness of humankind and leads us to God's righteousness. This is the revealed mystery proclaimed by Scripture. There are no other mysteries in the Bible (cf. Schmithals 1970b:85). In this way Schmithals wishes to define the Spirit in agreement with Scripture. The Spirit can only be formulated in accordance with Scripture. The Spirit required for the understanding of Scripture can only be found in Scripture (cf. Engelbrecht 1982a:63). Only the canon can be used to test the spirits.

The description of preaching as making the text a present actuality will not satisfy everyone; particularly those whose basic problem in homiletics is how preaching is or can be the word of God (cf. Dreyer 1989:350). It would help if the word of God is not understood to the exclusion of the human messenger and if God is not represented as being in opposition to humans in his speaking to them in judgment and grace. Rather, the real possibilities for their life should be shown to them, leading them away from their evil ways, their dead-end street. However, this does not solve the problem, because showing them real possibilities is not enough; they must be seized. Anthropologically speaking, the genuine possibilities can only become a reality in human existence. Dogmatically speaking, it is the work of the Holy Spirit who makes the listeners hear God laying claim to them and then induces them to surrender. Thus, the preacher is acquitted when it comes to the basic problem of homiletics. There is no way in which he or she can guarantee that the sermon will be the word of God. Preaching cannot be placed on the same level as the word of God. Trusting that God will intervene to make the word of the preacher God's word, the preacher only makes the text a present actuality. In this way the character of the word of God, as God's word, is left unsullied (cf. Schmithals 1967d:199).

The character of the word of the canon, namely that the truth was revealed in specific circumstances, forces us to keep in mind that humankind is continually confronted with the Biblical truth in history. The truth comes and goes; God is free to reveal himself when it pleases him. The truth is existential, *in actu*. In this way the word character of the word of God remain intact. Biblical truth does not have the same character as a timeless dogmatic truth. The crisis introduced into the church by historical critical scholarship is actually the crisis concerning the concept of truth. Truth as unhistorical objectivity should be replaced by historical truth. This truth becomes a reality in the history of humankind where people are converted to faith (Schmithals 1967d: 199, 207).

To summarize and round off: The term "dialectical theology" describes the insight of theologians that the truth is historical. The idea "that God is merciful" is no external truth, nor a direct truth. It is true in the human acceptance of God's act of grace (cf. Bultmann 1972:117; Schmithals

1972c:76). One could say that "dialectical theology" describes the insight into the nature of revelation, namely, that it is not absolute but *geschichtlich*. The expression that Schmithals prefers, "theology of the word," describes the insight into the manner of revelation, namely that the church and preaching form part of the events of salvation (cf. Schmithals 1972d:122). The gospel reaches one in a passing explanation. Formulation of the Gospel is always temporary, but it is still sufficient. The term "crisis theology" describes insight into the essence of the revelation, namely that God does not act according to human criteria; his judgment differs from ours. God brings us to a crisis, in which one is forced to search for an understanding of oneself (cf. Schmithals 1972g: 191, 195-196). All of these three terms throw light on the same matter. The insight into this matter precedes the historical critical work of the exegete, thus forming its foundation. Therefore it makes the exegete susceptible to what the text has to say (cf. Bultmann 1972a: 118; Schmithals 1970a:52-53).

To Schmithals the adequate homiletic question is a practical matter: How can I use this text in a sermon? Seen from Schmithals' preaching experience, it appears that he highlights and gives expression to the crisis that a particular text induces in the understanding of humans themselves. In this way, listeners are prompted to understand themselves anew as people under God's grace.

Schmithals (1986e) gave us an example of how the crisis of the human's understanding of himself or herself, can be induced by a specific text in the Bible. This is how he handled John 14:19b: "Because 1 live, you also will live."

He does not treat the text as a concrete claim to someone, but rather as a dogma in association with the Gospel of John. It has the possibility of becoming a claim in an actual congregation. The meaning of life does not lie in what people make of it; it is that life, in accordance with its original character, is lived as a gift. Life, a life like this, is the meaning of life in itself. The believer obtains certainty, where no certainty is visible. The human understanding of oneself as described by Dreyer (1972:61) is expressed in this way, "Can someone ever feel really secure and accept the meaningfulness of life and history, unless there is an objective validity and meaning?" This statement has been brought to a turning point. Security does not coincide with the discovery of some demonstrable meaning to life. It lies in surrender to the One who gave us life and whose message is that the meaning of life is life itself.

7.3 MEDITATION: THE LISTENER

Ascension Day owes its name to an outdated view of the world. People have doubts and questions concerning heaven and the ascension to heaven. Preachers are confronted with the question of whether they should make concessions to this outdated view of the world regarding Ascension Day or whether they should take their listeners seriously. Because this theme is so specifically linked to Ascension Day, it is advisable for them to take the bull by the horns and discuss this theme. Thus, Schmithals preached his sermon in such a way that it was obvious that he took the mentality of modem human beings seriously.

Schmithals makes no concessions to the mythological view of the world. He finds that the meaning for our faith does not lie in the representation of a change of place (cf. Schmithals 1979a:747). Schmithals does not wish to understand the ascension in isolation, but associates it with the Easter event. Together they form one event Jesus' exaltation and his investment with power (Schmithals 1982a:23; cf. 1988a:377). "Sat at the right hand of God" is added as an explanation in the oldest description of the ascension: "He was taken up into heaven and he sat at the right hand of God" (Mk 16:19).

The image of being seated at the right hand of God, implies that God rules the world through Christ. Ascension and the session at the right hand of God are realistic illustrations of the confession of the church that Jesus is Lord. The theme of the ascension is: Jesus is the Lord (Schmithals 1982b). In a similar way Bonhoeffer (1970:63) described faith in the ascension as being faith in Christ's rule of the world and of life.

Schmithals makes use of the insight of what is referred to as the theology of the word, which amounts to the insight that the gospel was, and constantly is, formulated in temporary forms. For people acquainted with the mythical view of the world, the Gospel could be formulated as ascension. But the explanation as ascension is not Gospel in itself, but a formulation of it. Consequently, Schmithals dissociates himself from formulating the Gospel as ascension. The Ascension is the expression of the Christ-event.

Van Selms (1955) took another route to arrive at the message of Ascension Day. We repeat the foundation and conclusion of his arguments:

> To put it clearly: Christ ascended to heaven as man. On Christmas Day, God descended to earth, but on Ascension Day, it is not God returning to heaven, but the divine man Jesus Christ. He takes his humanity with him from earth to heaven.

Therefore, humankind has a place in heaven and it is possible for humankind to exist there. People as we know them here, creatures bound by time and space, find a Father's house in eternity, beyond time and space. Human beings are not irretrievably abandoned to this world and its transience, but can find a place in the imperishable kingdom of God.

From this it is clear that Van Selms does not distinguish between the Gospel and its formulation; he sees the Gospel as identical to the formulation. It is not a temporary exposition of the Gospel, but a permanent one. The theology of the word plays no part in it. Van Selms' meditation formulates the objective deed of God, which is meaningful to humankind. Preaching does not form part of the act of God, but tells us about it. The manner of revelation is an objective deed, which took place between Jesus and God for the benefit of humankind. At the outset, these events take place outside the experience of human beings. Then they are brought within humankind's mental grasp by their formulation. Two different ways of believing are presumed here. The initial faith must believe in the report of the ascension of Jesus as a factual supernatural truth. In that a sign of hope can be seen. The next step in faith exists in hope itself, that is to say that people will hope (cf. Bultmann 1980:300).

Identifying the Gospel with the exposition of it must of necessity change the content of the Gospel. Preaching now confronts listeners with a crisis. As believers they must take cognizance of a heaven above the earth, which serves as the house of God. To their way of thinking, heaven above the earth is not a possibility, even though heaven is presented as higher than usual, "beyond time and space." However, when this vexed question is put before the listeners, it is not really a crisis, rather something uncomfortable. The only thing that is expected of them is to change their worldview to a much older one. It does not affect them in their perception of themselves. Thus, crisis theology is given an uncritical meaning and the content of the revelation is the mythological view of the world.

It is interesting to note that according to Van Selms the wretchedness of humankind consists of the following: From what must human beings be saved? "From the world and its transience." "World" is not understood here as being the world people build around and in themselves, where they put their trust in their own abilities, but as an objective estrangement from God. So one would call it a Gnostic or even apocalyptic representation of salvation rather than a Christian one. And once one has realized that there is "a place and the possibility of existence in heaven," one does not have to start all over and wait for God to have mercy on one; one already knows that one is part of the system of salvation. The moment of truth in which someone accepts God's imputed grace, so important in dialectical theology, is absent here.

From the preceding passage, it is clear that meditation is already present in exegesis. Understanding comes full circle, so that the end is already part of the beginning. If the theologian, fearing the uncertainty of historical existence, seeks certainty in an objective system, this search will determine the result of the exegesis. Where the theology of the word provides access to the message of the church, the sermon will do justice to people in their historical freedom and responsibility, as well as the impermanence of what they say about God. The fact that the hermeneutic process moves in a circle, is not a problem in itself. What is important is the question, with which approach or hermeneutic principle the circle is entered.

Van Selms presupposes an objective act of God, which makes the ascension meaningful to man. He distinguishes between Christology and soteriology. Christology forms the objective base from which salvation ensues. On the other hand, Schmithals understands God's act in Christ as a deed done to humankind and to their advantage from the beginning. The message not only proclaims the act of God in Christ, but is that act in itself. Because it is divine salvation, it cannot be shown objectively. In the word, which proclaims him, Christ is present as the Lord who lays claim to sovereignty over humankind. The external word that addresses people is the guarantee that the act of God precedes their acceptance in faith. However, in preaching, Christology and soteriology concur. Only in faith can people confess that Jesus is Lord.

Compared to Van Selms, Schmithals (1982c), sets about his task in a radical way. Right at the beginning of his sermon, he states that we can no longer visualize the ascension as depicted for the ancient world. Therefore, he relinquishes the image to get to the matter of importance. The matter must be explained. In addition, with this transfer to the matter, another problem apart from that of worldview arises. It is not the worldview that is adjusted; peoples' self-image is thrown into a crisis. The real problem with Ascension Day is that power and authority as well as mastery are no longer in demand. Schmithals explains this problem by pointing out that human beings can reject any kind of authority, but they cannot escape from themselves. People become their own "Lord." Moreover, for the person who has imprisoned himself or herself in his or her own prison, the liberation of being a child of God is offered in the message of the ascension, "Jesus is the Lord." In a natural way, Schmithals proceeds to refer to parental authority, because it is "father's day," which happens to fall on the same date. This authority is reflected in the lordship of Jesus Christ: only a man who has a Father, can be a father himself.

The above can serve as an illustration of how Schmithals meditates. It is not a separate, second step after the exegesis of the text, but in reality is interwoven with it. By understanding the ascension itself, he interprets it for modern people. As far as Van Selms is concerned, I do not wish to leave the impression that this one meditation of his represents the whole of his theology. This should be studied separately. Still, his meditation is representative of what one finds outside the theology of the word. Van Selms remained faithful to the orthodox view of the ascension (cf. Chantepie de la Saussaye 1874:13-15 for this point of view).

7.4 THE ROLE OF THE HISTORIC SITUATION OF THE TEXT IN PREACHING

The point of departure of historical-critical exegesis is that the words of Scripture are not addressed to present-day readers, but to readers of a past time in their particular circumstances. The people who were addressed originally must be kept in mind if the text is to be understood and explained correctly. Although this insight is more or less common knowledge in theology, it is seldom carried out with conviction. Although Bultmann worked as a distinguished believer in the historical-critical method, he did not always apply it consistently. By using Bultmann as an example to illustrate this defect, the tremendous challenge to the historical-critical exegete is shown. A sermon delivered by Bultmann on the Last Judgment (Mt 25:31-46) can serve as an example. In Matthew 25:31-33 we read:

> When the Son of Man comes in his glory, and all the angels with him, he will sit on his throne in heavenly glory. All the nations will be gathered before him, and he will separate the people one from another as a shepherd separates the sheep from the goats. He will put the sheep on his right and the goats on his left.

Bultmann (1962:48) takes a short cut between the text and the listeners of today. He explains the text as being an admonition for the listeners to come to a decision, without taking the situation in which it was written into account. He takes it for granted that the text has meaning for the modern situation. The listeners must identify with those who are blessed and those who are cursed, who are surprised and amazed by what they had done. The surprise comes from the fact that we are unaware of what we do. The story stresses the importance of the behavior of which we are not conscious. Bultmann realizes that this is a strange elucidation of a Biblical text, but goes on to say: "Usually the word of Jesus expects a decision from level-headed people, but today the text leads us to paying attention to the importance of our behavior of which we are not conscious." Bonhoeffer (1975:39-40) also uses the explanation that neither the congregation nor the Pharisees knew that they were doing good or evil. What is relevant, is that we are not conscious of the good or evil that we do.

After he has determined that the matter in hand is our unconscious behavior, he calls those people blessed who, however hard they try, can never do justice to the Christian way of life. The crux of the matter is not whether they succeed, but what they are in their innermost self. Furthermore he calls the undogmatic Christians fortunate. It also applies to the sick and the old people who can no longer accomplish much (Bultmann 1962:48-49).

The text is not only a consolation but is meant to be

a warning. The Pharisees, who prided themselves upon their conscious deeds, now have to learn that it makes no difference. What is judged, is the unconscious aspect of humankind (Bultmann 1962:49-50).

Bultmann (1962:50-51) associates the unconscious behavior of people with the readiness for each moment of life. When they relinquish their conscious calculation, they are exposed to the opportunity of the moment. Thus, Bultmann remains true to his finding: the message of the Bible is existential.

The unconscious life of the people being judged is identified by Bultmann (1962:51) as love, because all the unconscious good deeds mentioned here are deeds of love. Moreover, the source of our love is the message that God loves us. Thus the revelation correlates with human existence.

There is no sermon of Schmithals' available on this text; but he did publish the outline for a sermon (Schmithals 1985b; cf. 1985a:377) in which he offers suggestions on how to set about a sermon on this passage. He places the text in the circumstances of the *aposunagogos*. Jewish enmity towards the church has driven the congregation out of the judicial safety of Judaism.

Thus they are no longer absolved from the cult of emperor worship. Persecution originates primarily in religious motives. In these circumstances Matthew commands the congregation to turn the other cheek. This does not mean that they must flee from the scene. Like the city situated on a mountaintop, they have to live down the accusations made against them. "The nations," implying non-Jewish people, who sympathize with the one of the least of these, that is the Christians, will receive their reward. When they stand at the Last Judgement, they are amazed to discover that the Lord, who is worshipped by the least of all, is also the judge of the world and the king in God's kingdom. By means of the promise made in this narrative, Matthew encourages the church and then the church can pass this promise on to their helpers, especially the God-fearing gentiles. Schmithals recommends that a sermon, bound by a text, must introduce the listeners to the circumstances of those days. The purpose of this introduction is to prepare for the merging of the situation of that time with the present in the course of the sermon. One should note that the reconstruction of the situation should take place simultaneously with the interpretation for the present. Theoretically, one can differentiate between these two steps, but in the application they cannot be separated.

It becomes clear that Schmithals is convinced that historical exegesis is already present in matters concerning the preacher and the congregation. For that reason the congregation can be confronted with the historical text. The purpose of exegesis is not to understand the past. Exegesis is often presented in this way, without a sermon emerging from it. In that case the exegesis has failed. Biblical texts claim to be understood, here and now. If it is possible to understand the text, comparable phenomena of life will come to the fore which will bridge the gap between times gone by and today.

The factor which forms a link between the situation in times gone by and that of today, Schmithals finds in the dogmatic conclusion of the narrative, namely that the nations will be judged according to their behavior towards Christians. That means that the world exists for the sake of the church and not for itself. Christians do not live by their own human potential, but from the power given by God. In this sense Matthew coined the expression concerning the church: "You are the salt of the earth" and "you are the light of the world." The aim of the world is not for it to live in its own strength, but through the grace of God. Humankind is not the hope of the world. It will be futile to divide people into good and bad and expect the good people to save the world. Salvation comes from without, not from human beings. If Christians are called the light of the world, it refers exclusively to God's saving act for the world. Christians proclaim the message which the world itself cannot express, "My grace is sufficient for you." The situation in which persecution takes place already makes it clear that Christians are not referring to themselves and their own strength, but to the power of God. No elitist *theologia gloriae* is presented.

The situation of the listeners to the sermon is not determined by sociological analyses, but by the genuine understanding of the world, God, and themselves. The text is used against this understanding. Everyone is shown to be guilty: "See darkness covers the earth and thick darkness is over the peoples" (Isa 60:2a).

The text helps us to understand our present situation, in which we act as believers or unbelievers. In addition, this inducement is the promise of salvation. The promise of salvation constitutes the situation and the decision, which is reached, determines the situation. Believers see themselves in the light of the act of God and know that they are the "least of the brothers" of the Judge and King who awards the top priority to faith, hope and love, and not to power and achievement.

Schmithals is of the opinion that the ethical aspect can now also come into its own. People outside the church take pity on the persecuted ones, because "they may see your good deeds and praise your Father in heaven" (Mt 5:1 6b).

The good deeds are not the work of arrogant people, declaring themselves to be the salt of the earth, but the insignificant, the prisoners, those who are thirsty or naked; the deeds of people who realize their dependence on God; deeds of loving faithfulness and truth. Love, faithfulness, and truth constitute the very essence of Christian ethics, as seen by Matthew (cf. Schmithals 1985a:381). Even though circumstances may be more favorable for the church of today than for that of long ago, the only truly blessed way is that of love, faithfulness, and truth.

Thus the text, as explained by Schmithals, prevents faith from becoming ethical activity. No actual deeds are recommended. The answer to the question of what correct behavior is, can be found by referring to people who know how dependent they are on God. To live in love, faithfulness, and truth and to entrust oneself to God's care are two equivalent aspects of one Christian life. Ethics is dogmatics. The imperative is itself Gospel. People who put their trust in themselves and in their own deeds, no longer stand before God. The real goal is not something that must be done; salvation is the reality. It concerns the whole of human existence before God.

Schmithals thinks that it is not as easy to identify the "blessed of the Father" as it was for Matthew. In a probable reference to Bultmann (1962), he does not want to call unconscious Christians blessed, without further ado. The sermon is meant for the edification of believers and not to stress the importance of our unconscious inner life. Nevertheless, the congregation must know that God is greater than our hearts that condemn us. It would be best if each Christian were to see a "blessed of the Father" in every fellow human being and then to take heed of his or her own conduct in meeting with fellow-beings, so that this blessing can make a breakthrough to the glory of God.

7.5 CLOSING REMARKS

Bultmann's great contribution to the theology of the word lies in the fact that he meditated anew. In a surprising way, he brought the listener to the Christian message to the fore. The listener to the sermon was present, right from the start of his reading of the old Biblical text.

Schmithals agrees with this meditation and his contribution to modern theology lies further in that he renewed his exegesis. He succeeds, not only in depicting the situation within which the text originated, but also in using that situation to play a decisive role in the understanding of the text. The text was brought into being by the message of the church in particular historical circumstances. The historical facts are indispensable to the understanding of the text as developed by the author, because the text is a document, serving the message of the church in specific circumstances. One is impressed by the fact that Schmithals united historical and theological exegesis in a manner that has never before been so clearly articulated.

CHAPTER 8

Ethics

8.1 INTRODUCTION

In New Testament times, ethical problems were not as widely and broadly contemplated as they are in the church today. The social situation of the church meant that house rules and congregational ethics were adequate. To Schmithals, the "parable of the talents" (Mt 25:14-30; Lk 19:11-27) serves as an example of a self-sufficient congregation (Schmithals 1978a:148-152; 1991:322). All the energy in a congregation had to be used for the building up of the church. The talents that were not to be buried could have been official ones, like prophecy, teaching, pastoral work and care. They could also have included the conduct of all members of the congregation, using their talents of love, joy, peace, friendliness, et cetera.

Ever since World War II, ethical decision-making has largely been transferred to the political field. Political problems are the subject of discussion in church. Sermons and pastoral messages all make an attempt at giving guidance in political matters. The political responsibility of Christians and the church is highlighted from all angles. In his reflections on ethics Schmithals concentrates largely on the actuality of politics. Consequently, it is important to have a closer look at his approach to ethics as far as politics is concerned. The priority lent to political problems does not detract from his discussion of ethics in general, because the basic principles for ethical conduct are the same, whether on a social or personal level.

The fact that ethics is only discussed near the end does not imply that Schmithals saw the subject as one of lesser importance. In reality this chapter became a dogmatics in outline. To Schmithals it is important that Christians live their life in the freedom given to them by Christ. This implies that their faith is expressed in trying, as far as possible, to live out what is good and true and beautiful in life, to the best of their knowledge and with a clear conscience.

8.2 PUBLIC WORSHIP

To Schmithals (1978b:2) public worship is not merely the hub of the wider religious life of the congregation. He considers the church and public worship to be identical. In the New Testament the church perceives itself as being a congregation in public worship. The congregation consists of a "gathering" as described in the New Testament or "public worship" as we know it. Describing the congregation as a worshipping community is not a limitation of the term "congregation," for worship is not brought about by the congregation. The church has no previous existence, with public worship being organized as a second step. Essentially, the church appears as a congregation worshipping in public. The establishment of the church takes place where the gathering of the congregation is founded anew. Public worship forms the structure of the church. Even as far as the building up is concerned, one must not imagine the church as having a previous existence, which must be built higher. The structure is identical to the appearance of the congregation in worship.

Schmithals' point of view, considering public worship as constituting the church, differs radically from that of Beukes (1984:24-25). The latter sees the congregation as constituted beforehand and gathering for public worship. If the congregation has already been formed, what would be the purpose of public worship, which inspires faith and edifies the congregation? The eschatological character of the church and public worship was deliberately stressed by Schmithals, to preclude misunderstanding. Justice is not done to this attribute of the church if it is seen as an institution and mistakenly regarded as one of many organizations of the world. The church as public worship is characterized by word and faith; consequently its continuity cannot be taken for granted. Rather, it is a concrete event. In essence, public worship is new every time.

The church is the worldly sphere of certain events. What takes place there is, generally speaking, an attempt to fathom and conquer the world. In this context "world" refers to the reality that human beings create for themselves, when they expect their lives from the created, available reality. The world, which man come of age creates around himself, is exposed and he is liberated from it. In theological language, the church can be described as the place where judgment of man and his world is proclaimed and he finds grace (Schmithals 1978b:4).

Thus Schmithals (1971a:45-47) avoids the cultic misunderstanding of public worship, in terms of which human beings try to influence the Deity and set him in motion by their pious acts. According to the confession of the church, God has already acted and the church is founded on this act of Christ. Public worship corresponds to the eschatological events of salvation, namely the crucifixion and resurrection of Jesus. In public worship, Christ is present as the Lord (Schmithals 1979a:546). According to Schmithals (1979a:4), public worship forms an integral part of the saving events. What takes place in public worship is in reality an event of salvation (cf Schmithals 1979, 1:328, 547). The leper in Mark 1:40-45 accepts his admission to the public worship of the congregation as being reconciliation to God (cf. Schmithals 1979a:140-141). Moreover, the saying "no salvation outside the church" is true in the sense of "church" as eschatological church of salvation, but not when it means the church as instituted for this purpose. Salvation must be proclaimed to humankind, who must receive it in this way.

The church is typified by the reality of God's salvation. Therefore Schmithals does not hesitate to say (1972e:151) that no real distinction can be made between the church and the Kingdom of God. In the church there is peace and reconciliation. God rules through his word and the congregation overcomes the world by means of their faith. When referring to the above, Schmithals (1979a:189) speaks of the "eschatological foundation" of ethics.

The visibility of the church is equivalent to visibility of the word (Schmithals 1972e:152-153). The church is visible in public worship, where someone has been sent to proclaim the word. Here people gather to hear the word and try to comply with the word in their lives The church is *creatura verbi*. Around the actual words of the text, a fellowship of faith develops and from it a theory of the church must emanate. The word does not explain what the church already is, but bears the stamp of the events of God's presence. God establishes the church. The fact that this is his will lies outside the church and precedes its foundation. Any attempt to validate the concept of church without text and word dissociates the meeting with God from the category of "word." An example would be using a relatively independent idea of the covenant for this purpose. In this way the Nederduitsch Hervormde Kerk is shown as being independent, if it is said, "the church thinks in terms of the covenant, and not only in terms of the salvation of the individual" (Nederduitsch Hervormde Kerk van Afrika 1990:11). In this way the church is moving into a problematical area, where God's people are equated with the natural people, instead of following the New Testament message where the relationship with God is determined by faith.

How is the certainty of faith, which has been mediated by public worship, retained in the life of a believer? How does the believer keep his life in accordance with the word? Usually the life of faith is described in three steps: hear, believe, and do. By his works the believer convinces himself and others of his faith, because without works faith is dead. Schmithals (1983 1:173-174) concedes that this is a possible explanation. However, this is not the best way of linking the certainty and conservation of faith. The problem lies in the assumption that faith is already firm and certain and that works can follow. However, when will faith be firm and certain enough for conservation to be begun in works? When is the point of "then we do gladly" reached? We never get beyond: "I do believe; help me overcome my unbelief" (Mk 9:24). The believer cannot have the attitude of, "I believe, what more can I do?" Schmithals is of the opinion that the relationship between certainty and the conservation of faith can better be described as interaction. Certainty of faith needs to be conserved and conservation strengthens faith and makes it steadfast. Conservation cannot simply be added to certainty. Conservation is more important than that; it is an essential condition of faith. Conservation, seen only as a result of faith, is too inferior to conserve faith. Faith must at least be conserved by faith, by the experience of faith. This is the only way in which faith can be protected. Otherwise it could degenerate into the world, disconsolate with itself and its good deeds (Schmithals 1983 1:174-175).

Christian faith is not self-confidence or trust in what others can do, but putting your trust in God, that he remains faithful to his creatures and his creation. Faith is to relinquish oneself and commit oneself to God's care. A faith such as this cannot be detached from the existence in faith and the experience of faith (Schmithals 1983 1:175-176). Schmithals (1983 1:177) uses the example of parents, who in explaining to their children what faith is, find themselves again in their lived and experienced faith. Giving an account of one's faith conserves it. In this way, public worship not only moves from certainty to conservation, but also from explanation to new experiences.

Another warning by Schmithals (1983 1:178-179) is that faith is not just conserved in love. It could well happen that someone living a life of love experiences it as success. This could strengthen one's faith anew. This is why, on the one hand, love is called the greatest of faith, hope, and love. On the other hand, love is not the only element. It is associated with faith and hope. Therefore our distress concerning love that has failed (which is more common than grateful success) is not the end. Here faith is not conserved by love, but by faith itself; the faith that clings to the fact that God's love for us cannot fail, even though our love fails.

Schmithals (1983 1:182-184) explains that the correct concept of death is the source of the certainty of Christian hope. Death is understood as being the divine judgment on human sins, the self-aggrandizement of man against God. Hope is directed to a life beyond this exaltation of self, to life as a gift of God. Consequently death has been drawn into life as judgment, because that is where grace is present. The cry "Why have you forsaken me?" is an honest complaint so that man can receive life in the praise of "My God, my God." It is not the representation of what comes after death that keeps hope alive. In the confrontation with death itself, hope shows its strength. The believer hopes for what he has already received: grace through judgment. Therefore it is not important what the concrete expectations of the believer are, but that he hopes, hopes on God (Schmithals 1978a:537; 1983g:120; 1983 1:184).

In using the term "public worship" for religion inside and outside the meeting of the congregation, I wish to point out the close bond between the public worship of the church and the world as far as a believer is concerned. Schmithals (1971:45-46) does the same when using the term "worship." The two forms of public worship are mutually dependent. The movement towards and away from one another, must not be stopped, otherwise Christian life is endangered (Schmithals 1971a:44-45; 1983 1:184).

8.3 THE CHURCH AND THE CHRISTIAN.

The church has received the command to proclaim the gospel (Schmithals 1970a:36, 42; 1979a:324-325; 1983h: 131). In practice, the church has to preach. By the work of the church, salvation is brought to people and they are reconciled to God. This commission of the church is linked to church office and office bearers. Schmithals feels that is a good arrangement that official meetings of the church and office bearers should not take sides in political issues of the day. This is because office bearers are obliged to proclaim the gospel to all members of the congregation, regardless of their political convictions (Schmithals 1983h: 125).

Schmithals' point of view is not fully understood in a party political context. He did not mean that party politics divided the people, and that church meetings and office bearers should therefore abstain from it (cf. Pont 1985:41; cf. NHKA 1990:6). His reticence regarding politics goes much deeper. Schmithals is not concerned only about party politics, but about all politics. In the Old Testament, God's people and the people of the state were identical. As a result the prophets were also political prophets. Israel could not easily maintain this self-concept, because the prophets contradicted one another and each claimed that he was proclaiming the truth. In the New Testament this ambivalence is avoided by breaking up the unity between the people of the state and God's people. Each individual becomes a member of the congregation. The church does not see itself as being of political importance, but as the Kingdom of God, clearly distinguishable from the kingdoms of the world. Political prophecies, where the office bearer or bearers express their opinions on current political questions, wish to identify God's people with people of the state once more. This has always been rejected as sectarian by the church (Schmithals 1983a: 18-19; 1983d:73, 1983j: 147-148; 1983m). This sectarian tendency is seen in Rautenbach (1978:78-79) where he recommends political prophecy. He calls it "prophetic enlightenment of the political order by means of preaching, confession, witness, pastoral letters, messages from the pulpit, et cetera." This can only result in justifying political behavior on the strength of the gospel. The prophetic office of the church can have no other content but the proclamation of the Christ-event. After Jesus Christ there is no room for another prophet (Schmithals 1983a: 19).

The differentiation between people of the state and God's people is often seen as being typically Lutheran. In contrast, we have the reformed view in which the sovereignty of Christ also includes the people of the state. Schmithals (1983a:17-18) disagrees. He does not feel that the socio-ethical application of the sovereignty of Christ reflects the true reformed point of view. The Heidelberg Catechism would sooner formulate the Lutheran point of view as being Jesus Christ "reigns by Word and Spirit" over God's people. All efforts to justify political action Christologically are thus thwarted. Schmithals (1983a:15-16; 1983h:127) states that Barth eventually also engaged in finding a christological basis for political action.

According to Schmithals (1983d:73; 1983j:149; 1986a:33) the church should not attempt to present some or other political opinion with prophetic authority. On the one hand, it is the church's task to proclaim the message of the forgiveness of sin. That is what the world needs to hear from the church. No one else brings these tidings. On the other hand, political problems are solved by suggestions, which are acceptable to both Christians and non-Christians. These suggestions cannot have the status of infallible truth. The best way of dealing with such suggestions is to assess them in daily practice, with the realization that it will not be the end of problems and perplexities. The most suitable answer to these suggestions is not that this is a dependable word, as one says concerning the gospel. Referring to himself, Schmithals (1986a:33) says that as a teacher and in his ministry, he refrains from presenting his own political insight or, worse still, holding it up as being Christian. In his office he is expected to keep his political views to himself. As a matter of principle, he does not participate in voting when official meetings assume the right to give political advice or make binding demands on people in authority or on ordinary citizens. These suggestions could even correspond to his own views. However, he has his political point of view as a citizen and as a Christian, but not as a minister of the Word. As citizen and Christian, Bonhoeffer took part in the plot against Hitler (Schmithals 1983a:21).

The reticence shown by Schmithals concerning political problems of the day, must not be seen as an attempt on his part to escape responsibility. On the contrary, it is because of his insight into the nature of the gospel and his respect for the people listening to the sermon. They should not be overwhelmed and frustrated to the extent that the congregation becomes a pressure group. This cannot be the political service rendered to the world by the church. The church has a more profound task.

Where there is no clear distinction between the authority of the church to proclaim the gospel and the political maturity of the members of the church, there will continually be problems. When official meetings make political pronouncements, it casts doubt on the political maturity of the members. This position becomes untenable, and unintentionally it is admitted in the statement, "the members of the church will have to exert themselves seriously to keep hearing the voice of Christ in the official pronouncements of the church" (Nederlandse Hervormde Kerk 1965:31 = NHK 1965).

It will undoubtedly be contended that members of the church do not display political maturity. Such a judgment can be made on the strength of a particular political persuasion, in terms of which anyone who holds a different opinion is politically immature. In any case, Schmithals says, the church is not going to develop political maturity in its members by teaching them politics. Independent people are only freed for politics by the preaching of the gospel.

By means of the political diaconate (not political prophecy, cf Schmithals 1983 a:22) the church liberates Christians to accept their worldly political responsibility (Schmithals 1970a:39; 1972d: 123-124; 1979a: 129; 1983a: 21; 1983d:72; 1986a:33). In the world the believers serve mankind, life and humanity, but not parties and ideologies. Humanity is served, not because mankind is the ultimate value, thus making politics sacred, but because the Christian conserves faith in love. Believers cannot but be politically involved. They have the courage to participate in politics, because their plans need not be perfect, as though coming from God (cf. van Wyk 1987:410). Their intentions are not what God would intend. Even if their plans go wrong, the world is still in God's hand. Therefore, they can act as they see fit. Believers know that the kingdom within which they perform their deeds of charity is not the Kingdom of God. It is not even a forerunner of God's Kingdom, and this knowledge prevents them from becoming presumptuous. They build houses with walls that crack. Theirs is not the work of salvation. They disagree with the statement of the Nederlandse Hervormde Kerk "that politics has to do with truth and justice which belong to the kingdom of God" (NHK 1965:39). Pilate's question: "What is truth?" (Jn 18:38) is the acknowledgement that he, being a politician, has nothing to do with truth and justice. Truth and justice belong to the kingdom that is not of this world (Schmithals 1980c:150-151).

At the time of the celebration of the seven hundred and fifty years of existence of Berlin, Schmithals, himself a Berliner, delivered a sermon on Jeremiah 29:7: "if it (the city) prospers, you too will prosper." What will be best for the city? What we think? Perhaps, but it could also be what others think. Therefore, it is advisable to listen to one another and look at the interests of the city from all angles. People are not all the same and everyone would like to do things differently. On the same piece of land, one person would like to build a house, another a hospital and a third an Old Age Home. On one side of the wall, there is the onslaught on the human spirit by capitalism. On the other communist propaganda prescribes what is right. Neither of these two serves the best interests of the city. The different interests will have to be combined. Concessions are in the interest of the city. This applies to larger interest groups as well as to the individual. Although it might be necessary to make demands on others, it is still not the best. The best would be for each to do his duty.

Schmithals feels that it would be a good thing if the wall were to disappear, so that one Berliner is not shot by another. However, he realizes that the unity of the city will not be achieved easily. Therefore, the Berliners must use openings that exist in the wall to the best of their ability. The text in Jeremiah 29:7 continues: "Pray to the Lord for it (the city)." Further on it becomes clear that Schmithals understands Christian faith as providing man with the strength to live in conflict. The prayer for the city makes us realize that humans are powerless and that our cities are not in our hands. Prayer places the city in God's hands. At the same time it gives thanks for a habitable city where God also has his own people. It is best for any city to have people meeting in it who are on their way to the eternal city. They toil tirelessly for the progress and welfare of this transient city, always keeping the eternal one in mind. According to Schmithals (1970a:40-41), preaching the gospel with a view to liberating Christians to become politically active in the social-ethical field merely communicates opinions. It is not preaching of the gospel unless it can be accepted as such by people who hold different views. Any opinions expressed must not have an assertive color, but should rather be tentative. Accompanying commentary might be "If I am not mistaken" or "In this I am not covered by the authority of God's word" (cf. Schmithals 1983c:49, 55).

Another example of an opinion expressed by Schmithals (1983c:49-56) on the political course of events, has to do with peace. Schmithals distinguishes between the peace given by God, which passes all understanding, and the peace that must be maintained among people to the best of their political knowledge. The peace that is a gift from God gives the believer the impartiality to work for peace among men. In this service he will not be surpassed by anyone. The difference between peace and peace is important. The peace of God is independent of the degree of political peace that has been achieved. Political peace, which depends on move and countermove, can never be maintained without risk and apprehension (Schmithals 1980c:135).

Schmithals (1983c:51) points out that some people try to establish political peace by means of mutual trust, while others use deterrents. He denies that trust and reconciliation will be more peaceful and Christian, in the given human condition, than suspicion and mutual control. What is best in a particular set of circumstances will have to be settled in fear and trembling; there is no Christian demand that can be made. Could one in all fairness expect the communists to trust the system of the West or vice versa? We would all prefer to live without armament, but the superpowers arm themselves to survive. Peace in the world is armed peace (Schmithals 1983c:53).

To preach the peace of God is the mandate that the church has received. This peace consists in the justification of sinners. In spite of all man's burdens and the risks that he runs, he may know that he is borne up by God. This is the solace within which a Christian lives and this is how he serves peace. The constant admonition of the New Testament "to live in peace with everybody" is just as appropriate today. Christians must build mutual trust, despite political differences (Schmithals 1983c:54-55; 1983d: 74-75).

Schmithals (1972d:141-142) warns people not to misunderstand him. Although one is unsure of the correct thing to do in each case, Christians must be admonished, as brothers, to accept the world. It is the place where faith must be lived to the full and be conserved to make itself serviceable in love. We have no choice as to whether these ethical questions should be asked and answered. We are in the midst of this reality. It goes without saying that specific ethical norms and customs will be followed. This does not imply obedience to these norms and customs, but rather the obedience of faith, which is prepared even to oppose, accepted values.

On the one hand, the preaching of the gospel liberates people for their service to the world. On the other, a political sermon can assume a second form, when direct political utterances amount to proclaiming the gospel. It happens when, for example, the statement that Christianity must be defended with military force is contradicted. This very contradiction is, in fact, preaching of the gospel

(Schmithals 1970 a:40).

Although the church does not see itself as a sociological or political body, it might, on occasion, be necessary to speak on behalf of disenfranchised people (Schmithals 1970a:38; 1983a:21-22). It could in different ways be necessary in Eastern Bloc states and South Africa (Schmithals 1986a). However, Schmithals immediately adds that the Church must not overestimate its aid to the oppressed. This could be a hindrance to the Christians in the given circumstances and render them immature (Schmithals 1970a:38; cf. 1983a:22). The idea is that Christians should join groups, which can help to promote the welfare of these people. Here they operate with others in a worldly fashion and argue on factual grounds. There are no Christian prescriptions (Schmithals 1972d:124). The peace of the world is served as mundanely as possible. The Christian aims at righteousness and welfare for all, in short, a better world, together with other people. Moreover, Schmithals (1975b: 3) does not base this on Christ's direct sovereignty over the world or the social involvement of the Church in the world, because the improved world will always wait upon further improvement. The peace that Christians bring into the world is peace as the world gives it (Schmithals 1983d:77). Schmithals (1975b:3) bases the Christian's striving for a better world in a profane manner. He asks: What else would Christians strive for?

8.4 THE FOUNDATION OF ETHICS

A concrete example of how Schmithals expressed an opinion on the foundation of Christian ethics concerns the case of Cornelius Burghardt. Burghardt was found guilty of supporting the BaaderMeinhof gang of terrorists. On the radio Hellmut Gollwitzer voiced his appreciation of Burghardt: "The attitude apparent in this conduct is the correct attitude of a disciple of Jesus" (see Winterhager 1976:89-91; cf. Gollwitzer 1980: 58, 67, 72).

Schmithals (1974c:1, 3) analyses Gollwitzer's justification of Burghardt. He finds that for Gollwitzer the attitude with which is acted plays a decisive role. The nature of the deed and its results fall outside the field of vision; only the disposition should be judged. The attitude is important, while the deeds, in which the attitude is expressed, stand dangerously detached. Schmithals hold that such an ethic of attitude elevates man's conscience to the ultimate good, thus protecting man from the consequences of his deeds. However, the Bible never considers man's attitude as a foundation for his deeds. Through the urge to self-justification, the ethics of attitude is stealthily changed to ethics of merit on account of the noble attitude (Schmithals 1983 i: 137).

Schmithals (1983i:138; 1983j:150-151; 1983n) denies that ethical idealism can also be a Christian point of view. Here the conscience is viewed as man's innate ability to decide between good and evil, which provides the foundation of ethical behavior. We act to the best of our knowledge and according to our conscience, but we remain bound by the commandments of God; that means bound by the word of love. Thus bound, we are concerned not only with our own welfare but also with that of our neighbor, and would rather suffer injustice than act unjustly. We do not act against our better judgment, but realize that it is risky to act to the best of one's knowledge because we know only in part. This saves us from fanaticism. The people who differ from us are also acting to the best of their knowledge. In our struggle to find the correct course of action, we should convince one another by means of arguments and not use confessions and condemnation.

Schmithals (1974c:3) describes Burghardt's ethics as ethics with an objective in mind. The sacred value that he pursues is to create a new dispensation to replace the existing social structure. For this purpose he is prepared to use violence, even bombs. The deeds that are a means to the sacred end are good. Basing himself on the Bible, Schmithals contradicts this framing of a sacred end to be achieved by human, unholy means. Just as in the case of an ethics of attitude, Schmithals (1974:1, 3) respects the high moral ethos of an ethic of ends. In each case the deeds done in pursuit of the ethic must be able to stand up to the public scrutiny of means and ends. They should not be combined with the ethics of attitude to be justified on the strength of attitude. Whoever does not pass the test of public opinion, either with regard to ends or means, should repent. That is the Christian way.

To Schmithals (1975b:3; 1983e:78) repentance implies the rejection of the fallacy that man is almighty and can achieve anything. As an example we can take the conviction of terrorism that it can establish a perfect community. Repentance is the rejection of declaring profane values to be sacred. Repentance changes one from having to be almighty into a person living by grace. Only when we relinquish the fallacy that our work must be an act of salvation do we fall within the sphere of God's grace. In this sense, Schmithals (1979a:477-478; 1985c) also interprets the term "following of Christ" which usually plays an important part in Christian ethics. Christians follow the King who meekly rides into Jerusalem on a donkey, the King who teaches his subjects to distinguish between God's Kingdom and the kingdoms of the world. In addition, they can only enter the Kingdom of God prayerfully, while conceding their own powerlessness and trusting in his help. Jesus did not call violent men, from above or below, blessed; or the harsh men trying to improve the world. He says, "blessed are the meek" (Mt 5:5) and about himself he says, "I am gentle and humble in heart" (Mt 11:29)

What ethical guidance can be given to people from the message of the gospel? People in the field of decision-making and action wish to know; "Where can I find the norms which will determine my actions?" Schmithals (1970a:27; 1971a:44-45; 1979a: 189, 199; 1988a:425-434) sees Paul confronted with these fundamental questions in Romans 12:1-2:

> Therefore, I urge you, brothers, in view of God's mercy, to offer your bodies as living sacrifices, holy and pleasing to God, this is your

> reasoning worship. Do not conform any longer to the pattern of this world, but be transformed by the renewing of your mind. Then you will be able to test and approve what God's will is, his good, pleasing and perfect will.

Paul's answer to the question "What we ought to do?" is to refer the congregation to their relationship to God, urging them to take its consequences upon themselves. "You yourselves will know what to do if you give yourselves to God." God's saving act "in view of God's mercy," frees people from the power of sin; they surrender their self-righteousness, repent and live by grace. The congregation must exist as a congregation; then they can live properly and act correctly. The ground for the conduct of the congregation is not the problem of where to find their norms; it is a decision of faith. Norms are unnecessary, because the "renewing of your mind" will teach them what to do and how to do it.

Schmithals (1988a:429; cf. 1979a:464-465) explains that "offer your bodies as living sacrifices" calls the congregation into the present actuality of salvation. That amounts to "be what you are as eschatological church of God." This call is proclamation of the gospel. Here the commandment is gospel in itself. There is no interval between the mercy of God and the surrender of oneself, which follows. Rather, the mercy of God is fulfilled in the surrendering of oneself. The dialectic also applies to the following calls in the text, the imperative calls us into the indicative and together they form the promise of salvation. The renewal of the mind means repentance, to live by the forgiveness of sin. The congregation never reaches a stage where a recall to faith becomes unnecessary, because the grace of God is always a gift. Surrender to God enables Christians to know what to do. Now they can distinguish; not in a theoretical, dissociated way, but practically in what they do, as God wishes them to do (Schmithals 1988a:431-432). The fulfillment of the truth of their existence as a congregation depends on the deeds in which they discern the will of God. The nature of faith is not such that an activity must emerge from it or that it has to be applied. The surrender to God's mercy and the distinguishing of what is good and correct forms a unity that precedes the differentiation between theory and practice. Claim is laid to the whole person and so man cannot be seen as detached from his acts. The true unity between faith and deeds is preserved (Schmithals 1988 a:477).

Actually, the main question in New Testament ethics is not "What must I do?", but rather "Am I capable of doing?" (Schmithals 1988a:431-433; 1994a:267). Moreover, the message of the New Testament aims at qualifying us for action. This leads to the conviction that if we are qualified to do something, we will also know what to do. The virtuous person will also act. So the most important question of general moral theology, "What must I do?" is solved in principle for the New Testament. In faith the power of sin is broken. That means that man does not live of himself any longer and he cannot live of himself, and this is what becomes visible.

The fact that the believer knows the will of God does not mean that new and unheard of virtues will appear in the world along with Christian faith. Unbelievers do the same and practice the same virtues. Believers join in: "finally, brothers, whatever is true, whatever is noble, whatever is pure, whatever is lovely, whatever is admirable if anything is excellent or praiseworthy" (Phil 4:8). Schmithals (1988a:432; cf 1979a: 199) concludes that there can be no specific Christian ethics, not even in the sense of "dispositional ethics" where the character and the life-style of the believer are considered ethically and enable him to actualize ethical values (cf Engelbrecht 1982b: 67). To Schmithals the renewing of your mind is not meant ethically but soteriologically. The congregation is set free from the power of sin. Believers know that even though they fail in what they do, God will still always pardon them. We cannot justify ourselves by acting in an ethically correct way; we are still justified by God. Schmithals keeps to the Reformation insight. Whereas ethics commonly deals in "should," here we have a possibility made possible, a "may." With reference to this, Schmithals (1988a: 201; cf 1979a:495) understands the sanctification of the Christian life as a lived justification. Sanctification is not a second step after forgiveness; neither is forgiveness the inducement on which sanctification is based.

"The will of God," distinguished by the congregation, consists in the details of what he wants done in each specific situation; that which is sufficient and perfectly good here and at this moment (Schmithals 1988a:427). Faith works through love (Gal 5:6 see Schmithals 1983h: 130) and what is done in love is perfect, because it no longer requires forgiveness (Schmithals 1978a: 128; 1988a:475-476). Love fulfills the Torah; in other words, loving your neighbor does justice to the whole content of the law. Thus love is the yardstick and aim of moral guidelines and conduct. No moral commandment is transgressed in love (Schmithals 1978a:474). In faith man is part of the new creation and each moment becomes one of love and life (Schmithals 1978a:129; 1988a:476). Faith places man under the eschatological reality of "God's great mercy" and is therefore the only guarantee that ethics can be Christian. The only norm for Christian, ethical decision-making is love (Schmithals 1979a:543). Schmithals (1978a: 131-134; 1983 1:180; 1988a:478) stresses the fact that this love is passive and patient and does not wish to change and improve the neighbor by violent means. Yet, this tolerating love is highly active, because it overcomes enmity with friendship.

It is also clear that Schmithals is moving away from the Protestant approach to ethics as a relationship between the Bible and moral decision-making. According to this view, the Bible must serve as an authoritative source to provide instruction and ethical guidance (cf. Engelbrecht 1982b:61-63). This approach leads to ethical principles, claims and appeals. Schmithals agrees with Paul that the church must not be given subjective assurance of norms that they have satisfied. The church must take the risk of not trying to justify itself by means of deeds, but must entrust itself to God and do what comes to hand. The security of the believer remains the security of faith and does not come from acting according to certain guidelines.

In love the law is obeyed. Christ is the end of the law, also for the moral decision (Schmithals 1979a:543; 1988a:476; cf 1978e:33). Christ is also the end of the Ten Commandments; the Christian is not a slave to them; he is guided by love. Nevertheless, Schmithals (1986c) shows appreciation for the Ten Commandments in his writing. The Jews elucidated the ten and extended them to six hundred and thirteen commandments. This extension expresses the fact that man can never complete the task of loving God and his neighbor, but will always fail. The fact that there are only ten commandments means that they have an intermediate position, between the many rules regulating people's lives and the unrestrained life of the Christian, whose only restriction is that it must not be detrimental to love. Human life is not servitude, but it is clearly indicated what we may and may not do. The commandments point the way and a Christian cannot live without them; they also form part of the Christian catechism. However, Schmithals does not say that the law safeguards the believer in his faith. The believer is not protected by a high moral code.

Having noted Schmithals' appreciation for the law, his description of Christian ethics as ethics of situation cannot easily be misunderstood (Schmithals 1979a: 189). Love is the final norm for Christian conduct. What must be done in the immediate situation is not prescribed by a rule. Love must find for itself the right injunction among all the rest. In the search for and finding of what must be done now, love is guided by insight and experience in respect of what is best for man. The situation does not provide the norm, but once in the situation, love knows what is right. Because love does not know beforehand what has to be done, it, like the Good Samaritan, is prepared for the situation that arises. Meanwhile those who know in advance pass by (Schmithals 1979a: 189, 543; 1983a:24; 1988a:477). Schmithals (1983k:161) describes Bultmann's ethics as the ethics of love.

The explanation that Schmithals gives of the ethical question is supported by and founded on his understanding of the doctrine of dual order. He found this doctrine in Luther and other reformers in association with Augustine and the New Testament (Schmithals 1979a: 189, 530-533; 1981 d:75-83; 1983d:64; 1983f:91). Although there is more than one aspect to the doctrine of dual order, it is discussed here in connection with ethical decision-making (cf. Schmithals 1980c:113-114).

The Christian lives by virtue of his faith under the regime where God rules with his right hand; the Kingdom of Christ, the eschatological Kingdom, the new creation. This is the regime where God's grace and justice rule and man receives admission to this kingdom by means of penitence and faith, and here he receives forgiveness of sin. This kingdom is established "in view of God's mercy."

At the same time the Christian also lives under the regime where God rules with his left hand; the kingdom of the world, creation. This kingdom falls within the category of the law, and not the gospel. Here it concerns the physical welfare of people. Here the believer, side by side with all other people, strives for better conditions, a greater measure of justice, "whatever is good and praiseworthy." There is no principle that can be transferred from the Kingdom of the right to the Kingdom of the left. This would amount to a merging of the two kingdoms, while it is important to keep them apart. If these two kingdoms become intermixed, the result will be that the Kingdom of Christ will become profane and that of the world will be declared holy. God must receive his due, and Caesar his.

Schmithals (1981a:17; 1983c:50) concedes that it is not easy for the Christian to live in two kingdoms that converge in him and between which he must constantly distinguish. He lives within the peace of God and he concerns himself with the discord in life trying to make a peace that can never be maintained without fear and trembling. The believer's contribution to the world consists in an ability to associate with the affairs of the kingdom of the world in a particularly mundane and earthy way (Schmithals 1979a:532). The lesser evil that believers choose and the sensible and achievable things that they do are what are "good and praiseworthy."

Schmithals (1981a:17-18; 1983h:127-128) contends that the same problem that was named in the doctrine of dual order was solved in the early church in the doctrine of the Trinity. The church confesses the Trinity of God: God, the Father who can be distinguished from the Son, and the Holy Spirit who provides the insight into the distinction between the Father and the Son.

The distinction between the two kingdoms provides an answer to the distinction between the rule of God, the Creator, over the world and the rule of Christ over his Church, the new creation. God rules over the transient creation, and the empires of the world fall under the judgment of his sovereignty. Christ rules over the believers who receive grace. God sustains and Christ saves. Earthly welfare is part of the kingdom on the left and forgiveness of sins and divine salvation is the content of the Kingdom on the right.

Natural man cannot grasp that the distinction between these two kingdoms has to be made. He wants everything together, as something he can achieve and it must be readily available. To teach this man the difference between and the unity of the Father and the Son, he is faced in the Trinity with the Holy Spirit. The Spirit must make known to him the Kingdoms of the Father and the Son.

Schmithals (1981 a: 18) ventures still further in his explanation by pointing out that it was the Emperor who insisted on the Trinitarian formulae at Nicea in 325. By distinguishing between worldly welfare and divine salvation, Constantine was able to accomplish his secular task as Emperor, without the know-all intervention of the church. At the same time, the church was safeguarded against the error of a political theology.

With this interpretation of the Trinitarian dogma, Schmithals succeeds in explaining it as being anchored in history and allowing it to become the expression of the Christian understanding of life.

As an example of these important issues being brought up in different relationships, we find in the synodal report of the Nederlandse Hervormde Kerk:

> God rules. His Kingdom creates order among men. His deeds make sense of and give direction to history. Christ rules. To him the sovereignty has been given and entrusted. He has conquered the world by aligning it to the Kingdom. The Holy Spirit rules. He makes us mindful of the sovereignty of God and Christ and actualises them in the church and the world, both in individuals and community, in criticism and in form.
> (NHK 1965:11)

If Christ overcame the world by aligning it to the Kingdom, Christology serves as a ground for the social ethical point of view, in terms of which the Kingdom of God must be established by the most extreme revolutionary means if needs be.

The danger of "the adult responsible Christian systematically beginning to judge more and more things as he sees fit" (Engelbrecht 1982b:70) is not one that Schmithals fears. In this way life becomes liveable. Schmithals (1986b:127) even goes so far as to say that this is exactly the way in which people witness to the Gospel, namely that Christians live convincing and fully human lives. Convincing Christians need not be presented as little preaching evangelists who announce to everyone that they are Christians. Much rather, they are fully human in the kingdom of the world because they are included in God's great mercy." By acknowledging their own impotence, Christians are silent witnesses to the power of God (Schmithals 1982d: 230). In addition, God's strength lends them the courage to tackle a life of ambiguity, sorrow and death, with faith and in love.

8.5 CREATURE AND CREATION

Today there is a yearning for a "theology of nature," a system which embraces the whole of reality theologically. Buitendag (1986:694) expresses it in this way: "Dogmatics that links God, man and non-human creatures in such a way that exploitation is impossible." The text usually applied in this context is Romans 8:19-22:

> The creation waits in eager expectation for the sons of God to be revealed. For the creation was subjected to frustration, not by its own choice, but by the will of one who subjected it, in hope that the creation itself will be liberated from its bondage to decay and brought into the glorious freedom of the children of God. We know that the whole creation has been groaning as in the pains of childbirth right up to the present time.

For Schmithals (1988a:287-288) these word of Paul do not provide a basis for a systematic theology of nature. Paul is not concerned with the details of the manner and time of creation. Rather, he wishes his readers to hear the sound of the sighing of creation. Believers, meaning those who have already received the new life from God, hear and understand the sighing of creation, at the turning-point between the old and the new world, as an eager yearning for renewal. In this sighing the believer hears an indication of the coming liberation.

The content of the liberation of creation consists in its becoming part of man's salvation. Just as man involved creation in his fall and subjected it to his insignificance, it will be saved together with man. Man and creation are united in their destiny. Creation was made for man and man cannot exist without creation. What happens to man is decisive for creation. Schmithals (1986d) rejects the converse idea, that man will share in the liberation of the world, because then man would have to bring about the change himself; he would have to save the world and himself and he is unable to do it (cf. Schmithals 1976a:39). The unbeliever perceives a call to action in the sighs of the world; otherwise he becomes desperate. The believer knows that he does not have to and need not return the originality to creation, but where honor is given to God, the splendor of nature becomes apparent once more. God's grace to the sinner is also his grace to creation (Schmithals 1981 b:218; 1988a:286-287).

In Schmithals' dealings with the world one cannot speak of a "theology of nature" (Buitendag 1986:693-694; cf. Engelbrecht 1988:25). There could be no direct route from the basic doctrine of dual order to the theology of social problems. In the same way no direct theological pronouncement can be made concerning nature conservation. Christians who are involved in conservation are being led by their intellect. The word nature is no theological term; the wonder and gratitude to God that binds people to creation are missing. There is a tendency to concentrate on endangered nature, rather than on creation. As Buitendag formulates it: "what is necessary is a doctrine that unites God, man and non-human creatures to such an extent that exploitation would be impossible." In a meditation on a psalm concerning creation, Psalm 104, Schmithals admits that it is difficult to ignore man's disruption of nature, but we should not suppress the wonder and gratitude for creation in our hearts. The way in which we associate with creation depends on the stand we take: are we opposed to nature or are we in the midst of the created world, dependent on God?

In the midst of the created world, believers, being guilty, sigh together with creation. They know that the world suffers more from the good intentions than from the evil intentions of humankind. However, guilt does not have the last word. The sighing makes present to the believer the promise of a lost salvation restored (Schmithals 1986d).

From this exposition it becomes clear that the eco-ethic of Schmithals is also ethics of situation based on eschatology. Creation is not equated with the new creation (Schmithals 1981 b:218); the new creation shares in the grace which man receives. As far as the situation is concerned, Schmithals (1983c:49) fears that the attention given to the environment distracts the attention from a greater need, namely that nations should make political peace. Life itself, not nature only, is threatened by political conflict. Not only creation, but history too, is threatened by humankind.

8.6 CLOSING REMARKS

As far as ethics is concerned, Schmithals speaks as a theologian from the point of view of the doctrine of dual order. In theological history this is a recent term; it comes from the twenties of the twentieth century. The matter under discussion has, however, been part of the church from the beginning. Schmithals clarified it well by showing its connection with the doctrine of the Trinity in the early church. In his explanation of the matter, it is clear that the dual order doctrine is closely connected to the doctrine of justification of the Reformation. God's grace not only means that he will ignore the sins and mistakes of the past; it is much more. It allows human beings to know that in success or failure, they will be kept safe by God and will not be lost. Grace has nothing to do with what we consider success. Even failure can be ascribed to God and despite that the believer will still trust God. People are not destroyed by their failures, neither are they made by their successes; they receive there life from the hand of God (Schmithals 1978a: 100-101; 1988a:391). It becomes clear that the proponents of the so-called Reformed point of view, to be distinguished from the Lutheran, are no longer well informed as regards the Reformation doctrine of justification.

CHAPTER 9
Conclusion

The present theology is not really conversant with the theology of Bultmann. Despite the fact that he is generally considered to be the outstanding authority on the New Testament in our age, it is surprising how negligible the factual knowledge of his work remains. There are few authorities on and students of his work.

This state of affairs can be traced to the misunderstanding of the trend of his theology. It was already apparent in the Bultmann school. For example, he complains about the misunderstanding of his view of the main problem of New Testament theology. Referring specifically to his gifted student Ernst Käsemann, he says, "O Absalom, mein Sohn, mein Sohn!" (in Schmithals 1968:kol 262). If these misunderstandings were to continue, it would only be to the detriment of New Testament science. Schmithals must be given credit for the fact that he did justice to the theological intent of his tutor. He did not disregard the old problems, but considered them lucidly. This is what his work claims to be and his contribution must be judged accordingly. I know of no one who acquitted himself better of this task than Schmithals. This is what it is really all about: the thorough grasp of the Biblical reformational theology by means of the historical criticism. The true meaning of this method has never been as thoroughly examined as was done by Schmithals.

The time is past where the guideline of existential interpretation can be regarded as an inadmissible and forbidden adaptation to "modern man." This study may even serve to spell it out as support for those who wish to maintain the *sola Scriptura* in the preaching of the church.

Whoever wishes to follow in the footsteps of Schmithals and to understand him must immerse himself in the theologian's own work and not judge it on hearsay only. Klaus Schmitz, an assistant of Schmithals of many years standing, considers him to be at his best in the book *Die theologische Anthropologie des Paulus* (Schmithals 1980b). My first introduction to Schmithals, at his best, was his commentary on the gospel of Mark (Schmithals 1979a). However, the reader need not be influenced by Schmitz or me. Both these works concern dogmatic texts. These texts, from their very nature, are ousted from their historic definitiveness and are read in such a way that their theological quality is laid bare. The commentary is determined by the material. In other instances, Schmithals allows himself to be guided by the material. Then, as the case may be, he makes the theological assessment from the historical circumstances.

WORKS CONSULTED

Beukes, M. J. du P. 1984. "Vernuwing in die erediens." *HTS* 40, 7-35.
Boers, H. 1979. *What is New Testament Theology? The rise of criticism and the problem of the New Testament*. Philadelphia: Fortress. (Guides to Biblical scholarship: New Testament Series).
Bonhoeffer, D. 1970. *Widerstand und Ergebung: Briefe und Aufzeichnungen aus der Haft*. Neuausgabe. München: Kaiser.
— [1949] 1975. *Ethik* 8 Aufl. München: Kaiser.
Boshoff, P. B. 1987. "Eksistensiale verstaan van die Ou Testament: Die teologiese arbeid van Antonius H J Gunneweg." *HTS* 43, 352-373.
Buitendag, J. 1986. "Die skepping as gelykenis: 'n Beoordeling van die skeppingsleer van Karl Barth in die lig van die appèl van die ekologiese krisis." *HTS* 42, 674-695.
Bultmann, R. 1913. "Was lässt die Spruchquelle über die Urgemeinde erkennen?" *Oldenburgisches Kirchenblatt* 19/7, 35-37; 19/8, 41-44.
— 1926. "Die Frage der 'dialektischen' Theologie: Eine Auseinandersetzung mit Petersen," *ZZ* 4/1, 40-59.
— 1950. Leistungs-Zeugnis zur Bewerbung um Gebürenerlass für stud. theol. Walter Schmithals. Unpublished.
— 1954. Referat über die Dissertation des Pfarrers W Schmithals "Die Gnosis in Korinth" Unpublished.
— 1962. "Sermon," in Gollwitzer, H & Traub, H (Hrsg), *Hören und Handeln: Festschrift für Emst Wolf zum 60. Geburtstag*, 48-51. München: Kaiser.
— [1960] 1967a. "Das Verhältnis der urchristlichen Christusbotschaft zum historischen Jesus," in Dinkler, E (Hrsg), *Exegetica: Aufsätze zur Erforschung des Neuen Testaments*, 445-469. Tübingen: Mohr.
— 1967b. "Brief an die theologische Arbeitsgemeinschaft Philipps Haus, Marburg an der Lahn," in *Protokoll der Tagung "Alter Marburger,"* 3.-6. Januar 1983 und 2.-5. Januar 1984 in Hofgeismar, 32-33. Unpublished.
— [1941] 1968. *Das Evangelium des Johannes*, Göttingen: Vandenhoeck. (KEK.)
— [1933] 1972. *Glauben und Verstehen: Gesammelte Aufsätze, 1*. 7 Aufl. Tübingen: Mohr.
— [1928] 1972a. "Die Bedeutung der 'dialektische Theologie' für die neutestamentliche Wissenschaft, in *Bultmann* 1972:114-133.
— [1929] 1972b. "Die Bedeutung des geschichtlichen Jesus für die Theologie des Paulus," in *Bultmann* 1972:188-213.
— 1972c. "Die Christologie des Neuen Testaments" in *Bultmann* 1972:245-267.
— [1965] 1975. *Glauben und Verstehen: Gesammelte Aufsätze 1*. 3 Aufl. Tübingen:Mohr.

Bultmann continued
 [1961] 1975a. "Die Erforschung der synoptischen Evangelien," in *Bultmann* 1975:1-41.
 [1965] 1975b. "Antwort an Ernst Käsemann," in *Bultmann* 1975: 190-198
 [1925] 1975c. "Das Problem einer theologische Exegese des Neuen Testaments," in Strecker, G (Hrsg) *Das Problem der Theologie des Neuen Testaments*, 249-277. Darmstadt: Wissenschaftliche Buchgesellschaft (WdF CCCLXVII).
 [1921] 1979. *Die Geschichte der synoptische Tradition.* 9 Aufl. Göttingen: Vandenhoeck.
 1980. *Theologie des Neuen Testaments..* 8 Aufl. Tübingen: Mohr. (UTB 630).
 [1926] 1983. *Jesus.* Tübingen: Mohr. (UTB 1272).

Cadbury. H. J. 1933. "The Hellenists," in Foakes Jackson F J & Kirsopp Lake, D. D. (ed). *The beginnings of Christianity*, Part I, Vol V, 59-73. London: Macmillan.
Chantepie de la Saussaye, D. 1874. *De brief aan de Hebreën voor de gemeente uitgelegd*, 2e druk. Amsterdam: Hoveker & Zoon.

Dreyer, P. S. 1972. "Waarde en geskiedenis." *HTS* 28, 51-62.
Dreyer, T. F. J. 1989. "Poging tot 'n herdefinisie van die prediking binne die raamwerk van die Reformatoriese teologie." *HTS* 45, 350-369.

Engelbrecht, B. J. [1962] 1982a. Wat is die reg en die vryheid van die eksegeet? in *Versamelde opstelle, Deel* 2, 51-67. Pretoria: Universiteit van Pretoria. [Ook gepubliseer in *HTS* 42/3 (1986), 485-501].
 [1978] 1982b. Opmerkings rondom die basiese probleem van die Christelike etiek, in *Versamelde opstelle*, Deel 4, 61-72. Pretoria: Universiteit van Pretoria.
 1988. "Teologie en ekologie," *HTS* 44, 23-38.
Eicholz, G. 1960. "Was heisst charismatische Gemeinde? 1. Korinther 12," *ThEh, NF*, 77.

Geyser, A. S. 1951. "Die betrekking tussen Jesus en Johannes die Doper." *HTS* 7, 133-140
Goguel, M. 1949. *Les premiers temps de l'église.* Neuchâtel: Delachaux et Niestlé. (Manuels et précis de théologie XXVIII).
Graets, H. 1905. *Geschichte der Juden von den ältesten Zeiten bis auf die Gegenwart, III,225 I.* 5 Aufl. Leipzig: Leiner.
Gunneweg, A. H. J. 1978a. *Leistung.* Stuttgart: Kohlhammer. (Kohlhammer Taschenbücher: Biblische Kontrontationen, 1007).

Heim, K. 1955. *Die christliche Ethik: Tübinger Vorlesungen, nachgeschrieben und ausgearbeitet von Walter Kreuzburg.* Tübingen: Katzmann.

Jaspert, B. [Hrsg.] 1971. *Karl Barth - Rudolf Bultmann Briefwechsel 1922-1966.* Zürich: TheologischerVerlag. (Karl Barth Gesamtausgabe V, 1).

Käsemann, E. 1974. *An die Römer.* 3 Aufl. Tübingen: Mohr. (Hdb.8a).

Lichtenstein E. 1950/51. "Die älteste christliche Glaubensformel." *ZKG* 63, 1-74.
Lohse, E. 1962. "W. Schmithals Das Kirchliche Apostelamt: Eine historische Untersuchung." *ZKG* 73.140.
Lohmeyer, E. 1967. *Das Evangelium des Matthäus: Nachgelassene Ausarbeitungen und Entwürfe zur Übersetzung und Erklärung von E. Lohmeyer.* 4 Aufl. Göttingen: Vandenhoeck. (KEK).

Nederduitsch Hervormde Kerk van Afrika. Kommissie van die Algemene Kerkvergadering 1990. *Kerk en politiek: 'n Herderlike skrywe.* Unpublished.
Nederlandse Hervormde Kerk. Generale Synode 1965. *De politieke verantwoordelikkheid van de kerk.* 2e druk. 'S-Gravenhage: Boeckencentrum.

Oberholzer, J. P. 1990. "Ou-Testamentiese perspektiewe op die definisie van die prediking." *HTS* 46, 647-65S.

Pelser, G. M. M. 1984. "Die reformatoriese grondbeskouing oor die Christen as 'simul iustus et peccator' in die lig van Rom 7:14-25." *HTS* 40, 92-110.
Pont, A. D. 1985. "Die NHK se profetiese verantwoordelikheid teenoor die owerheid in die verlede en vandag." *HTS* 41, 29-48.
1991. "God zal het ons doen gelukken: Ons teologiese opleiding word 75 jaar oud." *Konteks* 2/4, 42-44.
Protokolle der Tagung der Marburger Theologen 20.10.53-23.10.53 in *Jugenheim an der Bergstrasse.* Unpublished.

Rautenbach, C. H. 1978. "Die toekoms van die kerk in die samelewing: Kollig op die sosiaal-etiese insluitende politieke afmetings van Christelike kerkbly in Suid-Afrika," in Vorster, W. S. (ed), *Church and society/Kerk en samelewing,* 68-97. Pretoria: Unisa.
Renan. E. [1863] 1864. *Het leven van Jesus,* uit het Fransch vertaald. 2de druk. Haarlem: De Erven Loosjes.

Schmidt, K. L. 1928. s v "Heidenchristentum." RGG.

Schmithals, W. 1953. "Die Bekehrung des Zachäus: Lk 19, 1-10." *RKZ* 24, 534-536.
1961. *Das kirchliche Apostelamt: Eine historsche Untersuchung.* Göttingen: Vandenhoeck. (FRLANT NF 61.)
1963. *Paulus und Jakobus.* Göttingen: Vandenhoeck. (FRLANT NF 85.)
1965. *Paulus und die Gnostiker: Untersuchungen zu den kleinen Paulusbriefen.* Hamburg-Bergstedt: Reich.
1965a. Die Häretiker in Galatien, in *Schmithals* 1965:9-46.
1965b. "Die Irrlehrer des Philipperbriefes," in *Schmithals* 1965:47-88.
1965c. "Die historische Situation der Thessalonicherbriefe," in *Schmithals* 1965:89-158.
1965d. "Die Irrlehrer von Rom. 16, 17-20," in *Schmithals 1965:* 159-174.
[1966] 1967a. *Die Theologie Rudolf Bultmanns: Eine Einführung.* 2. durchgesehene Aufl. Tübingen: Mohr.

Schmithals continued
1967b. "Zur gegenwärtigen Predigtnot und ihrer Überwindung." *KiZ* 3, 94-102.
1967c. "Kerygma und Heilstatsache: Kein anderes Evangelium." *KiZ* 11, 493-500.
1967d. "Die Wahrheit der Heiligen Schrift und das Konzil," in Hampe, J. C. (Hrsg), *Die Autorität der Freiheit: Gegenwart des Konzils und Zukunft der Kirche im ökumenischen Disput*, Bd.1, 197-208. München: Kösel.
1968. "R Bultmann, Glauben und Verstehen: Gesammelte Aufsätze IV, *ThLZ* 93/4, kol 260-262.
[1956] 1969. *Die Gnosis in Korinth: Eine Untersuchung zu den Korintherbriefen*. 3. bearbeitete und ergänzte Aufl. Göttingen: Vandenhoeck. (FRLANT NF 48.)
1970a. *Das Christuszeugnis in der heutigen Gesellschaft: Zur gegenwärtigen Krise von Theologie und Kirche*. Hamburg: Reich. (EZS 53).
1970b. "Sinn und Aufgabe der modernen Theologie." *Die Spur* 3, 80-85.
1970c. "Die Frage nach Gott im Neuen Testament." *Die Spur* 5, 176-185.
1971a. *Vernuft und Gehorsam: Zur Standortbestimmung der Theologie*. Hamburg: Reich. (*EZS* 58).
1971b. "Barth, Bultmann und wir: Zum Methodenproblem in der Theologie." *EZS* 59/60, 49-64.
1972. *Jesus Christus in der Verkündigung der Kirche: Aktuelle Beiträge zum notwendigen Streit um Jesus*. Neukirchen-Vluyn: Neukirchener Verlag.
[1970] 1972a. "Jesus von Nazareth in der Verkündigung der Kirche", in *Schmithals* 1972:9-35.
[1962] 1972b. "Paulus und der 'historische' Jesus," in *Schmithals* 1972: 36-59.
[1970] 1972c. "Das Bekenntnis zu Jesus Christus, in *Schmithals* 1972:60-79.
[1971] 1972d."Politische Theologie," in *Schmithals* 1972:118-143.
[1971] 1972e. "Die gesellschaftliche Verantwortung der Kirche und der Christen und das Problem der Macht," in *Schmithals* 1972:144-168.
[1968] 1972f. "Welchen Sinn hat das Bekenntnis zur Gottheit Jesus?227" in
Schmithals 1972:169-186.
---[1970] 1972g. "Erwägungen zur Didaktik des Theologiestudiums," in *Schmithals* 1972:187-205.
1973a. *Die Apokalyptik: Einführung und Deutung*. Göttingen: Vandenhoeck. (Sammlung Vandenhoeck).
1973b. "Die Gegenwart Jesu Christi in seiner Gemeinde." *Th Viat* 11, 217-233.
1973c. "Krise und Kritik des Religionsunterrichts." *Die Spur* 13, 120-127.
1973d. "Die Korintherbriefe als Briefsammlung." *ZNW* 64, 263-288.
1974a. "Theologie - Hochschule - Wissenschaft." *RKZ* 8, 82-84.

1974b. "Geisterfahrung als Christuserfahrung," in Heitmann, C. &

1974b. "Geisterfahrung als Christuserfahrung," in Heitmann, C. & Mühlen, H. (Hrsg), *Erfahrung und Theologie des Heiligen Geistes*, 101-127. Hamburg: Kösel.
1974c. "Im Dienst der Kirche?" *Berliner Sonntagsblatt/Die Kirche* 6, 1 und 3.
1975a. Predigt über Mk 10, 46-52. *Gemeinde-brief der Deutschen Evangelischen Gemeinde Rotterdam* 3,1-4.
1975b. Abkehr vom Wahn der Machbarkeit: Gedanken zum Busstag. *Der Tagesspiegel Berlin* 19.11.1975, 3.
1975c. "Jesus und die Apokalyptik," in Strecker, G. (Hrsg), *Jesus Christus in Historie und Theologie: Festschrift für Hans Conzelmann*, 59-85. Tübingen: Mohr.
1976a. "Meditationen zu Joh 3, 31-36." *GPM* 31, 37-42.
1976b. "Andacht über Mt 28, 18-20,", in Protokoll Bd 1 der Verlautbarungen der Regionalen Synode der Ev Kirche in Berlin-Brandenburg (Berlin-W.), 145-148.
--- & Gunneweg, A. H. J. 1978a. *Leistung.* Stuttgart: Kohlhammer (Kohlhammer Taschenbücher: Biblische Konfrontationen, 1007).
Schmithals 1978b. "Der 'Gottesdienst' im Licht des Neuen Testaments." *RKZ* 1, 2-4.
1978c. "Osterfreude. 1. Kor 15, 20." *Berliner Sonntagsblatt* 13, 2.
1978d. "Die Wiederkunft Christi." *RKZ* 11, 162-164; 12, 178-179.
1978e. "Zur Herkunft der gnostische Elemente in der Sprache des Paulus," in Aland, B. (Hrsg), *Gnosis*, 385-414. Göttingen: Vandenhoeck.
1978f. "Meditation zu Mt 3, 13-17." *GPM* 33, 75-81.
1979a. *Das Evangelium nach Markus*, 2 Bde. Gütersloh: Mohn. (*ÖTK* 2/1; 2/2; GTB-Siebenstern 502; 503.)
1980a. *Das Evangelium nach Lukas.* Zürich: Theologischer Verlag. (*ZBK NT* 3.1.)
1980b. *Die theologische Anthropologie des Paulus: Auslegung van Röm 7, 17- 8, 39.* Stuttgart: Kohlhammer. (Urban-Taschenbücher/ Kohlhammer Taschenbücher 1021.)
--- & Gunneweg, A. H. J. 1980c. *Herrschaft..* Stuttgart: Kohlhammer. (Kohlhammer Taschenbücher: Biblische Konfrontationen, 1012.)
1980d. "Kritik der Formkritik," *ZThK* 77, 149-195.
1981a. "Herrschaft und Sorge." *Epd Dokumentation* 30, 10-18.
1981b. "Meditation zu Lk 24, 36-45." *GPM* 35, 213-218.
1981c. "Von dem Sohne Gottes," in Selge, K. C. & Karzig Ch. (Hrsg), *Es wird bei uns gelehrt...: Berliner Predigten 1980 über das Augsburger Bekenntnis von 1530*, 22-27. Berlin: CZV-Verlag.
1981d. "Von den weltlichen Ordnungen", in Selge, K. C. & Karzig Ch. (Hrsg), *Es wird bei uns gelehrt.... Berliner Predigten 1980 über das Augsburger Bekenntnis* von 1530, 75-83. Berlin: CZV-Verlag.
1982a. *Die Apostelgeschichte des Lukas.* Zürich: Theologischer Verlag. (*ZBK NT* 3.2.)
1982b. "Auslegungen von 1. Kor 2, 1-10," in *Protokoll der Tagung 'Alter Marburger,'* 2.-5. Januar 1981 und 4.-7. Januar 1982 in Hofgeismar, 68-82.
1982c. "Himmelfahrt." Berliner Rundfunkpredigt, 20. Mai, als Ms. vervielfältigt.

Schmithals continued
1982d. "Meditation zu Kol 4, 2- 4 (5-6)," *GPM* 36, 225-231.
1982e. "Warum ist Geschichte so schwer zu verstehen?" *Criticon* 71, Mai/Juni, 120-121.
1982f. s v "Evangelien, synoptische." *TRE*.
1983. *Bekenntnis und Gewissen: Theologische Studien zur Ethik. Zum 60. Geburtstag herausgegeben von Hess*, H-E & Wildemann B. Berlin: CZV-Verlag.
[1980] 1983a. "Aufgaben und Grenzen einer christlichen Ethik des Politischen," in *Schmithals* 1983:12-24.
[1982] 1983b. "'Selig sind die Friedfertigen'- Was meint die Bergpredigt wirklich?" in *Schmithals* 1983:25-39.
[1981] 1983c. "Theologische und ethisch Überlegungen zum Problem des Friedens," in *Schmithals* 1983:40-56.
[1982] 1983d. "Zum Friedensauftrag der Kirche und der Christen," in *Schmithals* 1983:57-77.
[1975] 1983e. "Ist wirklich alles machbar?" in *Schmithals* 1983:78-83.
[1976] 1983f. "In Glaube und Freiheit verpflichtet," in *Schmithals* 1983: 84-105.
[1976] 1983g. "Utopie und Hoffnung," in *Schmithals* 1983: 111 -124.
[1982] 1983h. "Politische Ausserungen der Kirche und ihrer Amtsträger" in *Schmithals* 1983:125-134.
[1982] 1983i. "Vom Umgang mit dem christlichen Gewissen," in *Schmithals* 1983:135-138.
--- 1983j. "Das Bekenntnis der Gemeinde und das Gewissen der Christen" in *Schmithals* 1983:139-153.
[1979] 1983k. "Theologische Ethik Das Beispiel Rudolf Bultmanns," in Schmithals 1983:161 -171.
1983l. "Gewissheit und Bewährung," in *Schmithals* 1983:172-184.
1983m. "Jeremia 8, 4-7," in *Anregungen zur Predigt am Volkstrauertag 1983*, hrsg von VDK. Kassel: Hessen Druck.
1983n. "Berliner Rundfunkpredigt: Noch ist unser Wissen Stückwerk." 20. Februar 1983. *Ev. Rundfunkdienst in der Berliner Arbeitsgemeinschaft für Kirchliche Publizistik*.
1983o. "Judaisten in Galatien." *ZNW* 4, 27-58.
1984a. *Die Briefe des Paulus in ibrer ursprüngliche Form*. Zürich: Thelogischer Verlag. (Zürcher Werkkommentare zur Bibel.)
1984b. *Neues Testament und Gnosis*. Darmstadt: Wissenschaftliche Buchgesellschaft. (EdF; Bd. 208.)
1984c. "Gedanken zum Pfingstfest." *Der Tagesspiegel* 10. Juni 1984.
1984d. "2. Kor. 5, 1-10," in *Anregungen zur Predigt am Volkstrauertag 1984*, hrsg von VDK. Baunatal: Hessen Druck.
1984e. "The corpus Paulinum and Gnosis" in Logan, A. H. B. & Wedder burn, A. J. M. (eds), *The New Testament and Gnosis: Essays in honour of R .Mc L. Wilson*, 107-124. Clark: Edinburgh.
1984f. Ein Brief Rudolf Bultmanns an Erich Foester, in Jaspert, B. (Hrsg.), *Rudolf Bultmanns Werk und Wirkung*, 70-80. Darmstadt: Wissenschaftliche Buchgesellschaft.
1985a. *Einleitung in die drei ersten Evangelien*. Berlin: De Gruyter. (De Gruyter Lehrbuch.)

Schmithals continued
- 1985b. "Matthäus 25, 31-46," in *Anregungen zur Predigt am Volkstrauertag 1985*, hrsg von VDK. Kassel: Hessen Druck.
- 1985c. "Berliner Rundfunkpredigt: Wer ist dieser?" 31. März 1985. Ev. Rundfunkdienst in der Berliner Arbeitsgemeinschaft für Kirchliche Publizistik.
- 1986a. "Politisches Handeln verträgt kein Amen." *Der Tagesspiegel* 19.11.1986, 33.
- 1986b. "Wir haben hier keine bleibende Stadt," in *Protokoll der vierten Delegierten-Konferenz der Evangelischen Sammlung Berlin 1986*, 123-130, 27.-29.6.86.
- 1986c. "Andachten 1.-7. Juni," in *Brot für den Tag*. Berlin: CVZ-Verlag.
- 1986d. "Römer 8, 18-27 (28)," in *Anregungen zur Predigt am Volkstrauertag 1986*, 1986, 11-15, hrsg von VDK. Baunatal: Ahrend Inh.
- 1986e. "Berliner Rundfunkpredigt: Wir leben oder sterben - wir gehören Gott allein," 13. April 1986. *Ev. Rundfunkdienst in der Berliner Arbeitsgemeinschaft für Kirchliche Publizistik*.
- 1986f. "Meditation zu Phil 3, 7-11 (12-14)." *GPM* 40, 352-373.
- 1987a. "Berliner Rundfunkpredigt: 'Suchet der Stadt Bestes'," 26. April 1987. Ev. Rundfunkdienst in der Berliner Arbeitsgemeinschaft fur Kirchliche Publizistik.
- 1987b. "Psalm 104, 24," in *Gemeindebrief der Lindenkirche*, 10.87.
- 1987c. "Der betrügerische Verwalter: Lukas 16, 1-8," in *Anregungen zur Predigt amVolkstrauertag 1987*, 8-12, hrsg von VDK. Kassel: Hessen Druck.
- 1987d. "Der Konflikt zwischen Kirche und Synagoge in neutestamentlicher Zeit," in Oeming, M. K., Graupner, A (Hrsg), *Altes Testament und christliche Verkündigung: Festschrift für Antonius H. J, Gunneweg zum 65. Geburtstag*, 366-386. Stuttgart: Kohlhammer.
- 1988a. *Der Römerbrief: Ein Kommentar*. Gütersloh: Mohn.
- 1988b. "Eschatologie und Apokaliptik." *VuF* 33/1, 64-82.
- 1989a. "Paulus und die griechische Philosophie," in Abel, G. & Salaquarda, J. (IIrsg), *Krisis der Methaphysik: Wolfgang Müller-Lauter zum 65. Geburtstag*, 34-53. Berlin: De Gruyter.
- 1989b. "Reformation und Revolution," in *Vom Verlorenen Sohn: 450 Jahre Reformation in der Mark Brandenburg: Eine Festveranstaltung der Evangelischen Kirche in Berlin-Brandenburg (Berlin West) mit Unterstützüng der Hochschule der Künste*, Berlin, 7-18. Berlin: Wichern Verlag.
- 1989c. "Paulus als Heidenmissionar und das Problem seiner theologischen Entwicklung," in Koch, D-A, Sellin, G. & Lindemann, A. (Hrsg), *Jesu Rede von Gott und ihre Nachgeschichte im fruhen Chnstentum: Beiträge zur Verkündigung Jesu und zum Kerygma der Kirche: Festschrift für Willi Marxen zum 70. Geburtstag*, 235-251. Gütersloh: Mohn.
- 1989d. "Paulus und Jakobus ein theologischer Gegensatz?" in *Christliches ABC heute und morgen* 4, 19-29.
- 1990. "Erbe und Auftrag eine theologische Standortbestimmung: Ein Vortrag am 15.11.1989 aus Anlass der Einführung der Reformation an der Universität Greifswald 1539," in *ZKG* 3, 481-498.

Schmithals continued
1991. "Meditation zu Mt 25, 14-30. *GPM* 45, 318-322.
--- 1992a. *Johannesevangelium und Johannesbriefe: Forschungsgeschichte und Analyse.* Berlin: de Gruyter. *(BZNW* 64).
1992b. "Das Alte Testament als hermeneutische Problem," in *In memoriam Antonius H. J. Gunneweg*, 9-25. Bonn: Bouvier (Alma Mater 76).
1992c. "Die Bedeutung der E231vangelien in der Theologiegeschichte bis
zur Kanonbildung," in Van Segbroeck, F. et al, *The Four Gospels 1992: Festschrift Frans Neirynck.* Leuven: University Press.
1993a. "Bibliographie Walter Schmithals 1983-1992." *ThLZ*, 118. 12, Sp 1089-1095.
1993b. "Das Verhältnis von Juden und Christen in neutestamentlicher Zeit," in *Treffpunkt Matthäus, Evangelisches Gemeindeblatt der Matthäusgemeinde Steglitz*, 3-4.
1994a. *Theologiegeschichte des Urchristentums: Eine problemgeschichtliche Darstellung.* Stuttgart: Kohlhammer.
1994b. "Die Frage Nach dem historichen Jesus," in *ZGP* 12, 6, 13-16.
1995a. "Zum Problem der Entmythologisierung bei Rudolf Bultmann." *ZThK* 92, 2, 166-206.
1996a. "Zu Karl Barths Schriftauslegung: Die Problematik deVerhältnisses von 'dogmatischer' und historischer Exegese," in Trowitzsch, M. (Hg.), *Karl Barths Schriftauslegung*, Tübingen: Mohr.
1996b. "Das Alte Testament im Neuen: Zum Problem einer 'gesamentbiblischen Theologie'," in *Chnstliches ABC heute und morgen*, Gruppe 4, 247-284.
1996c. "Methodische Erwägungen zur Literarkritik der Paulusbriefe," in *ZNW* 87, 51-82.
1997a. "Probleme des Apostelkonzils (Gal 2, 1-10)" in *HTS*, 1 & 2, 53, 6-35.
--- 1997b."Vom Ursprung der synoptischen Tradition," *ZThK* 94, Heft 3, 288-316.

Valeton, J. J. P. [1894] 1907. "De 'historische Jesus' en de 'Christus der Kerk'," in Valeton, J. J. P. *Getuigenissen*, 1-26. Nijmegen Ten Hoet.
Van Rhijn, C. H. 1883. "De jongste litteratuur over de Schriften des Nieuwen Verbonds, III: De Handelingen der Apostelen." *Theologische Studiën* 1, 292-306.
Van Selms, A 1936. "Hoe lezen wij het Oude Testament?" *Onder Eigen Vaandel* 11, 10-27.
1955. "Hemelvaart." *Die Vaderland*, 19 Mei 1955, p. 9.
1951. "Leersuccessie als Gezagsvorm". *NTT* 5, 257- 276.
Van Wyk, I. W. C. 1987. "Das Theodizeeproblem als Orientierungspunkt der Kirchenpolitischen und theologischen Streiffragen: Eine Auseinandersetzung mit Jürgen Moltmann." Unpublished DTh-thesis, Universiteit van Pretoria.
Vinet, A. 1875. *Homiletiek of Theorie der Prediking.* Uit het Fransch vertaald en met aantekeningen voorzien door E. Moll. Tweede nieuw bewerkte druk. Tiel: Campagne.

Winterhager, W. E. 1976. "Berliner Kirchenkampf 1966-1976," in Motschmann, J. & Matthies, H. (Hrsg), *Rotbuch Kirche*, 76-94. Stuttgart: Seewald.

SCRIPTURE REFERENCES

Psalms
27:1 150
104 220

Isaiah
43:5 178
53 .... 144, 166
53:6 and 12 145
53:7 145
53:9 145
53:12 .... 145, 146
60:2a 193

Jeremiah
29:7 206-207

Joel
3:13 127

Amos
8:11-12 133

Matthew
1:23 83
2:11 86
3:14-15 83
5:5 211
5:1-6b 193
5:20 83
6:16-18 116
10:5-6 75
10:17-20 81
11:18-19 121
11:29 211
13:24-30; 36-43 169
18:15-17 82
25:14-30 197
25:31-33 190
25:31-46 190
28:19 168

Mark
1:9-11 166

Mark cont'd
1:14-15 34
1:15 178
1:40-45 108
2:9 199
2:18-19a 116
3:20-21, 31b-35 132
3:29 35
4:8 78
4:26-29 127
4:31-32 78
5:34 43
7:24-30 72
9:5 123
9:6 123
9:7 123
9:24 201
9:26-27 119
13 .... 77, 78
13:5-6 77
13:24-27 77
13:32 77
14:41 145
15:1 145
15:15 145
15:34 179
16:6 119
16:9 185

Luke
2:10-12 86
6:24-25 122
6:29 78
6:46-49 128
7:1-10 89
7:31-34 .... 76, 77
12:4-5 83
12:8-9 110
12:10 130
13:18-19 78
13:34 121
16:1-7 155
19:11-27 197

Luke cont'd
23:43 159

John
1:1 91
1:1, 2 94
1:17 94
1:18 140
1:29 91
1:33-34 .... 89, 90
2:11 89
2:13 91
3:6 93
3:8 93
3:10 99
3:13 92
4:46-47, 50-54a 89
5:6 90
6:35 103
6:63; 13:20-26a, 36-38
 16:12-13' 18:15-18,
 24-27; 19:24b-27;
 20:2-11a; 21:1-25 94
7:38-39 94
8:21 89
8:31 179
9:22 80
9:39 53
10:7b-8 67
13:3 91
13:23 95
14:3 89
14:6 89
14:14 94
14:16-17 .... 94, 98
14:19b 184
14:26 94
15:3 119
15:15 98
15:1-17 98
16:12-13 98
18:38 206
20:19 90
20:28 137
21:15-17 95
21:20-23 95

Acts
8:10 24
11:27-30 171
12:25; 13:5 165
15:1-34 171
16:23-25 83
16:36-39 83
18:25-26 79

Romans
1:3 31
1:3-4 129
1:3b-4a 115, 125, 138
1:3b-4 115
1:4 120
1:16 165
1:34 129
3:25 .... 38, 167
3:25-26a 167
4:24b-25 166
4:25 119
5:6 119
8:34 119
5:21 157
6:4 120
6:2-11 146
8:3-4 163
8:4 179
8:11 30
8:19-22 219
8:24 160
8:34 119
8:38-39 150
10:3 147
11:11-24 146-147
12:1-2 .... 142, 211
13:1-7 .... 85, 171
16:1-20 70
16:18 70

1 Corinthians
1:5-13a 161
1:8-20 162
1:12 18
1:17 7
1:17-2:5 10

1 Corinthians cont'd
1:18-25; 1:26b-29, 30...........11
2:1 34
2:2 159
2:6-3:3 15
4:1-3 7
5:1-10 21
6:11 168
6:12-20 19
6:13-14 ....19, 20
6:19 15
7:1-24 20
7:10 36
7:40 14
8:1 ....11, 18, 19
8:7 18
9:14 80
9:16 45
10:14-22 19
10:22 19
10:16b-17 26
10:28-30 19
11:2 6
11:2-16 21
11:10 20
11:16 20
11:19 7
11:20-22 26
11:23-25 36
11:26 167
12:1 14
12:1-3 ....7, 8, 9
12:3 35
12:7 16
12:9 14
12:12 25
12:13 162
13:5 168
13:8-13 11
14:12 ....28, 29
14:18 15
14:33b-36 21
14:34 21
14:37 29
15 ....13, 22
15:3 ....66, 92

1 Corinthians cont'd
15:3-5 37
15:4 119
15:9 162
15:12 ....7, 12
15:19 12
15:20 158
15:29 ....12, 27
16:15-18 71

2 Corinthians
1:20 148
3:1 16
3:14 147
3:17 17
4:2-5 16
4:5 67
4:7 ....12, 13
4:10 120
5:1 22
5:1-5 ....23, 24
5:1-10 22
5:3 22
5:6-8 23
5:9-10 24
5:10 159
5:14 120
5:16 ....29, 31, 32
5:17 ....107, 164
5:19 146
7:6-7 28
7:12-13a 7
10:1-10 15
10:7 17
10:18 17
11:4 10
11:4-6 11
11:5 ....8, 27
11:13 ....27, 69
11:22 8
12 71
12:1 28
12:3 38
12:6 28
12:9 178
12:9-10 13

2 Corinthians
12:11 27
12:12 28
12:16 28
13:3 17

Galatians
1:11-12 161
1:13 162
1:15-16 162
2:1-10 75
2:9 75
3:28 .... 21, 162
4:10 69
4:14 69
5:3 69
5:6 214
6:1 69
6:6 71
6:12 69
6:13 68
6:14 168
6:15 168
6:17 30

Ephesians
3:19 171
4:11-13 25
5:14 29

Philippians
1:23 159
2 114
2:5 108
2:6-11 .... 87, 163
2:29 71
3:2 69
3:6 162
3:9 169
3:10 120
3:19 70
4:8 213

Colossians
3:1 120

Colossians cont'd
3:10-11 162
4:10 165

1 Thessalonians
1:5 71
1:6 71
1:10 119
2:14-16 171
4:13-18 160
4:14 .... 119, 120
5:12-13 71

Hebrews
1:1 149

1 Peter
5:13 165

1 John
1:1-4 153
1:6 92
1:8, 10 93
2:12 94
2:13 91
2:22 9
4:1-2 35
4:2 9
5:1-13 90
5:6 9
5:16 93

2 John
5 93
10 93

3 John
5-8 93

Revelation
(e.g. 3:11) 97
19:16 87
22:13
  cf. 1:17-18 160

TOPIC REFERENCES

act of God	30,47,48,49,57,109,146,153,154,186, 188,193
adoption	114,138
antagonists	5,8,10,11,14,16,19,21,22,
anthropology	15,21
anti-Marcionite tendency	67
Antioch	72,74,75,87,145,156,165,166,168
apocalyptic	12,77,78,79,98,101,110,121,123,127,131, 141,142,143,147,148,150.154-161,187
apostle	8,9,10,12,13,14,15,16,18,21,27,28,36,37,54, 76,90
Apostles' Creed	37
apostleship	6,8,17,27,65,67,68
apostolate	65,66,67
aposunagogos	80,83,84,88,171,173
ascension	45,92,185-189
Ascension Day	185,186,188
baptism	9,12,27,79,90,91,120,129,130,138,168
beloved disciple	95-97
body	9-31,36,66,69,70,83,94,120,159,162
canon	40,46,47,49,97,98,144,175,177, 182,183
creatura verbi	200
Christ-event	180,186,203

christology	91,92,95,110,115,119,121,125, 129,132,134, 137-139,163, 164,166,188,218
chronology of Paul	161
continuity	10,106,107,110,111,117,118,136,160,182, 199
corpus permixtum	169
crisis theology	184,187
curse	9,10,81
dialectical theology	135,183,184,187
discontinuity	114,117,118
docetism	90,91,125
doctrinal method	61,62
doctrine of dual order	216,217,220,221
doctrine of justification	61,169,170,221
doctrine of satisfaction	151
doctrine of the Trinity	217,221
dogmatics	55,57,57,61,62,120,194
donum Spiritus Sancti	54
dualism	13,22,73,74,158,164,165
Early Christianity	3,32,65,71,72,99,145,149,161
Easter	158,185
Ebionites	76,112,121
ecclesiology	24
editors	144,171
ecclesia	75,162,169
encyclopaedia	59
emperor cult	85

eschatology	21,154,158,159,161,163,164, 220-221
Eucharist	26,36,167,168
evangelium	87
exegesis	2,21,33,39,40,41,49-51, 54,57-61,65,68,99,173, 174-176, 180, 181,185,189,192, 194, 195.
existential interpretation	1, 43,51,58,104,150,223
formulae	38,47,91,120,139,140,160,164, 166,170,217
fulfillment	38,116,118,131,132,148,154,156, 212
glossolalia	15
Gnosticism	3,5-18,24-26,65,67,73,143,162-165,171
gnosis	10,11,23,27,66,171
Hellenistic Christianity	72,99,111,112,122,124,166
Hellenistic and Gnostic Christianity	72
Hellenistic-Jewish Christianity	72,74,75,91,99,145
hermeneutics	50,59
historical critical exegesis	54,173
historical exegesis	2,40,51,58,59,99,174,180,192
Holy Spirit	33,35,37,108,125,129,130,138, 166,168,175,177,180-183,217,218
idolatry	18
Jewish Gnosticism	8,164
Judaism	112,153,164,191
literary analysis	6,155
Montanists	95,98,
once and for all	49,151,152

Palestinian Christianity	122,164
pneuma	13-18,20,25-29,31,66,67,71,73,92,162
politics	197,203,205,206
pre-Marcionism	148
Proto-Christianity	32,35,49
public worship	178,198-202
resurrection	7,12,13,21,22,30,42,45,79,104,110,114,115, 117,119-123,125,129,136, 138,146,158-160,166,199
revelation	41,43,71,94,97,98,110,118,137,141,147,149, 150,152,161,177,180,184,186,187,191
sola scriptura	49,177,223
solus Christus	49,177
sophia	10
theologia crucis	87,89,91,146,179
theologia gloriae	179,182,193
theology of the word	95,135,184,186,188,189,194
universalism	72,73,94,162,164,170
viva vox	46

BIBLIOGRAPHY: WALTER SCHMITHALS
1993 - 2000

This Bibliography is the continuation of the one of 1983-1992 in *Theologische Literaturzeitung* 118, 12, 1993, Sp. 1089-1095.

The Capital letters used in the Bibliography itemized:

    A Independent Publications

    B Essays and Lectures

    C Lexica etc.

    D Reviews

    E Meditations and Contemplations

1993

798 A *Die Schriftrollen vom Toten Meer. Die Essener von Qumran und das Urchristentum;* Deutsche Bibelgesellschaft, Stuttgart, 28 Seiten, also appeared in: *Ökumenische Informationen*, Kath. Nachr. Agentur. Nr. 12 vom 17.3.1993, S. 5-12, und Nr. 13 vom 24.3.1993, S. 6-11, also appeared in: *Christliches ABC Heute und Morgen*, Heft 1/1993, Neues Testament, S. 189-208.

799 B "The Pre-Pauline Tradition in 1 Cor 15,20-28", in: *Perspectives on Witness and Translation: Essays in Honor of John E. Steely*, Edwin Mellen Press, also appeared in: *Perspectives*, 20, Heft 4.

(475) B "Un témoignage: Le mouvement pacifiste ouest-allemand évalué par un théologien", in: *Risquer la Paix*, Edition Labor et Fides, Genève, 1992, S. 103-116.

800 B "Das Verhältnis von Juden und Christen in Neutestamentlicher Zeit," in: Treffpunkt Matthäus, *Evangelisches Gemeindeblatt der Matthäusgemeinde Steglitz*, März/April 1993, S.3-4.

801 D "Viel Lärm um Nichts. Zu: B. Mayer (Hg.), Christen und Christliches in Qumran," 1993, in *KNA, Ökumenische Information* 17 vom 21.4.1993, S.10-11.

802 D "Walter Bindemann, Theologie im Dialog. Ein traditiongeschichtlicher Kommentar zu Römer 1-11," 1992, in *ThLZ* 118, 1993, 919-922.

803 D "Henning Pleitner, Das Ende der liberalen Hermeneutik am Beispiel Albert Schweitzers," 1992, in *ThRs* 58, 1993, 222-223.

804 D Helmut Koester/François Bovon, "Genèse de l'écriture chrétienne," 1991, in *ZKG* 104, 1993, 86-87.

805 D Henning Paulsen, "Der zweite Petrusbrief und der Judasbrief," 1992, in: *RKZ* 134, 1993, 158-159.

806 D "Gerhard Barth, Der Tod Jesu Christi im Verständnis des Neuen Testaments," 1992. in: *Ebd.* 258.

807 D Peter Stuhlmacher, "Biblische Theologie des Neuen Testaments," Band 1: Grundlegung. Von Jesus zu Paulus," 1992, in: *Ebd.* 289-290.

808 D Peter Müller, "In der Mitte der Gemeinde. Kinder in Neuen Testament," 1992; in: *Ebd.* 321.

809 D Hans-Josef Klauck, "Der zweite und dritte Johannesbrief," 1991. in: *Ebd.* 352.

810 D Walter Jens, "Im Anfang war das Wort. Das Johannesevangelium," 1993, in: *Ebd.* 352-353.

811 D Hans Weder, "Einblicke ins Evangelium, in: *Ebd.* Theologische Beilage 3, 15-16.

812 E Andachten zum 13.- 19.10.1994, in Brot für den Tag," *CZV* Verlag Berlin.

1994

813 A *Theologiegeschichte des Urchristentums: Eine Problemgeschichtliche Darstellung.* Stuttgart: Kohlhammer.

814 B "Die Kollekten des Paulus für die Christen in Jerusalem," in: E. Axmacher und K. Schwarzwäller (Hg.), *Belehrter Glaube (Festschrift für Johannes Wirsching zum 65. Geburtstag)*, 321-352.

815 B "Die Entstehung des Neuen Testaments," in: *Christliches ABC Heute und Morgen,* Neues Testament, Gruppe 4, 231-245.

816 B "Das Gewissen und seine ethischen Normen," in: *Christliches ABC Heute und Morgen*, Gewissen, Gruppe 4, 33-48.

817 B "Die Frage nach dem historischen Jesus. Vor 300 Jahren wurde H. S. Reimarus geboren," in: *Zeitschrift für Gottesdienst und Predigt*, 12, 1994, Heft 6, 13-15.

818 B "The Pre-Pauline Tradition of 1 Corinthians 15, 20-28," in: *Perspectives in Religious Studies*, 20, 1993, Heft 4, 357 -380 (in Nr. 813).

819 B "Zum Problem der Entmythologisierung," in: *Protokoll der Tagung 'Alter Marburger'* 3-5.1.1994, 49-71.

820 C "Wunder," in: *Bibeltheologisches Wörterbuch*, 4 1994, Verlag Styria, 602-606.

821 D Markus Huppenbauer, "Mythos und Subjektivität," 1992, in: *ThR* 59, 1994, Heft 1, 108-109.

822 D Erich Grässer, "An die Hebräer." 2. Teilband, 1993, in: *RKZ* 135, 1994, Heft 9, 292-293.

823 D Wayne A. Meeks, "Urchristentum und Stadtkultur," 1993; Bruce Malina, "Die Welt des Neuen Testaments," in: *Ebd*. Heft 10, 343-344.

824 D Jürgen Roloff, "Die Kirche im Neuen Testament," 1993, in: *Ebd*. Heft 10, 343-344.

825 D Hans Dieter Betz, "2. Korither 8 und 9," 1993, in: *Ebd*. 12, 442-444.

826 D Ulrich Luz, "Die Jesusgeschichte des Matthäus," 1993, in: *Ebd*. Heft 12, 444-445.

827 D Hans Weder, "Gegenwart und Gottesherrschaft," 1993, in: *Ebd*. Heft 12, 445.

828 E "Quasimodogeniti. Kol 2,12-15," in *GPM* 48, 1994, Heft 2, 186-191.

829 E "16.Sonntag nach Trinitatis. Apg. 12,1-11", in: *GPM* 48, Heft 4, 364-369.

830 E "Zur Predigt am Sonntag Trinitatis. Eph 1,3-14," in: *Zur Predigt des Sonntags. Evangelische Sammlung Berlin, April - Juni 1994)* 45-48.

831 E "Andachten Zum 28.1.-4.2." in *Brot für den Tag*, CZV Verlag Berlin.

1995

832 A *La apocaliptica. Introducción e Interpretación.* Ediciones Ega, 1994. (Span. Übersetzung von Nr. 272)

833 B "Nation und Nationalismus," in: *Christliches ABC Heute und Morgen,* Gruppe 4, Staat, 593-617.

834 B "Gottesdienst im frühen Christentum" in: *Ebd.*, Gottesdienst, 53-90.

835 B "Zum Problem der Entmythologisierung bei Rudolf Bultmann," *ZThK* 92, 1995, 166-206 (in 819).

836 D Karolina De Valerio, "Altes Testament und Judentum im Frühwerk Rudolf Bultmanns," 1994, in: *ThRs* 60, 1995, 108f.

837 D Udo Schnelle, "Einleitung in das Neue Testament," 1994, in: *RKZ* 136, 1995, 189-191.

838 D H Frankemölle, "Der Brief des Jakobus," 1994, in: *Ebd., Theologische Literatur*, Heft 10, 1-2.

839 D Hartmut Löhr, "Umkehr und Sünde im Hebräerbrief," in: *Ebd.*, 2-3.

840 E "Markus 2, 23-28," in: *GPM* 49, 1995, 396-401.

841 E "Apg. 10,21-35," in: *GPM* 50, 1995, 97-103.

842 E "Zur Predigt am Karfreitag. 'Matth 27, 33-50 (51-54)'," in: *Zur Predigt des Sonntags. Evangelische Sammlung* Berlin, April - Juni 1995, 12-14.

843 E "Andachten 22.-28.12," in: *Brot für den Tag*, CZV Verlag Berlin.

844 E "Andacht 10.8," in: *Das tägliche Wort*, Jg. 54, Ludwig Bechauf Verlag, Bielefeld.

1996

845 B "Das Gewissen und seine ethischen Normen," in: *Das Menschenbild des Grundgesetzes* (Schriftenreihe der Guardini Stiftung, Band 6), 48-67 (vgl. Nr 816).

846 B "Methodische Erwägungen zur Literarkritik der Paulusbriefe," *ZNW* 87, 51-82.

847 B "Zu Karl Barths Schriftauslegung. Die Problematik des Verhältnisses von 'dogmatischer' und historischer Exegese," in: Michael Trowitzsch (Hg.), *Karl Barths Schriftauslegung*, Tübingen, 23-52.

848 B "Gekreuzigt, gestorben und begraben - Zum Symbol des Kreuzes und zur christlichen Botschaft vom Kreuz," in: *Christliches ABC Heute und Morgen*, Gruppe 4, Auferstehung, 41-61.

849 B "Das Alte Testament im Neuen. Zum Problem einer 'gesamtbiblischen Theologie' in: *Ebd., Neues Testament*, 285-305.

850 B "Die Weihnachtgeschichten. Ihr Ursprung und ihre Bedeutung," in: *Ebd., Neues Testament*, 285-305.

851 "Exegetische Beobachtungen zum Tagungsthema, ausgehend von Phil 2, 5-11," in: *Protokoll der Tagung 'Alte Marburger'* 2. bis 4. Januar 1996 in Hofgeismar, 81-96.

852 D K. Erdmann, "Naherwartung und Parusieverzögerung im Neuen Testament," in: *ThLZ* 121, 45-48.

853 D R. Bultmann, *Die Geschichte der synoptischen Tradition*. 10. Auflage. Mit einem Nachwort von G. Theissen, in: *RKZ* 137, 1996, Heft 3, Theologische Literatur, 2-4.

854 D Th. Kuchartz, "Theologen und ihre Dichter" in: *Ebd.*, Heft 12, Theologische Literatur, 9-10.

855 E "Zur Predigt am 13. Sonntag nach Trinitatis, Apg 6, 1-7," in: *Zur Predigt des Sonntags*. Evangelische Sammlung Berlin, Juli - September 1996, 31-33.

856 E "Andachten 13.-19.7," in: *Brot für den Tag*, CZV Verlag Berlin.

857 E "Andacht 25.4," in: *Das tägliche Wort*, Jg. 55, Ludwig Bechauf Verlag, Bielefeld.

1997

858 B "Vom Ursprung der synoptischen Tradition," in: *ZThK* 94, 1997, Heft 3, 288-316.

859 B "Literarkritik und Theologie," in: *Wege zum Einverständnis* (Festschrift für Christoph Demke), Ev. Verlagsanstalt Leipzig, 1997, 238-248.

860 B "Der Hebräerbrief als Paulusbrief. Beobachtungen zur Kanonbildung," in: *Die Weltlichkeit des Glaubens in der Alten Kirche* (Festschrift für Ulrich Wickert) Walther de Gruyter, Berlin, 1997, 319-337.

861 B Über Empfänger und Anlass des Hebräerbriefes," in: *Eschatologie und Schöpfung (Festschrift für Erich Grässer)*, Walther de Gruyter, Berlin, 1997, 321-342.

862 B "Probleme des 'Apostelkonzils' (Gal 2, 1-10)," in: *HTS* 53, 1997, Heft 1 & 2, 6-35.

863 B "Geisterkämpfe im Wüstensand. Warum aus neuen Textfunden keine neuen Erkenntnisse über den historischen Jesus zu erwarten sind." *Berliner Zeitung*, Nr. 74, 29./30. März 1997, Magazin III.

864 D K. de Valeirio, "Altes Testament und Judentum im Frühwerk Rudolf Bultmanns," Beilage zur *RKZ* 3, 1997,4, (in 836).

865 D K. Berger, "Theologiegeschichte des Urchristentums," *Ebd.*, 4-6.

866 D R. Riesner, "Die frühzeit des Apostels Paulus," *Ebd.*, 7-8.

867 D Chaim Cohn, "Der Prozess und Tod Jesu aus jüdischer Sicht," *Berliner Zeitung*, Nr. 239, 14.10.1997, Sachbuch XIII.

868 D R. Heiligenthal, "Der verfälschte Jesus," *Berliner Zeitung*, Nr. 160, 12./13.7.1997.

869 E 7. Sonntag nach Trinitatis - 13.7.1997. "Johannes 6, 1-15," *GPM* 51, 1997, 325-330.

870 E "Andachten 5.-11. April 1998," in: *Brot für den Tag*, CZV Verlag Berlin.

871 E "Andacht 14.11.1998" in: *Das tägliche Wort*, Ludwig Bechauf Verlag, Bielefeld.

872 E "Morgenandacht am 4.1.1997," in: *Protokoll der Tagung 'Alte Marburger'* 2.-4.1.1997 in Hofgeismar.

1998

873 A *The Theology of the First Christians*, Westminster John Knox Press, Louisville, 396p.

874 B "Literarkritische Analyse des Kolosserbriefes," in M. Trowitzsch (Hg.), *Paulus, Apostel Jesu Christi* (FS Günter Klein), Mohr Siebeck, Tübingen, S. 149-170.

875 B "Zu den Anfängen des niederrheinischen Postwesens und zu Johann Maurenbrecher," *Düsseldorfer Jahrbuch* 68, 1997, S. 77-87.

876 B "Gibt es Kriterien für die Bestimmung echter Jesusworte?" *Zeitschrift für Neues Testament* 1, 1998, Francke Verlag Tübingen, S. 59-64.

877 B "Die Sammlung der Paulusbriefe," in: *Jahrbuch der Berliner Wissenschaftlichen Gesellschaft*, 1997, 111-122.

878 B "Die Briefe des Apostels Paulus," in: *Christliches ABC,* 3/1998, Paulus, DIE Verlag, Bad Homburg, S. 33-50.

879 B "Vom Himmel hoch, da komm ich her," in: *Christliches ABC*, 6/1998, Kirchenjahr, DIE Verlag, Bad Homburg, S.37-46.

880 B "Von Jesus zur Weltreligion," in: *Christliches ABC*, 6/1998, Neues Testament, DIE Verlag, Bad Homburg, S. 307-328.

881 B "The Parabolic Teachings in the Synoptic Tradition," *The Journal of Higher Criticism*, 4, 1997, S. 3-32.

882 B "Példabeszédek a szinopticus evangéliunokban," in: *Benyik Gvörgv*

(Hg.), Példabeszédek, Szeged 1998, S. 151-173.

883 C "Abresch, Wilhelm," in: *Die deutsche Literatur*, Reihe IV, 1998, Friedrich Frommann, Stuttgart, Sp. 101-103.

884 D Karl Löning, "Das Geschichtwerk des Lukas," Band 1 (Urban Taschenbücher, 455), in: *ThLZ* 123, 1998, Sp. 480-481.

885 D Peter L., "Hofrichter, Modell und Vorlage der Synoptiker," in: *ThLZ* 123, 1998, Sp. 596-598.

886 D Ulrich Luz, "Das Evangelium nach Matthäus, Band 3, 1997, in *Theol. Literatur*, Beilage zur RKZ, 8/1998, S. 3.

887 D Ulrich Wilckens, "Das Evangelium nach Johannes" (NTD 4), 1998, in: *RKZ*, 8/1998, S. 4.

888 D Wolfgang Schrage, "Der erste Brief an die Korinther," Band 2, 1995, in: *RKZ*, 8/1998. S. 5.

889 D Klaus Berger, "Qumran," 1998, in: *Berliner Zeitung*, 300/1998, Magazin VI.

890 E "Römer 11, (32)33-36," in: *GPM* 52, 1998, 304-309.

891 E "Andachten 1.-7.8," in: *Brot für den Tag*, CCZ Verlag, Berlin.

892 E "Andacht 13.5., in *Das Tägliche Wort*, Jahrgang 57, Ludwig Bechauf Verlag, Bielefeld.

893 F "Der Partisan Gottes. Zum Tode Ernst Käsemanns," *Berliner Zeitung* 43, S. 10.

894 F "Zum Gedächtnis von Ernst Käsemann, in: *Protokoll der Tagung 'Alte Marburger'* 2.-4.1.1998, S. 6-8.

1999

895 B "Zur Geschichte der Spruchquelle Q und der Tradenten der Spruchüberlieferung. Das siebenfache Wehe Lk 11, 37-54 par." *NTS* 45, 1999, 472-497.

896 B "Der Konflikt zwischen Christen und Juden in neutestementlicher Zeit." *Christliches ABC* 1999, "Juden und Christen" 401-423.

897 B Sündige tapfer, glaube tapferer. Katholische Kirche und lutherischer Weltbund entscharfen einen zentralen Streitpunkt der Reformation." *Berliner Zeitung* Nr. 254, 30./31. 10. 1999.

898 D Alexander Demandt, "Hände in Unschuld. Pontius Pilatus in der Geschichte," Böhlau Verlag Köln/Weimar, 1999. *Berliner Zeitung* Nr. 266, 13./14.11, 1999

899 E "Andachten 26.3. - 1.4.2000," in: *Brot für den Tag*, CVZ Verlag Berlin.

900 E "Andacht 14.5.2000," in: *Das tägliche Wort*, Jahrgang 58, Ludwig Bechauf Verlag, Bielefeld.

2000

901 A "Evangelien aus dem Wüstensand. Das Thomas-Evangelium und andere apokryphe Evangelien." *Christliches ABC* 3/2000, Neues Testament, 329-348.

902 B "Der 'heilige Geist,' im Neuen Testament. Ein Kapitel aus der Theologiegeschichte des Urchristentums." *Christliches ABC* 2/2000, Geist, 11-37.

903 B "Weissagung und Erfüllung." *Christliches ABC* 6/2000, Juden und Christen/Israel, 425-441.

904 B "Die Zeit selbst wandelt sich. 2000 Jahre nach Christi Geburt." *Berliner Zeitung* Nr. 300, 23./26. 12.2000, S. 11-12.

905 D Klaus Berher/Christine Nord, "Das Neue Testament und frühchristliche Schriften," Insel-Verlag Frankfurt/Main, 1999. *Berliner Zeitung* Nr. 6, 8./9/1/2000, S.8.

906 E "Röm 9, 1-5.31 - 10,4" in: *GMP* 54, 2000, 357-364.

907 1 Thess 1,2-10, in: *GMP* 54, 2000, 393-398.

908 "Andachten 19. -24.3," in: *Brot für den Tag* 2001, CVZ Verlag, Berlin.

G 909 G "Eine geistige und geistliche Gemeinschaft. Zum Tod des Theologen Eberhard Bethge." *Berliner Zeitung* Nr. 72, 25./26.3.2000, S. 16.

910 "Grundlage für die Jesusforschung."*Berliner Morgenpost*, 23.7.2000, S. 18.

BS
2331
.B67
2001